Experience You!

The Puranjan Story

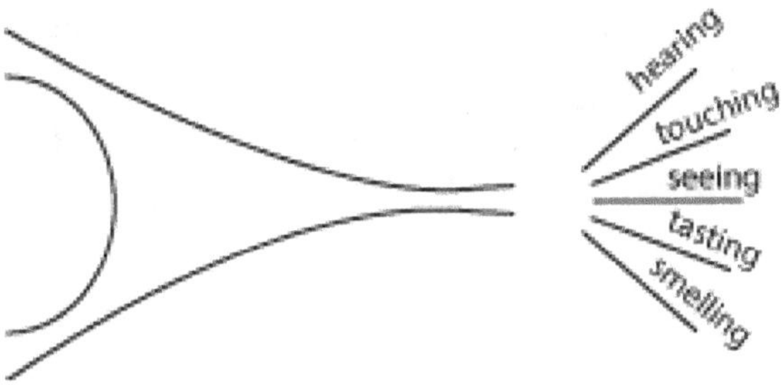

Michael Beloved

Original Sanskrit verse:

The Sanskrit text was adapted mainly from Göttingen Register of Electronic Texts in Indian Languages (GRETIL). That was a plain text transformation of

http://gretil.sub.unigoettingen.de/gretil/corpustei/sa_bhAgavatapurANa.xml (version: 2020-07-31)

Shiva Art: Sir Paul Castagna

Illustrations: Author

Correspondence:

Email: axisnexus@gmail.com

ISBN: 9781942887577

LCCN: 2024914616

Sanskrit Text

Transliteration Word-for-Word Meaning

ENGLISH TRANSLATION

Detail

Scheme of Pronunciation

Consonants

Gutturals:	क	ख	ग	घ	ङ
	ka	kha	ga	gha	ṅa
Palatals:	च	छ	ज	झ	ञ
	ca	cha	ja	jha	ña
Cerebrals:	ट	ठ	ड	ढ	ण
	ṭa	ṭha	ḍa	ḍha	ṇa
Dentals:	त	थ	द	ध	न
	ta	tha	da	dha	na
Labials:	प	फ	ब	भ	म
	pa	pha	ba	bha	ma

Semivowels:

य	र	ल	व
ya	ra	la	va

Numbers:

० १ २ ३ ४ ५ ६ ७ ८ ९

0 1 2 3 4 5 6 7 8 9

Sibilants:

श	ष	स
śa	ṣa	sa

Aspirate: ह

ha

Vowels:

अ	आ	इ	ई	उ	ऊ	ऋ	ॠ
a	ā	i	ī	u	ū	ṛ	ṝ
ए	औ	ओ	औ	ळ	ॡ	ं	:
e	ai	o	au	lṛ	lṝ	ṁ	ḥ

Apostrophe ऽ

A note on the diacritical marks and pronunciation:

A name like Krishna is accepted in common English usage. Its English spelling has no diacritical marks.

Sanskrit letters with a **dot** under them, should be pronounced while the tongue touches and is released curling slightly at the top of palate.

The **s** sound for **ś** carries an **h** with it and is said as the **sh** sound in **sh**e.

The **s** sound for **ṣ** carries an **h** with it and is said as the **sh** sound in **sh**un.

The **h** sound for **ḥ** carries an echoing sound of the vowel before it, such that **oḥ** is actually **oho** and **aḥ** is actually **aha**.

In many Sanskrit words the **y** sound is said as an **i** sound, especially when the **y** sound precedes an **ā**. For instance, **prāṇāyāma** should be **praa-nai-aa-muh**, rather than **praa-naa-yaa-muh**.

The **a** sound is more like **uh** in English, while the **ā** sound is like the **a** sound in **far**.

The **ṛ** sound is like the **ri** sound in **ridge**.

The **ph** sound is never reduced to an **f** sound as in English. The **p** sound is maintained.

Whenever **h** occurs after a consonant, its integrity is maintained as an air forced sound.

If the **h** sound occurs after a vowel and a consonant, one should let the consonant remain with the vowel which precedes it and allow the **h** sound to carry with the vowel after it, such that Duryodhana is pronounced with the **d** consonant allied to the **o** before it and the **h** sound manages the **a** after it. Say **Dur-yod-ha-na** or **Dur-yod-han**. Do not say **Dur-yo-dha-na**. Separate the **d** and **h** sounds to make them distinct. In words where you have no choice and must combine the **d** and **h** sound, as in the word dharma. Make sure that the **h** sound is heard as an air sound pushed out from the throat. Dharma should never be mistaken for darma. But adharma should be **ad-har-ma**.

The **c** sound is **ch**, and the **ch** sound is **ch-h**.

Table of Contents

How to use this book:

Make a casual reading page for page without becoming stressed about the concepts and ideas. Read to become familiar with the language style and presentation. If you read something of particular interest, make a mental note. Read on to get through the entire book.

Make a second reading pausing at areas of interest, where you feel you can grasp the material. Here and there, you may not follow the meanings but read on nevertheless.

Make a third reading with intent to grasp the concepts and methods.

Finally, make an in-depth study of this information.

Introduction

This is about you!

This story is from the *Srimad Bhagavatam*. It is a discourse between a supernatural yogi and a king named Barhi. This king was also known as *Prachinabarhi*. He was the son of some ascetic rulers, some brothers, who were named the *Prachetas*.

King Barhi indulged in Vedic religious sacrifices which involved killing animals and consecrating their carcasses. However, the king also killed animals which were prohibited from the procedures. To enlighten the king about the consequences, Nārad, a supernatural yogi, approached. The king recognized the great ascetic, treating him honorably.

When the pleasantries were completed, Nārad inquired of the king's welfare. He hinted that the monarch's actions, of killing so many animals, was self-destructive. Initially the king disagreed and cited that the priests who conducted the ceremonies were well-informed religious authorities, who if there was a fault in the king's actions, would alert the king, and even cease the sacrifices.

Nārad, for his part, told a story about someone named Puranjan, the City Person. This, he said, was an ancient king who slaughtered animals under the cover of religious offerings. This king faced certain existential penalties for the cruel actions against the victims.

There were unfavorable reactions during the life of that City Person. Then, during the hereafter, the deceased victims stabbed their horns into the subtle body of the king. This story was an allegory. King Barhi was impressed. He assumed that King Purañjan was in a royal lineage. Barhi asked Nārad to give information about the ancestry and descendants of that king.

Nārad then stated that Purañjan, the City Person, was a fictitious man, whose description was similar to Barhi's. It was an allegory, which Nārad continued to explain part by part. King Barhi was enlightened about his faulty actions which were recommended by misinformed indulgent priests.

In the book, *sex you!,* I detailed the birth process. In *death You!*, the course taken when one is permanently bared the use of the physical body, is featured. In this book, *Experience You!,* what happens between birth and death is pictured. Nārad detailed the existential situation of a human being.

Chapter 1
Purañjan meets a Queen

This discourse begins in verse 9 of chapter 25 of the fourth canto of *Srimad Bhagavatam.* It is completed in chapter 29 of the same canto. This yields five chapters in this book. The verse numbers are from the *Srimad Bhagavatam.*

To activate the deep meanings of the allegory, I used the assigned Sanskrit name of the actors but with their English equivalents.

नारद उवाच
अत्र ते कथयिष्ये ऽमुम् इतिहासं पुरातनम् /
पुरञ्जनस्य चरितं निबोध गदतो मम (४॥२५॥९)

nārada uvāca
atra te kathayiṣye 'mum
itihāsaṃ purātanam /
purañjanasya caritaṃ
nibodha gadato mama (4.25.9)

nārada – Nārada, uvāca – said, atra - now, te – to you, kathayiṣye – I will describe, 'mum = amum = about this, itihāsaṃ - history, purātanam – ancient, purañjanasya – concerning someone names City Person), caritaṃ - biography, nibodha – be informed, gadato = gadataḥ = said, mama – by me

Nārad said.
Now I will describe to you an ancient history, the biography of someone named Purañjan City Person. Be informed by me. (4.25.9)

Detail

Nārad will admit to King Barhi that this is a fictious story, which is based on the real life of any coreSelf. Barhi was a king during the Vedic era. He was habituated to sacrificing animals in religious ceremonies but he killed even animals which were not approved. Worse was the fact that Barhi paid no attention to the long-ranged objectives of the ceremonies, and the related restrictions.

Nārad told this fictitious story to give the king a warning, regarding what would happen in the life hereafter, where the tides would turn to make Barhi a sacrificial victim. In the afterworld, the king would be disadvantaged just as the animals were in this world. The roles of predator and prey would be reversed. The king would be hurt instead.

King Barhi attentively listened to Nārad. The king wanted to hear the histories of previous kings of his own or of other dynasties. It was a way to be entertained. This was the narration about a certain Purañjan, the City Person. This was not any person but a specific someone who was an adventurer in need of a well-furnished, properly-staffed city.

King Barhi had no idea that the narration was fictitious, nor that it ran parallel to his lifestyle. After Nārad rendered the story, he alerted the king to this. In the days of Barhi only a handful of people in a kingdom were literate. Most could neither read nor write. In fact, stories were not penned to be shared in books. They were composed by a scribe and spoken to one or two persons who were of high status.

Suspecting that this story was about someone he did not know, and thinking that it would be well worth the while hearing of it, Barhi listened keenly.

It was not an ancient history, except in the allegoric way. Hence Nārad was misleading at the onset. He would later correct this by explaining that there was no King Purañjan, the City Person, except for Barhi himself whose activities were duplicated in the narration.

Puran + jan gives the dual compound as Purañjan, which literally is Puran (City) + jan (person). The significance of this is that there is a psychological environment which is inhabited by a coreSelf. To some extent that self transcends the environmental container or psyche.

आसीत् पुरञ्जनो नाम राजा राजन् बृहच्-छ्रवाः /
तस्याविज्ञात-नामासीत् सखाविज्ञात-चेष्टितः (४॥२५॥१०)

āsīt purañjano nāma
rājā rājan bṛhac-chravāḥ /
tasyāvijñāta-nāmāsīt
sakhāvijñāta-ceṣṭitaḥ (4.25.10)

āsīt – there was, purañjano = purañjanaḥ = City Person, nāma – so named, rājā – king, rājan – O King, bṛhac-chravāḥ = bṛhat (great) + śrāvaḥ (hearing of), tasyāvijñāta= tasyā (his) + avijñāta (invisible person), nāmāsīt - name was, sakhāvijñāta = sakhā (friend) + avijñāta (Not-Recognized), ceṣṭitaḥ - movements

O King, there was a king named Purañjan City Person. He is great to hear of. His friend, whose movements were imperceptible, was named Not-Recognized (Avijñāta). (4.25.10)

Detail

Nārad breaks the news about this fictitious king but the listener to the story has no idea that there was no such person, and that the story has symbolism which relates directly to King Barhi.

Whatever Nārad would depict was relevant to the life of Barhi. It was a critique of Barhi's self-destructive lifestyle. It was spoken as a remedy for Barhi's vices, which were emotional indulgences and violent behavior.

The fascination about this story is that the focus was on Barhi's psychological actions, not his physical behavior. While initially as Nārad spoke of it, one is drawn to the moral conduct and excessive indulgences, still when Nārad sorts the instances, he brings it to one's attention that it is the inner theatre which is described.

They were two persons of prominence but there was another, a beautiful and resourceful woman, a queen. The first two persons were male beings. The third person was the female. Of the two males, one was Purañjan, the City Person. The other was Not-Recognized (Avijñāta). He was the superior of the three. However, this one is hardly mentioned except at the beginning and ending of the narration.

The reason is that Not-Recognized (Avijñāta) was invisible. He did not impose himself on the circumstances of life. He was detached and alert. During the City Person's stay in the city where the queen ruled, Not-Recognized remained invisible and inaudible, such that Purañjan, had no recall of him.

The question about Not-Recognized (Avijñāta) is. Who did not recognize him? The alarming issue is that King Barhi did not interrupt the story to get information about the invisible one. Barhi believed that Not-Recognized (Avijñāta) was Purañjan's friend. That was more reason to get the information as to why a dear friend of Purañjan was not recognized.

सो ऽन्वेषमाणः शरणं बभ्राम पृथिवीं प्रभुः /
नानुरूपं यदाविन्दद् अभूत् स विमना इव (४॥२५॥११)

so 'nveṣamāṇaḥ śaraṇaṃ
babhrāma pṛthivīṃ prabhuḥ /
nānurūpaṃ yadāvindad
abhūt sa vimanā iva (4.25.11)

so = saḥ = he, 'nveṣamāṇaḥ = anveṣamāṇaḥ = searching, śaraṇaṃ - accommodation, babhrāma – touring, pṛthivīṃ - earth, prabhuḥ - gentleman, nānurūpaṃ = na (not) +anurūpaṃ (not suitable to his taste), yadāvindad = yadā (when) + avindad (he found), abhūt – was, sa = saḥ = he, vimanā – depressed, iva – so it was

While touring the earth, the gentleman searched for accommodations. He found nothing that was suitable to his taste. Eventually he was depressed. (4.25.11)

Detail

This mythical king, Purañjan, the City Person, happen to wander from place to place, rather from dimension to dimension. He had a need for accommodations. He had no idea about what he really wanted but he knew that once he saw a desirable place, he would recognize it. This was due to his strong confidence in the senses, the subtle instruments whose judgement and prejudices he trusted.

Nārad really meant that the coreSelf felt incomplete at the onset of its emergence in this creation. It was nervous and felt undone. It needed adjuncts for completion and to have the upper hand as an exploiter of the environment.

The coreSelf spend millions of years, in fact countless eras, shifting here and there in search for *who-knows-what.* Still, it continued this quest. It could not pin what it desired. All the same the urge for fulfilling its needs was felt.

It was perplexed. It wondered what it should do to cause its presence in a desirable environment. It mused to itself. "If there is no fulfillment of my urges, why was I happened into existence?"

While touring the dimensions which it could perceive, the City Person searched for accommodations where it could relax and rest its weary self. After some time, it found nothing that was to its liking. Up to that point, there was no place where it could fully enjoy itself.

न साधु मेने ताः सर्वा भूतले यावतीः पुरः /
कामान् कामयमानो ऽसौ तस्य तस्योपपत्तये (४॥२५॥१२)

na sādhu mene tāḥ sarvā
bhūtale yāvatīḥ puraḥ /
kāmān kāmayamāno 'sau
tasya tasyopapattaye (4.25.12)

na - not, sādhu – suitable, mene – contentment, tāḥ - them, sarvā = sarvāḥ - all, bhūtale – on earth, yāvatīḥ - many, puraḥ - residences, kāmān – desirable things, kāmayamāno = kāmayamānaḥ = desiring, 'sau = asau = that one, tasya – his, tasyopapattaye = tasya (his) + upapattaye (wanting)

In all the residences on this earth, he found none which was suitable for his contentment, not one desirable location. (4.25.12)

Detail

The coreSelf, who is depicted as Purañjan, the City Person, existed time and again. It tried and tried to find adjuncts which could subsidize what it could not produce to satisfy itself. It searched and searched here and there. It was unsuccessful. Despite the frustration, it could not cease looking.

A living being could surely assume that its quest for position is eternal. Its needs for sensual access is perpetual. Even if it becomes unconscious, if it again becomes aware, it will desire certain basic needs and will also have urges for some non-basic fulfilments.

This requires the use of adjuncts. Without adjuncts the living being may subjectively exist but not as a grasping self, only as a radiant something which unknown to itself, shines on and on with no idea of self.

The City Person contacted many features of life, which were unsuitable, or which could cause an alliance for exploitation of the environments. It seemed that every such adjunct was a mismatch. Nothing fitted suitably. And still, Purañjan kept searching.

This indicates that despite using various bodies, besides the human one, the coreSelf feels undone, as if it should be facilitated even more. It also suggests that Nature rarely gives one the opportunity to be the presiding tenant in a human form.

स एकदा हिमवतो दक्षिणेष्व् अथ सानुषु /
ददर्श नवभिर् द्वार्भिः पुरं लक्षित-लक्षणाम् (४॥२५॥१३)

sa ekadā himavato
dakṣiṇeṣv atha sānuṣu /
dadarśa navabhir dvārbhiḥ
puraṃ lakṣita-lakṣaṇām (4.25.13)

sa = saḥ = he, ekadā – once it happened, himavato = himavataḥ = of the Himalaya Mountains, dakṣiṇeṣv = dakṣiṇeṣu = south, atha – then, sānuṣu – scenic with ridges, dadarśa – discovered, navabhir – with nine, dvārbhiḥ - entrances, puraṃ - city, lakṣita – noticed, lakṣaṇām – adequate

Once it happened that he was on the Southern Himalayas, a place with scenic ridges. There he discovered a city which had nine entrances. He noticed its adequate accommodations. (4.25.13)

Detail

By sheer chance, after going here and there, following his intuition, Purañjan, the City Person, found a place to his liking. This one location seemed the most suitable place he experienced in his travels over the earth. This signified the discovery of his psyche as it is represented and formatted in the human species.

The coreSelf is itself preformatted just like the various bodily forms which it may use but the lower species do not accommodate it suitably as does the human body.

The human situation is a special existential niche which accommodates the versatile format of a self. It is rare and unique. It is not acquired in every case of every searching self.

At the top of the items advertised in the evolutionary catalog, is the human being. It is the best format which was produced by Nature.

The human facility is a bit lower than the Northern Himalayas where the celestial beings reside, but it is the highest species of what was available which was south of that mythical mountain range. Humans are lower than the celestial beings but higher than any other species which exploit the earth.

Purañjan, the City Person, was relieved to find this place which was a fully enclosed city with nine gates. It allowed sensual access. Through the senses, one could reach out and procure what was needed.

प्राकारोपवनाट्टाल- परिखैर् अक्ष-तोरणैः /
स्वर्ण-रौप्यायसैः शृङ्गैः सङ्कुलां सर्वतो गृहैः (४॥२५॥१४)

prākāropavanāṭṭāla-
parikhair akṣa-toraṇaiḥ /
svarṇa-raupyāyasaiḥ śṛṅgaiḥ
saṅkulāṃ sarvato gṛhaiḥ (4.25.14)

prākāropavanāṭṭāla = prākāra (walls) + upavana (parks) + aṭṭāla (towers), parikhair = parikhaiḥ = with canals, akṣa – windows, toraṇaiḥ - arched doorways, svarṇa – golden, raupyāyasaiḥ = raupya (silvern) + āyasaiḥ (with iron), śṛṅgaiḥ - with domes, saṅkulāṃ - congested, sarvato = sarvataḥ = everywhere, gṛhaiḥ - with residences (4.25.14)

It had walls, parks, and towers, with canals, windows, and arched doorways. There was gold, silver, and iron domes on residences in every place.

Detail

When compared to the lower species, a human body is excellent. It has many environmental and situational advantages which are not afforded to the species below it. However, some of the situations of the human have less capacity than that of particular lower lifeforms.

As for instance, an eagle has keener vision than a human. A horse has faster mobility. But these advantages, when gaged collectively, set the human apart as the superior facility. Purañjan already used the major lower species. He felt that the human one was the selected utility.

There is a subtle self which transmigrates from a near dead lifeform in some species to another newly produced lifeform in some other or in the same species.

Like different cities with similar or dissimilar accommodation, the various bodies function as residential quarters for the transmigrating self, such that it can reside in a psychological niche for a limited time. Either by choice or by influence, the transmigrating basic self must, on occasion, shift from one form to another.

This self is not an absolute principle in these operations. It relies on adjuncts, which are psychological instruments which provide for the self, various contrasting perceptions.

That self has a physical and psychological structure but only when it has a living physical appearance. When it is psychological only, it has only a subtle form or psyche. That is a psychic apparatus which is like a container or complex city.

When categorized as a physical principle, the self has a skin which encloses its city-like apparatus. When regarded as a psychological something, it has a psychic gossamer which encloses its essential parts.

As there are walls, parks, towers, canals, windows, and arched doorways in a fortified city, so in the structure of the physical body and in the subtle form as well, there are enclosed glands, bones, veins, arteries, eyes, cartilage, and other compositions which are special areas where certain functions operate.

The subtle body, and the physical one, are interspaced aptly. The physical one is designed on the basis of the subtle framing, which is used by Nature in the composition of the physical system.

The coreSelf does not supervise the construction of its physical body. The core does not know every technical aspect. It is unable to properly maintain the physique. In addition, because the core craves experience, it rarely takes the time to study how the physical body should be maintained. Even though the self is present during the construction of the sperm and ovum, still it does not observe every detail of the embryonic formation. This puts it at a disadvantage, which it overlooks as it becomes preoccupied with various experiences.

As there may be gold, silver, and iron domes on residences, so in the subtle body there are various qualifying influences. These are energy states which are graded as are metals, as per usage and quality.

As domes are seen from far away, so the behavior of a person may be determined by his/her conduct, which is supported by an energy state, either as clarifying, motivating, or depressing. Sometimes someone enters a building voluntarily. At another time, he/she may be confined in a building involuntarily. Someone may be influenced by a state of mind or may go under that spell voluntarily.

नील-स्फटिक-वैदूर्य- मुक्ता-मरकतारुणैः /
क्लृप्त-हर्म्य-स्थलीं दीप्तां श्रिया भोगवतीम् इव (४॥२५॥१५)

nīla-sphaṭika-vaidūrya-
muktā-marakatāruṇaiḥ /
kḷpta-harmya-sthalīṃ
dīptāṃ śriyā bhogavatīm iva (4.25.15)

nīla – sapphire, sphaṭika – quartz, vaidūrya – diamonds, muktā - pearl, marakatāruṇaiḥ = marakata (emerald) + aruṇaiḥ (with ruby), kḷpta – constructed, harmya - palace, sthalīṃ - floor, dīptāṃ - illuminated, śriyā – irresistible, bhogavatīm – excitement city or the realm of iridescent snakes, iva - like

The floors of the palaces were constructed with sapphire, quartz, diamond, pearl, emeralds, and rubies. It was illuminated and was irresistible, just like Bhogavatī, Excitement City, or the realm of the iridescent snakes. (4.25.15)

Detail

As everything moves on the floors, and are supported in some way by the foundation, which is the base of a building, so in the psychic body there is a gossamer which is littered with subtle nerve endings which provide feelings of various types. These are like sapphire, quartz, diamond, pearl, emeralds, and rubies, in the sense that the feelings vary, according to the response registered by visual, tactile, or other perception.

In the time of King Barhi, there was a legend about a place called Bhogavatī, the realm of the iridescent snakes. The movement of the reptiles and their coloration was such as to bewilder and hypnotize the mind. Bhogavatī when literally translated means Excitement City.

Nārad wanted to bring to King Barhi's attention that as a coreSelf, Barhi somehow acquired a human body, which is a lifeform or existential location, which allows the experience of various sensual challenges.

There is much fascination for a self, when it assumes the facilities which Nature provides as a human body. One enjoys the body as an amusement park for the self, and even to one's detriment. Some selves notice the sensual bewilderment and avoid the tendency to exploit. Instead, those yogis use the higher functions to discover transcendental access to higher dimensions.

The human body, like Bhogavatī, the colorful heavenly subterranean place, is full of desirable and undesirable excitements which enthrall the self. This stuns discrimination and postpones the search for a transit to a better place, to a body which is superior even to the human species.

When he set out to find a suitable place with suitable social relations, Purañjan did not design the facilities architecturally. He searched. He relied on his sensual detecting, according to whatever was available for sensing in such a body.

सभा-चत्वर-रथ्याभिर् आक्रीडायतनापणैः /
चैत्य-ध्वज-पताकाभिर् युक्तां विद्रुम-वेदिभिः (४॥२५॥१६)

sabhā-catvara-rathyābhir
ākrīḍāyatanāpaṇaiḥ /
caitya-dhvaja-patākābhir
yuktāṃ vidruma-vedibhiḥ

sabhā – assembly building, catvara – court yard, rathyābhir = rathyābhir by streets, ākrīḍāyatanāpaṇaiḥ = ākrīḍa (sport arenas) + āyatan (resort) + āpaṇaiḥ (by malls), caitya – monument, dhvaja – flag, patākābhir = patākābhiḥ = partitions, yuktāṃ - orderly arranged, vidruma - coral tree, vedibhi - with ceremonial areas

The city was designed with assembly buildings, court yards, streets, sport arenas, resorts, malls, monuments, flags, and partitions. This was orderly arranged. It had coral trees and ceremonial areas. (4.25.16)

Detail

Purañjan was so astonished to discover this place, that he failed to query about it. He was eager to enjoy it. He felt that his good luck caused it to be there. He did not consider its designer. As a lifeform assumes itself to be a certain type of body, living in some place, where it came to exist, so Purañjan assumed that as he existed, so did this place.

The city was orderly arranged with positioned coral trees and ceremonial areas. It had assembly buildings, court yards, streets, sport arenas, resorts, malls, monuments, flags, and partitions. “What a wonder?” he thought. “I will certainly take this. For whom other than my honored self was this place created.”

Like Purañjan, the coreSelf is all too eager to be equipped with facilities for experiencing whatever there is, anywhere and everywhere. Naturally, that self feels that it deserves to be accommodated in the most pleasant way, with whatever circumstances it would require, either physically and/or psychologically.

Even though, it discovered itself to be existing just a short time ago, within one hundred years or so, still it feels that whatever produced this environment, should afford the maximum fulfillment for its needs.

पुर्यास् तु बाह्योपवने दिव्य-द्रुम-लताकुले /
नदद्-विहङ्गालि-कुल- कोलाहल-जलाशये (४॥२५॥१७)

puryās tu bāhyopavane
divya druma latākule /
nadad-vihaṅgāli-kula-
kolāhala-jalāśaye (4.25.17)

puryās = puryāḥ = of the city, tu – but, bāhyopavane = bāhya (outside) + upavane (in a park), divya – heavenly, druma – tree, latākule = latā (vines) + ākule (filled with), nadad = nadat = sounding, vihaṅgāli = vihaṅga (birds) + ali (bees), kula – groups, kolāhala – huming, jalāśaye – water reservoir

Outside the city, there were parks, trees, and vines, near a heavenly place. This was filled with the sounds of birds and humming bees near a water reservoir. (4.25.17)

Detail

Any well-furnished city may have pleasant surroundings which are either in the city limits, or adjacent to it. There may be forests, gardens, farmlands, and resorts. Bhogavatī, Excitement City, was such a place.

Beyond the skin of the physical body and exterior to the gossamer membrane of the subtle form, there are environments which are experienced through sense perception.

The physical body may have its healthy or unhealthy inner condition. It must respond to the conditions of the physical environment, which is exterior to it. There are similar considerations for the subtle form.

However, while there is one environment which is usually encountered by the physical senses, there are multiple situations, which are experienced by the subtle ones.

हिम-निर्झर-विप्रुष्मत्- कुसुमाकर-वायुना /
चलत्-प्रवाल-विटप- नलिनी-तट-सम्पदि (४॥२५॥१८)

hima-nirjhara-vipruṣmat-
kusumākara-vāyunā /
calat-pravāla-viṭapa-
nalinī-taṭa-sampadi (4.25.18)

hima – icy, nirjhara – jagged mountain, vipruṣmat – with water spray, kusumākara = kusuma (flowering) + ākara (season), vāyunā – by breeze, calat – moving, pravāla – sprout, viṭapa – branch, nalinī – lotus flower, taṭa – shore, sampadi - posh place

From the icy jagged mountain, during the flowering season, there was water spray, carried by the breeze to the sprouts and branches, which were on the shore of a lotus lake of that posh place. (4.25.18)

Detail

This may be compared to the climatic situation within the body of a human being. The temperature is regulated mainly by the food eaten and the air absorbed. When one part of the body overheats, cooler energy flows through it to convey the excess to some other place, either to the lungs or the skin of the body. This prevents organ malfunction.

That happens involuntarily but it is monitored and adjusted by the lifeForce in the body. That is a secretive mystic energy. Correspondingly, there is a subtle body which is the psychic coordinator of the physical one. This subtle form mimics the condition of the physical system. There is feedback between the two systems.

The coreSelf observes this. It may or may not comprehend a certain operation, but it responds to whatever climatic condition there is.

From the brain, nerve instructions are sent to the lower parts of the body, even to the lowest part of the trunk, to the thighs, legs, and feet, even to the arms, forearms, and hands. This is like water spray which spread from mountain peaks, and descend to the flowering bushes, which feed from lakes.

नानारण्य-मृग-व्रातैर् अनाबाधे मुनि-व्रतैः /
आहूतं मन्यते पान्थो यत्र कोकिल-कूजितैः (४॥२५॥१९)

nānāraṇya-mṛga-vrātair
anābādhe muni-vrataiḥ /
āhūtaṃ manyate pāntho
yatra kokila-kūjitaiḥ (4.25.19)

nānāraṇya = nānā (many) + araṇya (forest), mṛga – animal, vrātair = vrātaiḥ = with herds, anābādhe - no violent behavior, muni-vrataiḥ = like disciplined yogi-philosophers, āhūtaṃ - invited, manyate – felt, pāntho = pānthaḥ = person walking by, yatra – where, kokila – cuckoos, kūjitaiḥ - by cooing

Various herds of forest animals exhibited no violent behavior there. They were like the disciplined yogi-philosophers. People walking by, felt invited, especially by the cooing of the cuckoos. (4.25.19)

Detail

When the body works to a self's satisfaction, when there is no disease evident, when the mind has just enough stress to motivate desire and fulfillment, that is like when one is in a park which has no vicious animals.

This is like the mind and lifestyle of a disciplined yogi philosopher, who is at peace internally and who somehow is facilitated by Nature for a relatively simple lifestyle. This person is carefree. He is a function of Nature just as everyone else, but he is facilitated by it, and is spared abject conditions.

The environment outside the physical body could be daunting or inviting, where someone is discouraged from experiencing it, or someone may be eager to enjoy it. With the help of the senses, the coreSelf can detect enjoyable objects outside his physical body. Through hearing, touching, seeing, tasting, and smelling, he can retract from and avoid those features which bring no delight. These may occur individually or collectively and may be complexly experienced; where for example, one object which produced an enjoyable sound, may also be visually unappealing.

That is how the coreSelf may become inextricably involved in an experience, where it is trapped, and cannot extricate itself from the incidence. Some experiences involve the use of one sense detecting a particular object which only that sense can appreciate. Some other experience which is more compelling, may involve more than one sense being interlocked into an object, whereby the core feels forced to involve itself with the flow of energy which comes from the object.

This participation may be ruinous. Usually, a self investigates what is outside of its container, beyond its psyche. It procures sense objects which it can enjoy. It is of the opinion that its form should procure pleasures through each of the senses.

When the pleasures are experienced, there is an interpretation which reads that the pleasures are desirable or unpleasant. Some conclusions are incorrect. That causes bafflement, anxiety, and disappointment.

यदृच्छयागतां तत्र ददर्श प्रमदोत्तमाम् /
भृत्यैर् दशभिर् आयान्तीम् एकैक-शत-नायकैः (४॥२५॥२०)

yadṛcchayāgatāṃ tatra
dadarśa pramadottamām /
bhṛtyair daśabhir āyāntīm
ekaika-śata-nāyakaiḥ (4.25.20)

yadṛcchayāgatāṃ = yadṛcchayā (somehow) +āgatāṃ (came), tatra – there, dadarśa – he saw, pramadottamām = pramadā (attractive woman) + uttamām (most), bhṛtyair = bhṛtyaiḥ = with male attendants, daśabhir = daśabhiḥ = with ten, āyāntīm – coming, ekaika = eka (one) + eka (one), śata = hundred, nāyakaiḥ - with manager

Somehow, as he came there, he saw the most attractive woman who had ten male attendants who managed hundreds of other employees. (4.25.20)

Detail

By chance, somehow, as if it was a fortunate coincidence, Purañjan, the City Person, saw the most attractive woman who was catered by attendants. Discovering that place with the well-furnished city and inviting surrounds, was a fortune. Meeting a beautiful woman who had no husband but who had servants, was all the more auspicious.

This reinforced the City Person's pride. It verified that despite his searching everywhere on earth, everywhere beside this city with the outer zones, the circumstances led to this great event; his meeting with a fascinating lady.

When the coreSelf is first attracted to a psyche, that happens spontaneously. The core does not plan this. It finds itself in the vicinity of an enclosure, a psyche. Outside of that existential enclosure, it senses an intellect which has accessory powers and functions.

Because of the cooperation of the intellect with the core, that intellect is similar to an agreeable woman who renders cooperation most frequently. To booth, the aristocratic lady had a staff which catered to her needs.

पञ्च-शीर्षाहिना गुप्तां प्रतीहारेण सर्वतः /
अन्वेषमाणाम् ऋषभम् अप्रौढां काम-रूपिणीम् (४॥२५॥२१)

pañca-śīrṣāhinā guptāṃ
pratīhāreṇa sarvataḥ /
anveṣamāṇām ṛṣabham
aprauḍhāṃ kāma-rūpiṇīm (4.25.21)

pañca – five, śīrṣāhinā = śīrṣa (head) + ahinā (by a snake), guptāṃ - protected, pratīhāreṇa- by a bodyguard, sarvataḥ - all around, anveṣamāṇām – looking for, ṛṣabham – sexual partner, aprauḍhāṃ - not sexually experienced, kāma-rūpiṇīm = having the form of sexual display

She was protected on each side by a five-headed snake, her bodyguard. It seemed that she needed a sexual partner. Even though she was not sexually experienced, she was the form of sexual display. (4.25.21)

Detail

The lady had a security service which efficiently protected her from assaults which came from any direction. However, it seems to Purañjan that she lacked a sexual partner.

He was encouraged though. He too needed a lover. It was his luck. Even though her bodyguard was present, he did not prevent Purañjan, from approaching to her.

A coreSelf discovers itself to be in this creation, and to be with a set of adjuncts, which are psychological tools for accessing the objects it encounters. In the allegoric rendering, Nārad revealed that the lady was the equivalent of the intellect. Her attendants were the accessory senses.

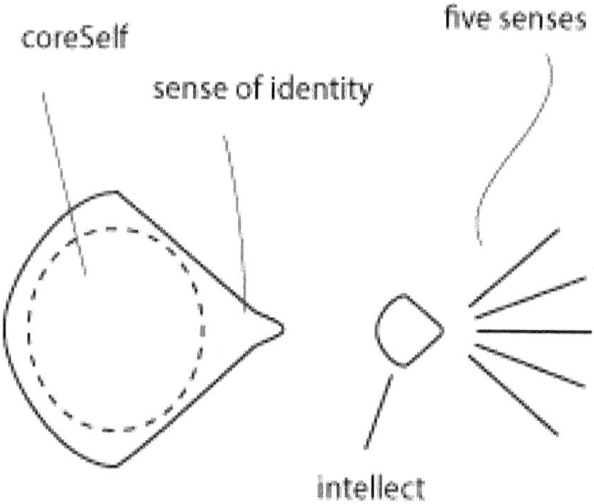

Regardless of the gender of the body, the core is represented as a male being in this analogy. The intellect appears as a female which has male and female attendants.

The amazing event was that everything was preconstructed to meet the needs of Purañjan. Even the people, not just the environment, suited his fancy.

How does someone appear in a place which is properly designed for his convenience? How could one arrive in an environment which has personnel facilities?

सुनासां सुदतीं बालां सुकपोलां वराननाम् /
सम-विन्यस्त-कर्णाभ्यां बिभ्रतीं कुण्डल-श्रियम् (४॥२५॥२२)

sunāsāṃ sudatīṃ bālāṃ
sukapolāṃ varānanām /
sama-vinyasta-karṇābhyāṃ
bibhratīṃ kuṇḍala-śriyam (4.25.22)

sunāsāṃ- nice nose, sudatīṃ - beautiful teeth, bālāṃ - young, sukapolāṃ - nice forehead, varānanām - beautiful face, sama – matching, vinyasta – artistically placed, karṇābhyāṃ - both ears, bibhratīṃ - dazzling, kuṇḍala – earings, śriyam - beautiful

Her nose and teeth were beautiful. She was young with a nice forehead. Her beautiful face was adorned with matching, dazzling earrings, which were artistically placed. (4.25.22)

Detail

Even though, when analyzed from a scientific angle, the adjuncts which are furnished for the coreSelf, are part of a psychic device, from the emotional view they are agreeable or disagreeable, being lubricated with subtle feelings.

So, it was! Purañjan, the City Person, rated the woman and her entourage to be pleasing. He was thrilled beyond expectation. He was so satisfied that he could hardly make a comment. The woman had beautiful nostrils and teeth. Her pretty face was adorned with matching, dazzling earrings which were artistically placed.

Such is the situation. Normally, the core lacks the discrimination and cannot rate the psychic operations in its psyche. Instead, its judgements are based on emotional shifts and interruptions. By itself, the core lacks discrimination, which is necessary for precise rating. This means that only some of its decisions and consents, facilitates its interest.

पिशङ्ग-नीवीं सुश्रोणीं श्यामां कनक-मेखलाम् /
पद्भ्यां क्वणद्भ्यां चलन्तीं नूपुरैर् देवताम् इव (४॥२५॥२३)

pišaṅga-nīvīṃ suśroṇīṃ
śyāmāṃ kanaka-mekhalām /

padbhyāṃ kvaṇadbhyāṃ calantīṃ
nūpurair devatām iva (4.25.23)

piśaṅga – yellow, nīvīṃ - sari, suśroṇīṃ - beautiful hips, śyāmāṃ - blueish complexion, kanaka – golden, mekhalām - belt, padbhyāṃ - with feet, kvaṇadbhyāṃ - by tinkling, calantīṃ - walking, nūpurair = nūpuraiḥ = with ankle bells, devatām – goddess, iva - like

She wore a yellow sari, which accentuated her beautiful hips. Blue was her complexion. Her belt was golden with blackish highlights. As she walked, ankle bells tinkled at her feet. She was like a goddess. (4.25.23)

Detail

In actuality, the woman was a psychic device, a supernatural roboton. But its operations delicately mimic a human lady. Purañjan had no idea of her situation. He assumed that she was on par with him, except that she was the female of his species. She indulged him. Her psychic energy was so similar to his feelings that he could not distinguish the difference.

The intellect of the coreSelf is flashy, colorful, and enticing. From the onset, the core has a trusting relationship with it. The intellect is seductive. It provides services which the core cannot render. This makes the intellect indispensable. The core depends on the intellect's opinions.

The woman had a blue complexion which suggested her deep imaginative and calculative capacity. With that the coreSelf fathomed many perplexities. However, when the intellect was influenced within the depths of the psyche by the tainted sensual energies, it drew the wrong conclusions. That caused the core to consent to faulty actions, which produced distressful outcomes.

To convince the core to consent to unrequested schemes, the intellect flashes attractive ideas, wishful thinking, which is similar to when a beautiful woman appears in public with a golden belt which has a blackish background.

Thus, the self becomes enamored. It renders its approval for the execution of faulty actions. But these result in unwanted repercussions.

A coreSelf which cannot determine when the intellect is incorrect, will consent to detrimental behavior. The core should have a method of determining when the intellect makes a faulty conclusion.

Just as Purañjan was reliant on the beautiful woman whom he met outside the city, the responsibility of the core is hampered by its reliance on the intellect.

Purañjan carries the liability for all actions. This is why the coreSelf must be vigilant. It should not assume that its adjuncts, the psychic machinery, carries the responsibility.

स्तनौ व्यञ्जित-कैशोरौ सम-वृत्तौ निरन्तरौ /
वस्त्रान्तेन निगूहन्तीं व्रीडया गज-गामिनीम् (४॥२५॥२४)

stanau vyañjita-kaiśorau
sama-vṛttau nirantarau /
vastrāntena nigūhantīṃ
vrīḍayā gaja-gāminīm (4.25.24)

stanau – breasts, vyañjita – indicated, kaiśorau – young adult, sama-vṛttau = matched breasts, nirantarau – challenging each other, vastrāntena – by the fabric, nigūhantīṃ - hiding. concealing, vrīḍayā – modesty, embarrassment, gaja – elephant, gāminīm - strolling

Her breasts indicated her young adult age. They were equally matched as if challenging each other. Being embarrassed, she concealed them with the end of her sari. She strolled like an elephant. (4.25.24)

Detail

Regardless of if one is male or female, this allegory about Purañjan, applies. Still, one should keep in mind, that the coreSelf is indicated as a male being. The intellect is presented as a female person, the queen of Bhogavatī.

One should bear in mind that the core in the psyche functions with masculinity or directiveness. The intellect functions more like a female. There is this love affair between the core and its intellect. There is some *give and take* between the two, but the core carries the full liability, such that mistakes made by the intellect, are charged to the core.

Even females are required to control, monitor, and discipline their intellects. Otherwise, there will be regret and hardship.

The woman in the analogy, the person who Purañjan met, was both sexually untouched and sexually charming. This indicates that at the onset, when the core was equipped with an intellect, it, the core, could not resist being allied with that adjunct.

The intellect was so irresistible, that Nārad compared it to a graceful elephant. When the core first met the intellect, it was like a young man, a hero, meeting a sexually mature virgin whose breasts were equally matched as if challenging each other. At first, she was embarrassed to be appreciated by a male suitor. Her modesty took control.

ताम् आह ललितं वीरः सव्रीड-स्मित-शोभनाम् /
स्निग्धेनापाङ्ग-पुङ्खेन स्पृष्टः प्रेमोद्भ्रमद्-भ्रुवा (४॥२५॥२५)

tām āha lalitaṃ vīraḥ
savrīḍa-smita-śobhanām /
snigdhenāpāṅga-puṅkhena
spṛṣṭaḥ premodbhramad-bhruvā (4.25.25)

tām – to her, āha – he spoke, lalitaṃ - affection, vīraḥ - adventurer, savrīḍa – with shyness, smita – smiling, śobhanām – beautiful, snigdhena – by love, apāṅga – emotional impulsion, puṅkhena – by impetus, spṛṣṭaḥ - affected, premodbhramad – exciting love energy, bhruvā – by the eyebrows

To that beautiful shy woman who smiled lovingly, Purañjan, the adventurer, spoke with affection. He was affected with the impetus of emotional impulsion which came from her eyebrows with exciting love energy. (4.25.25)

Detail

The conjunction of Purañjan and the beautiful woman seemed to be predestined. There was no chance of Purañjan, the adventurer, rejecting the young lady. He could not bring himself to criticize her.

This was due to his being seduced by the format of her existence. It was not that she was flawed or flawless. The issue was his ability to resist and his tendency to objectify himself from the circumstance. The situation was preset by time, a power which was greater than his discrimination.

The coreSelf is hoodwinked by the intellect, to such an extent that their communication is private, so much so that the core does not know how it is seduced.

This happens because of the core's not being equipped to illustrate everything it needs. As an adventurous man needs a capable woman, who is pretrained and has emotional intelligence, so the coreSelf (Purañjan, the City Person,) requires an intellect to function as its analytical advisor and illustrator. But such a need of the core, may imperil it, and cause it to become responsible for faulty actions.

The romantic notions which flash between the core and the intellect, are enjoyed by the core. And yet, this relationship may cause regret and fatigue to it.

Purañjan was infatuated by the look of the aristocratic woman. His discrimination was totally subdued. He could not make a decision because the love energy from the damsel's eyebrows held him in a spell. This gives some idea of how the coreSelf consents to every decision made by the intellect.

Instead of carefully checking the conclusions, the self accepts those views as valid actions which it supports. The fact is that some are correct. Some are erroneous. Regardless, the core carries the liability. Even though the intellect compliments the core, still it is the core which is tagged for the actions.

Purañjan felt incomplete. He could not function fully without a female companion. That was a hint given by Nārad, that the coreSelf all by itself cannot fulfill its tendencies. It needs adjuncts. It is not independent. It has needs, which if not fulfilled, makes it a wandering adventurer.

का त्वं कञ्ज-पलाशाक्षि कस्यासीह कुतः सति /
इमाम् उप पुरीं भीरु किं चिकीर्षसि शंस मे (४॥२५॥२६)

kā tvaṃ kañja-palāśākṣi
kasyāsīha kutaḥ sati /
imām upa purīṃ bhīru
kiṃ cikīrṣasi śaṃsa me (4.25.26)

kā – who, tvaṃ - you, kañja – lotus, palāśākṣi = palāśa (petal) + ākṣi (eyes), kasyāsīha = kasya (whose) + asi (you are) + iha (in this place), kutaḥ - where, sati – sexually untouched woman, imām – this, upa – near, purīṃ - city, bhīru – shy lady, kiṃ - what, cikīrṣasi – wanting to acquire, śaṃsa – explain, me – to me

(Purañjan inquired.)
Who are you, person with lotus-shaped eyes? Whose daughter, are you? Why are you in this place? Where do you go, you sexually untouched woman? What do you want at this place near the city? Explain your situation to me. (4.25.26)

Detail

Even though Purañjan was happy to meet the woman, he suspected that there would be conditions for his assuming the young lady as the sexual partner. To get to the details, he inquired. This means that initially when the coreSelf discovered its conscious self, it began seeking an environment and a suitable companion, with whom it could live in harmony.

This had to be someone who was capable from the onset. This required someone who was pretrained. Purañjan had pressing urges to fulfill. Now that he met a woman whom he felt strongly attracted to, whatever he would have to do to live with her, he would certainly complete. That was the urgency.

In this verse, the curiosity and presumption of the coreSelf is displayed. This gives insight into the nature of the self, as to its assumption that it has a right to demand explanations, about whatever it is confronted with in this existence.

Even without knowing anything about its origin, this adventurous self feels that everything is accountable to it. Just like Purañjan, the self queries about its endowed intellect, to know what it is, what functions it has, and who created it. The self loves the intellect, which to it, is similar to a female with lotus-shaped eyes.

The self compares the intellect to someone's young but suitable daughter. It wants the intellect to explain its existence and origin. The self expects that the intellect will give insight about why it is located in the mind, and why it disappears now and again, and then reappears instantly.

क एते ऽनुपथा ये त एकादश महा-भटाः /
एता वा ललनाः सुभ्रु को ऽयं ते ऽहिः पुरः-सरः (४॥२५॥२७)

ka ete 'nupathā ye ta
ekādaśa mahā-bhaṭāḥ /
etā vā lalanāḥ subhru
ko 'yaṃ te 'hiḥ puraḥ-saraḥ (4.25.27)

ka – who, ete – these, 'nupathā = anupathā – attendants, ye – they, ta – you, ekādaśa – eleven, mahā – powerful, bhaṭāḥ - bodyguards, etā - these, vā – or, lalanāḥ - women, subhru – having beautiful eyebrows, ko = kaḥ = who, 'yaṃ = ayam = this, te – your, 'hiḥ = ahiḥ = snake, puraḥ - preceding, saraḥ - going

Who are the attendants, each with eleven powerful bodyguards? O person with beautiful eyebrows, who are the women with you? O lotus-eyed one, who is this snake which precedes you? (4.25.27)

Detail

Even in the womb of the mother, there is questioning and research done by the embryo. It wants to know what it should do in such a predicament as such a someone, a unit identity. It tries to move itself. It expresses itself in successful or failed attempts to move its body, make sounds, experience perceptions, hear noises, track vibrations, taste apparent flavors, sniff its environment, and respond to movements of what surrounds it in the form of gases, liquids, bones, and flesh.

Purañjan seductively interrogated the young lady. He could not afford to alienate her. He needed the companionship and services. She had a kingdom with the social trappings which are required for a ruler. It was a perfect situation for him. Even though he did not know her father, nor the city planner, he suspected that it did not matter.

If he could convince the young lady to espouse him, the city and a government staff was available to him. Here was the perfect arrangement for a touring aristocrat like him.

The significance of this is that the coreSelf, when it was all to itself, sometime back in the hoary past, before it was linked with an intellect, it lacked certain functions and facilities.

Somehow, it understood that it needed company and environment. This happened when it was made to be aware that other features of existence were present. It perceived some objects in that environment. It instantly felt the need for some of these things, even some psychic functions.

Purañjan queried the young lady. He wanted her to explain her status, retinue, and residence. If he was to indulge, he needed information about the attendants and security force.

Since it was not a political relationship, he spoke with romantic overtones and commented about the woman's beautiful eyebrows. For him, this young lady was heaven-sent.

The relationship between the coreSelf and the intellect is a political one but the core rarely considers it in that way. To soften the impact of the hard bargain it has with its adjuncts, the core pretends that it has an agreeable alliance.

त्वं ह्रीर् भवान्य् अस्य् अथ वाग् रमा
पतिं विचिन्वती किं मुनिवद् रहो वने /
त्वद्-ङ्घ्रि-कामाप्त-समस्त-कामं
क्व पद्म-कोशः पतितः कराग्रात् (४॥२५॥२८)

tvaṃ hrīr bhavāny asy atha vāg ramā
patiṃ vicinvatī kiṃ munivad raho vane /
tvad-aṅghri-kāmāpta-samasta-kāmaṃ
kva padma-kośaḥ patitaḥ karāgrāt (4.25.28)

tvaṃ - you, hrīr = hrīḥ = dignity personified, bhavāny = bhavāni = Bhavani, goddess of the world, asy = asi = you are, atha - or, vāg = = goddess of learning, ramā = goddess of fortune, patiṃ - husband, vicinvatī – pursuing, kiṃ - what, munivad = munivat = like a yogi philosopher, raho = rahaḥ = remote place, vane = in the forest, tvad = tvat = your, aṅghri – feet, kāmāpta = kāma (wanting) + āpta (achieved), samasta – all, kāmaṃ - desirable things, kva – where, padma-kośaḥ = lotus flower, patitaḥ - fell, karāgrāt – from the palm of the hand

Are you Hrī, dignity personified? Are you Bhavāni, goddess of the world? Are you Vāk, the goddess of learning? Are you Ramā, the goddess of fortune? Are you searching for a husband in this remote forest, which is suitable for a yogi philosopher? Otherwise, having you, a partner already achieved all desirable things. Where is the lotus flower which fell from the palm of your hand? (4.25.28)

Detail

The young woman, queen of the Bhogavatī, Excitement City, seemed so complete, that Purañjan rated her as being on par with the most famous goddesses of his time. She reminded him of Hrī; a goddess who is dignity personified. She caused him to remember the legendary Bhavāni, goddess of the world, the spouse of Lord Shiva. He rated her with Vāk, the goddess of learning? She caused him to recall Ramā, the goddess of fortune, the wife of God Vishnu.

Considering her innocence and the companion vacancy which she expressed, he confronted her about the need for a husband. If she had a male companion, she would not be anxious to find someone in that remote forest.

This description of the young woman who was the center of attention in Bhogavatī, tells a story of a coreSelf which was needy for an intellect, and which once it was paired with one, got its lack of certain skills supplemented. The dependence was a handicap for the core. Initially it did not have everything it needed. It had to be assisted, not just with an intellect as described but with other assistants to the intellect. Somehow, the intellect was supplemented before it was paired with the core.

नासां वरोर्व् अन्यतमा भुवि-स्पृक्
पुरीम् इमां वीर-वरेण साकम् /
अर्हस्य् अलङ्कर्तुम् अदभ्र-कर्मणा
लोकं परं श्रीर् इव यज्ञ-पुंसा (४॥२५॥२९)

nāsāṃ varorv anyatamā bhuvi-spṛk
purīm imāṃ vīra-vareṇa sākam /
arhasy alaṅkartum adabhra-karmaṇā
lokaṃ paraṃ śrīr iva yajña-puṃsā (4.25.29)

nāsāṃ - na (not) + āsāṃ (of those), varorv = varoru = great person, anyatamā – special someone, bhuvi-spṛk = touching the earth, purīm – place, imāṃ - this, vīra – honored person, vareṇa – distinguished, sākam – with, arhasy = arhai = you deserve, alaṅkartum – to decorate, adabhra – copious, karmaṇā – actions, lokaṃ - world, paraṃ - best, śrīr = śrīḥ = goddess for wellbeing, iva – as if, yajna – religious ceremony, puṃsā – personfication

O special one, because you touch the earth, you are neither of the women I mentioned. But as you are an outstanding person, you deserve to be with me, who is distinguished. You fully decorate this world as if you were Śrī, the goddess for wellbeing, who matches the personification of religious ceremony. (4.25.29)

Detail

Purañjan was anxious to exploit the beauty, poise, and accommodations of the woman. He was anxious to indulge. He did not need to know her origin. He did not check with the authority who controlled her. He found it convenient that there was no authority present.

Wandering and wandering over the earth, he was relieved to stumble on this queen of the Excitement City.

He knew that she was not a supernatural being. That was convenient because he was an earthly being just the same. The indication is that the coreSelf is so eager to experience, that it readily is attracted to an intellect and related adjuncts.

यद् एष मापाङ्ग-विखण्डितेन्द्रियं
सव्रीड-भाव-स्मित-विभ्रमद्-भ्रुवा /
त्वयोपसृष्टो भगवान् मनो-भवः
प्रबाधते ऽथानुगृहाण शोभने (४॥२५॥३०)

yad eṣa māpāṅga-vikhaṇḍitendriyaṃ
savrīḍa-bhāva-smita-vibhramad-bhruvā /
tvayopasṛṣṭo bhagavān mano-bhavaḥ
prabādhate 'thānugṛhāṇa śobhane (4.25.30)

yad = yat = why, eṣa = eṣaḥ = this occasion, māpāṅga = mā (me) + apāṅga (by glances), vikhaṇḍitendriyaṃ = vikhaṇḍita (agitated) + indriyam (senses), savrīḍa = sa (with) + vrīḍa (bashfulness), bhāva – feelings, smita – smiling, vibhramad = vibhramat (bewildering), bhruvā – with eyebrows, tvayopasṛṣṭo = tvayā (by you) + upasṛṣṭaḥ (molested, influenced), bhagavān – lord, mano-bhavaḥ = god of love, prabādhate – invaded, 'thānugṛhāṇa = atha (thus) + anugṛhāṇa (render kindness), śobhane – lovely woman

Why was this occasion afforded to me, this event with your glances which agitate my senses? With your bashfulness, feelings, smiles, and eyebrows, I am bewildered. The lord of love invaded me. Render kindness to me, O lovely woman. (4.25.30)

Detail

This is an admission of Purañjan's helplessness. His search for a suitable companion and furnished residence was completed. He abandoned the adventure.

Once the core meets its intellect, it becomes wedded for the run of its existence. It will now experience in reference to that adjunct.

Whatever that core lacked for full exploitation of time and circumstance, may be supplied by the intellect directly or indirectly through the servants and security force.

Amidst this will be an undercurrent of relationship between the core and the intellect, with the core giving appreciation directly to the intellect, and also to its assistant adjuncts.

Purañjan, the adventurer, was finally fortuned to meet a young woman who pleased his heart. He had no kingdom. The woman had one. It was fully staffed.

He wondered about his good luck. Was there some supernatural or natural being who created the circumstance? Anyway, since it happened that he met the young lady, and she was furnished with accommodations and security, there was nothing to do but to bond with her.

He would not have to organize an army, build a city, staff a government, and have a treasury.

त्वद्-ाननं सुभ्रु सुतार-लोचनं व्यालम्बि-नीलालक-वृन्द-संवृतम् /
उन्नीय मे दर्शय वल्गु-वाचकं यद् व्रीडया नाभिमुखं शुचि-स्मिते
(४॥२५॥३०u१)

tvad-ānanaṃ subhru sutāra-locanaṃ
vyālambi-nīlālaka-vṛnda-saṃvṛtam /
unnīya me darśaya valgu-vācakaṃ
yad vrīḍayā nābhimukhaṃ śuci-smite (4.25.31)

tvad = tvat = your, ānanaṃ - face, subhru – with compelling eyebrows, sutāra – with attractive pupils, locanaṃ - eyes, vyālambi – exciting, nīlālaka = nīla – blue, alaka – hair, vṛnda – ample, saṃvṛtam – surrounded, unnīya – lifted, relate, me – to me, darśaya – show, expose, valgu – pleasing, vācakaṃ - speech, yad = yat = which, vrīḍayā – by shyness, nābhimukhaṃ = na (not) + abhimukhaṃ (face to face), śuci – bright, smite - smile

With its compelling eyebrows, attractive pupils, and eyes, being surrounded with the exciting, ample, blue hair, your face excites me. Relate yourself with pleasing speech, O lady, whose shyness does not allow a face-to-face communication, which would expose your bright smile. (4.25.31)

Detail

A mutual focus between the coreSelf and the intellect, usually results in the core being indulged by the intellect. This frequently results in the core being subjugated, where it consents to suggestions which it endorses but which carry consequences which the core is subjected to and is liable for.

As an adventurous man rarely can avoid looking head on at a beautiful woman whom he meets, so Purañjan could not resist that queen of Excitement City.

Despite being completely under her influence, he craved her all the more. He wanted to view her head on. He sensed that such exposure would diminish his objectivity. Since she was modesty personified, he made an appeal. He requested her pleasing speech.

नारद उवाच
इत्थं पुरञ्जनं नारी याचमानम् अधीरवत् /
अभ्यनन्दत तं वीरं हसन्ती वीर मोहिता (४॥२५॥३२)

nārada uvāca
itthaṃ purañjanaṃ nārī
yācamānam adhīravat /
abhyanandata taṃ vīraṃ
hasantī vīra mohitā (4.25.32)

nārada – Nārada, uvāca – said, itthaṃ - on this, purañjanaṃ - Purañjan, the City Person, nārī – lady, yācamānam – requesting, adhīravat – as excited, abhyanandata – she responded, taṃ - him, vīraṃ - adventurer, hasantī – smiling, vīra – hero, mohitā –fascinated with

Nārad said.
On this basis, Purañjan made that request of the lady, who was excited just the same. She responded to that adventurer. She smiled. For her part, she was fascinated with him. (4.25.32)

Detail

There was need on every side, some for the adventurer, others for the wealthy fully-staffed lady. Purañjan was excited beyond belief. He knew that this was his desire fulfilled. It was the same for the queen too.

The challenge of this in terms of the analogy, where the adventurer is the coreSelf, and the queen is the intellect, is that both the core and the intellect craved matching factors. One needed the other mutually. The intellect existed with a need for unity with a self. To become active to exploit this creation, either one needed the other.

Being in existence is one factor. Being involved and active with desires and purpose, was the issue for that adventurer, and the woman he met.

King Barhi listened intently to this narration about Purañjan. Barhi had no idea it was an allegoric tale which applied directly to the condition of the coreSelf and the intellect in the psyche.

Nārad explained the truth of this to Barhi later in the discourse. Barhi will also be told that his life is similar to that of Purañjan. Barhi was over-dependent on his intellect and failed to consistently act in a way which empowered the coreSelf.

न विदाम वयं सम्यक् कर्तारं पुरुषर्षभ /
आत्मनश् च परस्यापि गोत्रं नाम च यत्-कृतम् (४॥२५॥३३)

na vidāma vayaṃ samyak
kartāraṃ puruṣarṣabha /
ātmanaś ca parasyāpi
gotraṃ nāma ca yat-kṛtam (4.25.33)

na – not, vidāma – know, vayaṃ - we, samyak – precisely, kartāraṃ - maker, puruṣarṣabha – best of persons, ātmanaś = ātmanaḥ = of self, ca - and, parasyāpi = parasya (of another), + api (also), gotraṃ - family, nāma – identity, ca – and, yat – which, kṛtam - agent

(The woman replied.)
"O best of the persons, it is certain that we do not know the producer of ourselves, or of any other person. I have no idea about the identity of my lineage, nor agency. (4.25.33)

Detail

The young lady accurately appraised Purañjan as the best of persons. Of what could be taken or mistaken for personality in the psyche, the coreSelf was the highest factor. If there is more than one self to be recognized or addressed, then the core is the principal.

The young lady, the intellect, admitted that it had no way of determining who produced herself, nor any of the attendants who catered to her needs, nor anyone who existed elsewhere.

She had no information about the identity of her lineage, nor that of her agency. What she knew was that she existed. So did her assistants and even their visitor, the adventurous Purañjan.

In the existential environment, the core may sometimes look to the intellect for an explanation of the mysteries of existence. The self may inquire within itself. It may also seek explanations from other psyches. But has anyone ever heard of an intellect querying its coreSelf about an origin?

It seems that the inquiring tendency is particular to a core. It is never expressed by the intellect nor by any other adjunct.

The inquiring tendency is a markup for each core where one can distinguish itself from any other core. The objective feature of one, puts it into a specific perspective which gives it the ability to denote itself to itself, and to feature itself to other selves who are in communication with it.

The intellect which is a reality on to itself, was honest enough to admit to the core, that it was unaware of its parents. It did not know who produced it, nor did it have any understanding about a producer of anything else. It seemed that whatever there was, just appeared spontaneously. The intellect could not explain its existence. Now that it saw the core, and was irresistibly attracted to it, that intellect wanted to begin their history as lovers in a relationship.

इहाद्य सन्तम् आत्मानं विदाम न ततः परम् /
येनेयं निर्मिता वीर पुरी शरणम् आत्मनः (४॥२५॥३४)

ihādya santam ātmānaṃ
vidāma na tataḥ param /
yeneyaṃ nirmitā vīra
purī śaraṇam ātmanaḥ (4.25.34)

ihādya = iha (here) + adya (at present), santam – existing, ātmānaṃ - selves, vidāma- we know, na - not, tataḥ param = beyond that, yeneyaṃ = yena (by whom) + iyam (this), nirmitā – created, prepared, vīra – great person, purī – city, śaraṇam – suitable for residence, ātmanaḥ - of selves, ourselves

"We know that we exist presently but we know nothing beyond that. O great person, we have no idea of the one who created this place for our residence. (4.25.34)

Detail

A feature of trust is there in the intellect, where the coreSelf relies on the intellect because it draws conclusions based on the information it collects from the senses and the memory. This however is faulty. And yet, it is the best that the intellect can do.

Its method is to enlist the services of the senses to procure information about interesting subjects. This input is analyzed, and memories from the past are recalled. That is contrasted to the new information. A conclusion is drawn, which is presented to the core.

Once a conclusion is announced, the coreSelf may object or approve of it. If the opinion is allowed, an action is executed either mentally, emotionally, or physically. The action may be a combination activity which occurs simultaneously on those three levels.

The young woman, the queen of Excitement City, was totally honest at the onset. This was admired by Purañjan. It was one of the reasons why he was irresistibly attracted to her.

She admitted her ignorance initially. She did not pretend to know her origin. She said she had no idea of the person who created the Excitement City. As she existed, seemingly in a causeless way, so did the place.

In addition, she never challenged Purañjan. She did not inquire about his pedigree. She trusted her feelings which indicated that he was the perfect spouse to derive her attention and services.

As the queen knew nothing beyond the fact that she, her attendants, and her city with its surroundings, existed, as they had no information about who or what caused them to be, so the intellect cannot inform the coreSelf about how the intellect was created, nor the assistant senses, nor even the psyche. This was enigmatic.

Initially, in the very beginning of their conjunction, there was an agreement between the core and the intellect, that the intellect would serve the core with accommodations and authority.

The responsibility to explain how anything was produced, rests with the core only. Though she had domestic skills and assistants at her command, the queen could not see the origins.

Initially, Purañjan, wanted to know her parentage. He asked about it. He inquired about the security detail which protected the woman on all sides.

She alerted him however that she was not informed. This shows a difference between the intellect and the core. When all is said and done, the core will be unable to pass the responsibility for knowing the origins, to the intellect.

Actually, the person who would know about it, is the one listed previously as Not-Recognized (Avijñāta). He was with Purañjan, from the beginning of the City Person's awareness of himself. Purañjan however did not realize this about his perpetual friend. Instead, Puranjan looked to the queen for information about origins, something which she admitted ignorance of, from the onset.

The psychology of the intellect, like that of the queen is to acquire information, compare it to memories and give conclusions which may or may not be put into action by the body.

Purañjan, had expectations of the queen, where no matter what, he expected that she would render perfect non-erring conclusions. This tendency caused Purañjan to be short-sighted even in instances where the queen did her very best to render well-calculated views. One can do the best but if one does not perceive the remote origins, one's ideas will, more than likely, be faulty.

The invisibility of Not-Recognized (Avijñāta) is the cause of the Purañjan's inability to access this great friend, who knew the origins. Not-Recognized

(Avijñāta) is not for the convenience of Purañjan. Only the queen is. She is required to fulfill his needs. For his part, Purañjan was preset for the services of an agreeable woman. He was not inclined to submit to someone who was superior and had transcendence perception into origins.

एते सखायः सख्यो मे नरा नार्यश् च मानद /
सुप्तायां मयि जागर्ति नागो ऽयं पालयन् पुरीम् (४॥२५॥३५)

ete sakhāyaḥ sakhyo me
narā nāryaś ca mānada /
suptāyāṃ mayi jāgarti
nāgo 'yaṃ pālayan purīm (4.25.35)

ete – these, sakhāyaḥ - male friends, sakhyo = sakhyaḥ = female friends, me – my, narā – men, nāryaś = nāryaḥ = women, ca – and, mānada – honored person, suptāyāṃ - sleeping, mayi – I am, jāgarti – awake, nāgo = nāgaḥ = snake, 'yaṃ = ayam = this, pālayan – securing, purīm - city

"These men and women who are with me are my male and female friends. Honored person, while I sleep, the snake remains awake and secures the city (4.25.35)

Detail

In terms of what service, she could provide, those activities would be done by her attendants, and the security official, which was a sleepless snake. The serpent's continuous awareness did not include perception of the origins. Like the queen, the reptile had limitations.

It did its best to protect her from danger. This service extended to Purañjan as well, but it did not include extrasensory perception about the origins. That was a significant limitation.

The serpent, Nāga, was an energy Power Central for the Bhogavatī Excitement City and for its environs. Purañjan, appreciated the reptile but due to its species, he was also uncertain about it.

First of all, the creature was responsive to the queen, not to Purañjan. Whatever security it would provide would be in relation to the queen. Since she was in love with Purañjan, since she committed herself and staff to him, the snake took it as his responsibility to protect Purañjan.

When this is applied to the psyche, it is that the intellect is provided with information by the sensual energies which are a conjoint security force which is controlled by the kundalini lifeForce Power Central. There is a commitment between the intellect and the lifeForce. When the intellect is given information about whatever would inconvenience the psyche, this information is used to construct plans, which the kundalini makes every effort to institute.

The core for its part is reliant on the intellect and the services of the intellect's assistants and the protector. As some senses are aggressively active and some are passively receptive, so some of the queen's attendants were male and some female. They were matched to the services they skillfully performed.

दिष्ट्यागतो ऽसि भद्रं ते ग्राम्यान् कामान् अभीप्ससे /
उद्वहिष्यामि तांस् ते ऽहं स्व-बन्धुभिर् अरिन्दम (४॥२५॥३६)

diṣṭyāgato 'si bhadraṃ te
grāmyān kāmān abhīpsase /
udvahiṣyāmi tāṃs te 'haṃ
sva-bandhubhir arindama (4.25.36)

diṣṭyāgato = diṣṭyā (lucky me) + agataḥ (came), 'si = asi = you are, bhadraṃ - the best situation, te – to you, grāmyān – natural, kāmān – desirable things, abhīpsase – craving, udvahiṣyāmi – I will give, tāṃs = tān =them, te – to you, 'haṃ = aham = I, sva – my, bandhubhir = bandhubhiḥ = with friends, arindama – subduer of hostility

"It is lucky for me that you came. It is the best situation. O subduer of hostility, my friends and I will give you whatever is desirable which you crave. (4.25.36)

Detail

The young lady, the queen of Excitement City, admitted her fortune in meeting the wanderer, the adventurous Purañjan, the City Person. What is the use of an intellect if it is not connected to a coreSelf? As a woman naturally needs a man, so the individual intellect needs a core as its paired faculty.

As a man needs a woman, so a core needs an intellect to interpret events and institute plans for exploiting whatever it may discover in this creation.

Both were happy, the adventurer and the queen, the coreSelf and the intellect. They met. It was mutual fortune.

The young lady admitted that the presence of Purañjan, caused harmony and increased the sense of security in her city. She addressed him as *arindama,* a subduer of hostility. They met accidentally. She already felt that her attendants and even the sleepless serpent were awed by the wanderer, and would render even more service and cooperation, through his charismatic presence.

She pledged that her friends and herself would give him whatever was desirable which he craved. When applied to the existential situation, the intellect, on its own, without being coerced, wanted to satisfy the core in every possible way. It would influence the other adjuncts, like the senses, the kundalini lifeForce and the memories even, to serve Purañjan to the utmost.

Nārad portrayed the intellect as a woman. He presented the coreSelf as a male wandering adventurer who felt the need for a spouse and extravagant accommodations. The chauvinistic one was the core, while the servile one was the analytical function.

This suggests that regardless of the gender of a body, the observing coreSelf is the directive principle. The calculative function is the more submissive assistant feature. Theoretically, the core should make requests, while the intellect should comply.

Is that the situation, where the core dictates to the intellect, which in turn harnesses its assistants and security staff, to make things happen, which were requested by the core?

What happens when the intellect fails to produce what is requested by the core? Does the intellect, represented as the queen, ever refuse to service the core, which is featured as Purañjan?

Ideally when a mayor of city is unfulfilled or dissatisfied, his consort and her servants do everything possible to please that lord of the place. Does this mean that when the coreSelf wants something the intellect will immediately to provide it?

What about the security chief, the snake which is sleepless and which protects the young lady and her staff? Would the reptile give its very life to protect the lady, her staff and Purañjan?

इमां त्वम् अधितिष्ठस्व पुरीं नव-मुखीं विभो /
मयोपनीतान् गृह्णानः काम-भोगान् शतं समाः (४॥२५॥३७)

imāṃ tvam adhitiṣṭhasva
purīṃ nava-mukhīṃ vibho /
mayopanītān gṛhṇānaḥ
kāma-bhogān śataṃ samāḥ (4.25.37)

imāṃ - this, tvam – you, adhitiṣṭhasva – stay at this place, purīṃ - city, nava – nine, mukhīṃ - entrances, vibho – powerful man, mayopanītān = mayā (by me) + upanītān (furnished), gṛhṇānaḥ - taking, kāma – desire, bhogān – sensual experience, śataṃ - one hundred, samāḥ - years

"This is for you. Stay at this city with its nine entrances, O powerful man. It will be furnished by me. Take this opportunity to fulfill your desire for sensual experience for one hundred years. (4.25.37)

Detail

The queen informed Purañjan that the situation was at his disposal. Never mind that the queen had no idea about her origins and did not know about the source of anything else anywhere. Still her sense of possession was so defined that she guaranteed that the adventurer would be serviced by her and her staff in Bhogavatī Excitement City, a place that she did not construct and did not know its architect.

By intuition alone, the queen declared Purañjan, as the king of the city, as her lover-man. He was to fulfill his desires for sensual experience for one hundred years, an arbitrary span of time, except that it was declared so by her intuition.

The parallel to this in the psyche, is that the intellect exist with its assistants which are the senses, the kundalini lifeForce Power Central, and the memories. Before the arrival of the core, the intellect and its assistants were already in operation in a subtle enclosure. These formed an environment which was much desired by the core, which lacked the conveniences which the intellect could provide.

There was a hitch however, in that the queen declared that one hundred years was the limit for these conveniences. We may assume that the intellect, even though it was unaware of its origin, knew that there was a limit to its serviceability. She informed, that he could benefit from the people and the place for a limit of one century.

If the adventurer was perceptive, he would anxiously arrange his needs so that within one century he would no longer need the queen and her assistants. However, as we will hear, Purañjan did nothing to offset the closure of the service he would be deprived of, after the stipulated time.

कं नु त्वद्-न्यं रमये ह्य् अरति-ज्ञम् अकोविदम् /
असम्परायाभिमुखम् अश्वस्तन-विदं पशुम् (४॥२५॥३८)

kaṃ nu tvad-anyaṃ ramaye
hy arati-jñam akovidam /
asamparāyābhimukham
aśvastana-vidaṃ paśum (4.25.38)

kaṃ - to whom, nu – then, tvad = tvat = than you, anyaṃ - other, ramaye – I will enjoy, hy = hi = certainly, arati-jñam = no idea of sexual pleasure, akovidam – inexperienced, asamparāyābhimukham = asamparāya (no insight about the afterlife) + abhimukham (expecting), aśvastana-vidaṃ = one who cannot interpret life's events, paśum - animal

"Other than yourself, with whom should I enjoy? The others certainly have no idea of sexual pleasure. They are inexperienced with no insight about what to expect for the afterlife. Like an animal, they cannot interpret life's events. (4.25.38)

Detail

A particular woman with specific domestic and administrative skills chanced to meet the lone wanderer, the one known as Purañjan, the City Person. As far as they were concerned, it so happened by sheer luck. However, it may be argued that it was predestined as part of the layout of time.

Correspondingly, a specific coreSelf meets and becomes irresistibly unified with a specific intellect, such that both features seem perfectly suited to the other. There are trillions of cores and more than sufficient intellects which are slated to live in individual psyches. Does this happen by chance? Is this produced by a deity, an unseen, undetected super personality?

The lovely woman seemed to be on the same footing as a personality, capable of relational coordination with Purañjan.

It begs the question as to if the intellect is on the same footing as the core. Previously we discussed that the intellect felt incomplete due to not having a male partner, but all the same the core felt insufficient without the intellect. How does the two factors compare?

The queen addressed Purañjan. She said, 'Other than yourself, with whom should I enjoy?' She ridiculed other male beings as inferior in reference to the newfound hero. She declared that other men have no idea of sexual pleasure.

The males in her retinue did not have the capacity for sexual intercourse. They could not relate to her intimately by sexual penetration. They lacked certain organs and the corresponding abilities. They did not think about an afterlife. Thus, they could not prepare for being shifted from physical existence. They were like animals which cannot interpret events to anticipate the future.

This clarifies that the intellect rates the coreSelf and the adjuncts. It determines that the adjuncts are inferior to the core, mainly because the core can utilize conclusions to determine actions, which may benefit it hereafter.

As in life, we experience that some persons have qualities and skills which others lack. The core and its adjuncts have particular displays which differentiate one from the other.

धर्मो ह्य् अत्रार्थ-कामौ च प्रजानन्दो ऽमृतं यशः /
लोका विशोका विरजा यान् न केवलिनो विदुः (४॥२५॥३९)

dharmo hy atrārtha-kāmau
ca prajānando 'mṛtaṃ yaśaḥ /
lokā viśokā virajā yān
na kevalino viduḥ (4.25.39)

dharmo = dharmaḥ = righteous behavior, hy = hi = certainly, atrārtha= atra (here) + artha (sufficient livelihood), kāmau – striving for desire, ca – and, prajānando = prajānandaḥ = pleasure of reproducing children, 'mṛtaṃ = amṛtaṃ = heavenly happiness, yaśaḥ - fame, lokā = lokāḥ = realms, viśokā = viśokāḥ = without regret, virajā – without disease, yān – which, na – not, kevalino = kevalinaḥ = lone yogis, viduḥ - know

"It consists of righteous behavior, for certain, along with sufficient livelihood, striving for desire and getting pleasure by reproducing children. It yields heavenly happiness, fame, and transfer to the realms in which one experiences neither regret nor disease. Except that lone yogis can never understand this. (4.25.39)

Detail

The young woman spoke about those who lived with no understanding about the life hereafter. She presented herself as being informed about the ways and means of physical existence, such that by certain behavior, a person could live the life on earth in happiness, and then transit when the body dies, and shift to even more happiness as a result of selected behaviors.

She earmarked righteous conduct, sufficient livelihood, striving for desire, and getting pleasure by reproducing children. To her view this was the ticket to heaven, when by time's unfavorable swipe, one is deprived of physical existence.

This is interesting because this same youthful woman stated previously that she had no idea of the origins. She could not identify who build the Excitement City.

Why does she know about reproducing children but have no idea about how she was produced. Who told her that certain physical behavior would yield heavenly happiness, fame, and transfer to the realms in which one experiences neither regret nor disease? She declared that lone yogis who pry into the psychic underbasis of this world, can never understand this?

The technical aspect of this is that the intellect has preconceived notions which are inconsistent with reality. If the core relies solely on the intellect, if that core does not inspect and rate the verdicts derived, it will find itself with liability for faulty actions.

What is defined as righteous behavior by intellect, may not be rated as such by Nature. Having sufficient livelihood may be undermined by how the person acquired it. Striving for desire may prove to be harmful, if the means of fulfillment causes others to be imperiled. Getting pleasure by reproducing children has its inherent fault which is addiction to sexual indulgence.

Can the intellect determine the correct methods for attainment of the worlds which have no regret nor disease? Does the coreSelf lack insight, such that it is reliant on the intellect for every conclusion?

The young woman was of the view that lone yogis cannot understand the means of success, which would result in attainment of the highest of the heavens hereafter. Any confidence Purañjan had about the superiority of yogis was uprooted by the woman.

पितृ-देवर्षि-मर्त्यानां भूतानाम् आत्मनश् च ह /
क्षेम्यं वदन्ति शरणं भवे ऽस्मिन् यद् गृहाश्रमः (४॥२५॥४०)

pitṛ-devarṣi-martyānāṃ
bhūtānām ātmanaś ca ha /
kṣemyaṃ vadanti śaraṇaṃ
bhave 'smin yad gṛhāśramaḥ (4.25.40)

pitṛ - departed ancestors, deva – supernatural rulers, ṛṣi – accomplished domestic yogis, martyānāṃ - of humans, bhūtānām – of the living beings, ātmanaś = ātmanaḥ - of the self, ca – and, ha – for sure, kṣemyaṃ - beneficial, vadanti – they assert, śaraṇaṃ - shelter, accomdation, bhave – in the being, 'smin = asmin = this, yad = yat = this, gṛhāśramaḥ - parenting life

"Departed ancestors, supernatural rulers, accomplished domestic yogis, even humans and living beings in general, and even the self, assert the benefit and accommodation provided by the parenting lifestyle. (4.25.40)

Detail

Even though Nārad was a lone yogi of the highest order, even though the queen uprooted the reputation of yogis, Nārad gave her opinion with no alteration.

For the coreSelf, that was the opinion of the intellect. Despite its usefulness, regardless of it being indispensable, still the intellect draws some wrong conclusions and impresses itself upon the core. This causes the core to be responsible for errors made in consenting to actions which are detrimental to the self.

From the onset, Purañjan fell under the influence, to such an extent, that he could not determine when the intellect indulged in unjustified conclusions, which were faulty and speculative.

As the adventurer needed a capable woman and municipality, so the coreSelf needed an intellect and a psyche. But that did not mean that the adventurer should give itself over and not use its discrimination.

The young lady declared that departed ancestors, supernatural rulers, accomplished domestic yogis, even humans and living beings in general, even the self, asserted the benefit provided by the parenting lifestyle. That was true but the implication is a distortion which was designed to steer Purañjan from realizing that the value of the queen was limited.

Something may have worth, and still not be useful in all circumstances. When the accounting is done, it will be that the adventurer would be liable for the actions of the psyche. Hence, he should check every suggestion of the queen.

Should Purañjan trust the lovely woman? Yes, he should. Otherwise, how will there be harmony in the household. Trust should be expressed but a reservation about decisions should be present. That will cause the adventurer to intercept any questionable conclusions, which were derived from false information, rendered by the queen's assistants, or by her security officer, the snake.

The lady never told Purañjan that if he did not trust her in every instance, she would reject him. To the contrary without his demanding it, she committed herself and her staff to accommodating him.

The coreSelf should accept the services of the intellect, but it should apply discrimination, and should always remember that it, the core, carries the full liability. Even though it was her city, her attendants, her serpent protector, still, once he accepted the conditions of the relationship, he was the liable factor.

As for the parenting lifestyle, nearly every human being, and even people who only register on a psychic level, appreciate and are grateful for it. Where would any human be, if that person was not nurtured in infancy. Dead people whose brilliant or ghostly forms are on the astral planes, wish for new parents.

Even the supernatural rulers, and some domestic yogis, even the self, assert the benefit and accommodation provided by caring parents.

Still, family life is subjected to criticism because when serviced with undue attachment, it causes unwanted inconvenience. The queen did not understand this. Her instinct was to ridicule celibate anti-social yogis. She appreciated the domestic yogis who even though they were aware of the danger of undue interest in family life, remain involved in it.

The queen was of the opinion that there was no need to cultivate and apply detachment at any stage of life. She felt that one would get to heaven hereafter by remaining attentive to family concerns.

These conclusions, were flawed. Purañjan did not consider this. He was too happy to have the wonderful woman who had the accommodations he dreamt of. He was not concerned to consider the limits of time, which would undermine the security she shared with him. Time does sponsor. The same time deteriorates.

The queen could service Purañjan but for how long? He was an idealist. The queen herself was one as well. They were prone to disappointment.

When one considers this in terms of the psyche, there is the coreSelf with the intellect and its assistants. If the core does not instruct, monitor, and control them, there will be problems for which the core will be liable.

Purañjan was a great person, an adventurer. He travelled everywhere on earth until at last he reached the southern Himalayan mountains. The queen, the love of his life whom he happened to meet, was a special person. She was beautiful. She had an entourage of servants and a security official. And still, neither Purañjan, nor that queen, created this world.

In fact, as the queen admitted, she had no idea of how she came into existence. Purañjan also, could not declare his pedigree. If anything, he was a wanderer who needed a family and kingdom.

Either should have concluded that things may be upset in the future. They should have researched the origins. Instead, their interest was immediate. They had no interest in preparing for the future when the duration of one-hundred years would expire.

का नाम वीर विख्यातं वदान्यं प्रिय-दर्शनम् /
न वृणीत प्रियं प्राप्तं मादृशी त्वादृशं पतिम् (४॥२५॥४१)

kā nāma vīra vikhyātaṃ
vadānyaṃ priya-darśanam /
na vṛṇīta priyaṃ prāptaṃ
mādṛśī tvādṛśaṃ patim (4.25.41)

kā – who, nāma – in name, vīra – great man, vikhyātaṃ - famous, vadānyaṃ - generous, priya-darśanam = pleasing to see, na – no, vṛṇīta – accept, priyaṃ - pleasing, dear, prāptaṃ - acquired, mādṛśī – like me, tvādṛśaṃ - like you, patim – male partner

"O great man, who, like me, will not accept a male partner like you, someone who is charismatic, generous, and pleasing to see? (4.25.41)

Detail

The adventurous man found the beautiful woman who was wealthy. In turn the beauty, a queen by class, found a handsome adventurous man.

The lady accepted the proposition of the wanderer. She stated that a woman would be a fool not to accept his proposal. He was charismatic, generous, and pleasing to see.

The intellect, though not rated as a person in full, has a sense of selfhood nevertheless. It estimated that the coreSelf was the perfect match. The core was alone with no visible escort, no sovereignty, no attendants, and no security. The only thing the core had was itself which included desire energies. The core needed accommodation, sexual company, servants, and protection.

कस्या मनस् ते भुवि भोगि-भोगयोः
स्त्रिया न सज्जेद् भुजयोर् महा-भुज /
यो ऽनाथ-वर्गाधिम् अलं घृणोद्धत-
स्मितावलोकेन चरत्य् अपोहितुम् (४॥२५॥४२)

kasyā manas te bhuvi bhogi-bhogayoḥ
striyā na sajjed bhujayor mahā-bhuja /
yo 'nātha-vargādhim alaṃ ghṛṇoddhata-
smitāvalokena caraty apohitum (4.25.42)

kasyā – whose, manas – mind, te – you, bhuvi – here, bhogi - (having curves), bhogayoḥ - body like snake, striyā = striyāḥ = of woman, na – not, sajjed = sajjet = becomes, bhujayor = bhujayoḥ by the arms, mahā-bhuja = great muscular person, yo = yaḥ = who, 'nātha = anātha = without protection, vargādhim = vargā (set of) + adhim (no security), alaṃ - enough, ghṛṇoddhata = ghṛṇā (compassion) + uddhata (impulsive, motivated), smitāvalokena = smita (smile) + avalokena (by smiling), caraty = carati = travel, apohitum – to remove

"Here in this place, whose mind would not be attracted to your curvaceous body which is like that of a snake? O muscular person, with your smiling appearance, you are motivated with compassion. It is sufficient to provide protection and remove a woman's insecurity. You travelled here for that only." (4.25.42)

Detail

The woman did not attribute the adventurer as being motivated by discrimination. She recognized his compassionate nature instead. Without discrimination how was Purañjan to rate her suggestions. This flaw of the adventurer would prove to be his undoing.

He did not take into account that regardless of what the queen suggested, he was responsible for her behavior.

Even though there was no evidence that the adventurer could provide security, except for his looks, still the queen was so infatuated, and anxious to be officially partnered with him, that she imagined he would provide adequate protection.

It was however the snake which protected. She took the snake for granted. She over-rated the wandering hero.

To the intellect, the coreSelf is all-attractive and all-capable. But the fact is that the core was less than the rating it was given by the intellect.

Perceptually, the intellect saw the core as having an attractive curvaceous body? The intellect declared that the core was a muscular person, with a smiling appearance, who was motivated by compassion. Feeling secure in its presence, the intellect rated the core as giving sufficient protection which would remove a woman's insecurity. The intellect thought that the core was the perfect compliment.

नारद उवाच
इति तौ दम्-पती तत्र समुद्य समयं मिथः /
तां प्रविश्य पुरीं राजन् मुमुदाते शतं समाः (४॥२५॥४३)

nārada uvāca
iti tau dam-patī tatra
samudya samayaṃ mithaḥ /
tāṃ praviśya purīṃ rājan
mumudāte śataṃ samāḥ (4.25.43)

nārada - Nārada, uvāca – said, iti – it was natural, tau – they, dam-patī = female and male partners, tatra – there, samudya – same enthusiasm, samayaṃ - commited to each other, mithaḥ- mutual, tāṃ - that, praviśya – entering, purīṃ - city, rājan – O King, mumudāte – they enjoyed, śataṃ - one hundred, samāḥ - years

Nārada said.
It was natural that with equal eagerness, the female and male partners were committed to each other. Thus, they entered the city, O King. They enjoyed together for one hundred years. (4.25.43)

Detail

The meeting and union of the adventurer and the queen, was predestined. How long ago did the earth begin? Who or what created it?

Certainly, the queen had no idea. Purañjan was ignorant as well. He never named his parents. He never said that he was a god from another domain.

Despite their ignorance and lack of interest in prying for origins, they had equal eagerness and were mutually committed. Having met outside the walls of Excitement City, they entered and enjoyed whatever they could for one hundred years.

One's curiosity is kindled, to know what happened in the meantime. Where did they go? What did they do?

Correspondingly, the intellect and the coreSelf entered the psyche which was represented as Excitement City. When the queen entered, she did so with her security officer, the lifeForce, and with her sensual procurements and memory. In the end, after one hundred years, were these expelled from the place?

What was the relationship between the coreSelf and the kundalini Power Central which was represented as a snake in the story?

Even at this point, this far into the tale of Purañjan, King Barhi has no idea that his life is parodied. His was a mirror image of the incidences. Running parallel is the internal situation of the psyche of King Barhi or of any other person who uses a physical body.

उपगीयमानो ललितं तत्र तत्र च गायकैः /
क्रीडन् परिवृतः स्त्रीभिर् ह्रदिनीम् आविशच् छुचौ (४॥२५॥४४)

upagīyamāno lalitaṃ
tatra tatra ca gāyakaiḥ /
krīḍan parivṛtaḥ strībhir
hradinīm āviśac chucau (4.25.44)

upagīyamāno = upagīyamānaḥ = mentioned positively, lalitaṃ - nicely, tatra tatra = here and there, ca – and, gāyakaiḥ - by singers, krīḍan – enjoying playfully, parivṛtaḥ - surrounded, strībhir = strībhiḥ = by women, hradinīm – in a river, āviśac = āviśat = entered, chucau = śucau = uncomfortable

Here and there, that king was mentioned positively by professional singers. Enjoying playfully and being surrounded by women he entered a river when the weather was uncomfortable. (4.25.44)

Detail

Besides enjoying oneself with agreeable people like a beautiful or handsome spouse, while being served and being protected, there was no work for Purañjan to do.

He enjoyed and made himself available for royal privileges. The coreSelf feels that it should be entertained. It should have an intellect which can display, discriminate, plan, remember and illustrate events and desires.

Here and there, the core was attended by the accessory powers of the intellect. This was experienced by intellect as a soothing flow of energy from a particular sense, sense object or memory. The core enjoyed this. It was like when on a hot day, a king enters the cool water of a river. He may, with some women, enjoy playfully.

To stress the cooperation that the coreSelf received from its adjuncts, Nārad depicted the queen and her attendants as doting on, surrounding and readily responding, to the needs and moods of Purañjan. Whatever he could think of, was provided as per his wishes.

सप्तोपरि कृता द्वारः पुरस् तस्यास् तु द्वे अधः /
पृथग्-विषय-गत्य्-र्थं तस्यां यः कश्चनेश्वरः (४॥२५॥४५)

saptopari kṛtā dvāraḥ
puras tasyās tu dve adhaḥ /
pṛthag-viṣaya-gaty-artham
tasyāṃ yaḥ kaścaneśvaraḥ (4.25.45)

saptopari = sapta (seven) + upari (up), kṛtā – made, dvāraḥ - gate, puras = puraḥ = of the city, tasyās = tasyāḥ= that, tu – but, dve – two, adhaḥ - down, pṛthag-= pṛthak = different, viṣaya – facilities, gaty-arthaṃ = purpose of getting, tasyāṃ - that, yaḥ - who, kaścaneśvaraḥ = kaścana (whoever) + Īśvaraḥ (mayor of the city)

The gates of the city were designed with seven on the upper storey. Two were at the lower level. Each give access to different facilities for that mayor of the city. (4.25.45)

Detail

Excitement City was created by someone but its architect was neither the queen nor the wandering adventurer. Whosoever made it, selected a prime territory. It was fortified with a wall which protected it from invasion. To allow access to its surroundings, there were nine gates which limited what could enter or depart.

The constructor took security into account when he/she/it planned the complex. It was all the more satisfying to Purañjan, the queen, her security officer, and staff.

In the evolutionary outlay of Nature, senses were designed according to the species, beginning with the uni-cellular systems, to the complex animal forms with millions of individual cells comprising glands, organs, tissues, muscles, and bones. The development of the human species is special and extraordinary.

Purañjan wandered everywhere until he reached the southern side of the Himalayas. There he found a special woman who owned a plush city. This is symbolic of the human body. Purañjan represented the coreSelf which seeks a suitable lifeform for its need to exploit environments.

With adjuncts, beginning with the intellect, the core can experience environments. It does so through the seven entrances of the five senses. However, since it has to reproduce, consume food and expel waste, it requires more than seven orifices.

The city was constructed with two lower gates, one for excreting urine and the other for evacuating solid waste. Of these two, the urine has an accessory line for sexual access. It is interesting that the designer of the human body, constructed the reproductive organ near to the urine expulsion tubing.

Since there were only two gates on the lower level, and there was a total of nine entrances, we should account for the remaining seven. Beginning at the highest area, we find two gates which are widely space but which are patterned to be equally spaced from the center of the face. These are the two eyes which give access through the sight sense. From these two gates, Purañjan looked out and consumed visually.

Lower than the eyes are the ears, through which Purañjan, the City Person, could access sounds from without and within the city.

Lower yet and facing forward with one to the left and one to the immediate right, were two nostrils, which gave access to odors. Below the nostrils was the mouth, through which the adventurer could consume food, cough, and express speech.

It should be noted that the wall of the city was continuous, surrounding everything. It did not allow enemies to penetrate easily. That is reminiscent of the skin which encloses the body. It is a waterproofed enclosure. It serves as an alarm to alert of anything which attempts to penetrate the body.

The opinion of Purañjan, was secretive. He did not relay it to anyone. He felt however that this situation was paramount for his sensual and mental satisfaction.

Purañjan felt that this place was appropriate for a great person. It did not matter who or what created the situation, whether Nature did it in the sequence of its eons-old development, or if it was a creatorGod who conceive of it, and whose powerful mind engineered it. What mattered was that the place was enjoyed to the fullest by the fated person, himself.

This signified a quality of the coreSelf which is that it rarely stops to consider if someone else created the world or itself. It should recognize that causal agency. Instead, a self is mostly involved in *me, me, me,* endlessly clutching objects.

पञ्च द्वारस् तु पौरस्त्या दक्षिणैका तथोत्तरा /
पश्चिमे द्वे अमूषां ते नामानि नृप वर्णये (४॥२५॥४६)

pañca dvāras tu paurastyā
dakṣiṇaikā tathottarā /

paścime dve amūṣāṃ te
nāmāni nṛpa varṇaye (4.25.46)

pañca – five, dvāras – gates, tu – but, paurastyā – front side, dakṣiṇaikā = dakṣiṇā (right side) + ekā (one), tathottarā = tathā (also) + uttarā (to the left), paścime – back side, dve – two, amūṣāṃ - of them, te – to you, nāmāni – names concerning, nṛpa – O King, varṇaye – I will tell

But five gates were to the front. To the right there was another, as well as one to the left and also two to the rear area. To you I will tell the names of the entrances, O King. (4.25.46)

Detail

Whosoever or whatever created Excitement City, designed it efficiently, and after much experience in biological construction. This is due to the fact, that it takes millions of years for Nature to produce the first human body, something that is so complicated, that many trial-and-error experiments were conducted by Nature, in its creation of rudimentary forms, to more complex biological apparatus, in a step-by-step process.

The skin of a body is the main wall which surrounds it. That surface has hairs for touch sensitivity. The importance of touch is that in this environment, a lifeform should sense when it is contacted by any other surface. In this environment, there is a principle of eating other lifeforms. This implies that a form must be equipped with sensitivity, so that if it is sensed by another body, it can relocate before that other species procures it as a meal.

An enclosure like the skin should have controlled entrances. As Purañjan was told by Nārad, the Excitement City had nine entrances. Besides that, there was no entry to the place. Each entrance was equipped with sensors.

Any threat to the inhabitants could be detect and blocked from entering. Seven of the nine gates were to the front. These consist of two eyes, two nostrils, one mouth and two ears.

The senses use various entrances. Of these the two nostrils were always open. Their sensors are odor alarms. Their procurement is air which is the main diet of the kundalini lifeForce Power Central. The nostrils inhaled fresh air which is the main fuel for the lifeForce. They exhaled used air which was a pollutant in the body.

The two eyes procured colors. This was used for enjoyment and for determining the format of threats to the body. Many of these threats were other lifeforms which considered the human form to be edible.

When a color was contrasted with some other hue, the eyes sent information to the intellect, which determines if that object is desirable. The coreSelf regard the eyes as its windows into the external environment. When the intellect determines that a color is undesirable, it alerts the lifeForce, and suggests a conclusion to the coreSelf. This results in a command to cease the effort to contact the unwanted object.

Of the seven gates to the front, the lowest is the mouth. This organ has unique functions. It supplements the nostrils on occasion. This happens when the nostrils are blocked or when for some reason, the breathing system is impeded. Then the mouth draws fresh air and expels stale air, just as the nostrils do.

The standard functions of the mouth are to eat and speak. Food is part of the energization force. It is second only to air in that respect. The mouth however has lips which function like a double door. In design, the lower door moves up or down.

As Nature would have it, the energy ingestion engine uses two sections, one for burning air fuel, the other for processing food. Both are important but the air fuel mechanism is the lungs which are more vital than the other, which is the stomach-intestines-colon complex.

There are sensors in the nostrils such that if an offensive gas is detected, the olfactory nerves send signals which cause the body to move to a safe area. In the mouth there are taste and temperature sensors which issue alerts about the condition of food.

Besides the five gates on the front of the face, there are two gates which are on each side of the face. These are the ears. Their specialty is hearing. They procure sounds and send conclusions to the intellect, which analyzes and then relays information to the core, which gives permission for an evasive or supportive action.

खद्योताविर्मुखी च प्राग् द्वाराव् एकत्र निर्मिते /
विभ्राजितं जनपदं याति ताभ्यां द्युमत्-सखः (४॥२५॥४७)

khadyotāvirmukhī ca prāg
dvārāv ekatra nirmite /
vibhrājitaṃ janapadaṃ yāti
tābhyāṃ dyumat-sakhaḥ (4.25.47)

khadyotāvirmukhī = khadyotā (glow-worm) + āvirmukhī (peep hole), ca – and, prāg = prāk = to the front, dvārāv = dvārāu = two gates, ekatra – in one structure, nirmite – were placed, vibhrājitaṃ - captured forms, janapadaṃ - suburbs, yāti – went, tābhyāṃ - by them, dyumat – vision, sakhaḥ - friend

Glow-Worm (Khadyotā) and Peep-Hole (Āvirmukhī) were the two gates in one structure on the front side. Through these the King went to the city of Captured Forms (Vibhrājitaṃ) with his friend named Vision (Dyumat). (4.25.47)

Detail

Two special gates of the city which were in the upper part, were the ones used to reveal color. Purañjan went through those exits to visit the city of Captured Forms. He took an assistant, a friend named Vision.

By himself, the adventurer was blind but when he was accompanied by Vision, he saw colors and forms.

For the coreSelf, vision was experienced as attention only. But if the attention was allied with the vision sense, the coreSelf visualized colors and saw forms.

Roaming about the earth previously, Purañjan lacked a means of seeing physical things. As soon as he made an agreement to stay with the queen, who acted as his intellect, he enlisted the services of Vision and could enjoy the city of Captured Forms (*Vibhrājitaṃ*).

नलिनी नालिनी च प्राग् द्वाराव् एकत्र निर्मिते /
अवधूत-सखस् ताभ्यां विषयं याति सौरभम् (४॥२५॥४८)

nalinī nālinī ca prāg
dvārāv ekatra nirmite /

avadhūta-sakhas tābhyāṃ
viṣayaṃ yāti saurabham (4.25.48)

nalinī – right nostril, nālinī – left nostril, ca – and, prāg = prāk = front, dvārāv = dvārāu = two gates, ekatra – in one structure, nirmite – located, avadhūta – smell urge, sakhas – friend, tābhyāṃ - by two, viṣayaṃ - enjoyment place, yāti – went through, saurabham - suburb of fragrance

Right-Nostril (Nalinī) and Left-Nostril (Nālinī) were two gates to the front. These were located in the same structure. With his friend, named Smell-Urge (Avadhūta), he went through the gates to enjoy in Fragrance City (Saurabha). (4.25.48)

Detail

Before he met the queen of Excitement City, Purañjan was terribly handicapped. He lacked a luxurious territory. He lacked assistants and a security agent. The queen was endowed with that staff, which she shared with him, once they were committed.

Right-Nostril and Left-Nostril afforded two important services which were acquirement of continuous air supply and detection of odor. The main assistor was a person called Smell-Urge. This one continually procured air. He was known as Avadhūta, the lone checker. This person worked to keep the lifeForce fueled continuously. This service was so important that if Purañjan was deprived of it, the city would collapse immediately.

Sometimes, to find desirable odors in Fragrance City, Purañjan enlisted the services of Smell-Urge.

मुख्या नाम पुरस्ताद् द्वास् तयापण-बहूदनौ /
विषयौ याति पुर-राड् रसज्ञ-विपणान्वितः (४॥२५॥४९)

mukhyā nāma purastād
dvās tayāpaṇa-bahūdanau /
viṣayau yāti pura-rāḍ
rasajña-vipaṇānvitaḥ (4.25.49)

mukhyā – Prominence, nāma – called, purastād = purastāt = to the front, dvās -= dvāḥ = gate, tayāpaṇa = - tayā (by that) + āpaṇa (Consuming), bahūdanau = Food Variety, viṣayau – two senses, yāti – went, pura-rāḍ = king of the city, rasajña- Taste-Knowler, vipaṇānvitaḥ = vipaṇa (Vocal Chord) + anvitaḥ (with)

Through Prominence (Mukhyā), a front entrance, he went to Consuming Food Variety (Āpaṇa Bahūdana). His companions for this, were Taste Knower (Rasajña) and Vocal Cord (Vipaṇa). (4.25.49)

Detail

The official public entrance through which many physical things passed into the body, and through which many expressions were issued, was a gate called Prominence. This was the mouth of the city. Purañjan went through that gate with his friends Taste Knower and Vocal Cord. They went to a suburb known as Consuming Food Variety (*Āpaṇa Bahūdana*).

Purañjan had no taste if he travelled without those friends. He could neither eat nor speak if they were absent.

The coreSelf must take assistance from the intellect, the sensual energies, the kundalini lifeForce and the memories. However, this assistance is direct only for the intellect. The lifeForce is supervised by the intellect but if that force overpowers the intellect, it gains control of the psyche for a time.

The sensual energies are part of the lifeForce Power Central psychic apparatus. Thus, the intellect finds it a challenge to control the senses and to direct them.

The two companions Taste Knower (Rasajña) and Vocal Chord (Vipaṇa) are ruthless operators. Their actions are subtle and specific. When Taste Knower (Rasajña) wants to possess a certain food, it will command the lifeForce to acquire that substance. If the intellect presents evidence from memory or from its observation, that a commodity will result in painful feelings, the Taste Knower may undermine the resistance of the intellect.

The Vocal Chord (Vipaṇa) is a reckless operator which in conjunction with the tongue may produce sounds which may be harmful either to the body or to someone else.

Purañjan has a task to monitor the queen and her assistants. The security official is the one indispensable member of the queen's staff. Purañjan is challenged to maintain an informed relationship with the creature.

पितृहूर् नृप पुर्या द्वार् दक्षिणेन पुरञ्जनः /
राष्ट्रं दक्षिण-पञ्चालं याति श्रुतधरान्वितः (४॥२५॥५०)

pitṛhūr nṛpa puryā dvār
dakṣiṇena purañjanaḥ /
rāṣṭraṃ dakṣiṇa-pañcālaṃ
yāti śrutadharānvitaḥ (4.25.50)

pitṛhūr – called Ancestral Ritual, nṛpa – O King Barhi, puryā – of the city, dvār – gate, dakṣiṇena – rear, purañjanaḥ - City Person, rāṣṭraṃ - country, dakṣiṇa – right side, pañcālaṃ - religious ritual, yāti – went. śrutadharānvitaḥ = śrutadhara (named Hearing Container) + anvitaḥ (escorted by)

O King Barhi, Ancestral Ritual (Pitṛhū) was a gate on the right side. Through it, Purañjana went to the country known as Religious Text (Pañcālaṃ). He was escorted there by his friend named Hearing Container (Śrutadhara). (4.25.50)

Detail

Even though Purañjan had no relatives, still the tendency for attending his ancestors was active. The beautiful and capable lady openly declared that her parents were unknown. She was unfamiliar with any relatives of her staff. Still, her employees functioned as if they were related to her.

To listen to scriptural statements about the status of deceased people, the coreSelf makes exits and entrances through the right ear. Purañjan could not do this alone. He was escorted by the Hearing Container (Śrutadhara), the right ear, whose main focus was Ancestral Ritual (Pitṛhū).

Like Purañjan who was dependent on the young lady and her staff, when the coreSelf could not access the services of the intellect and senses, it is like a handicapped person.

देवहूर् नाम पुर्या द्वा उत्तरेण पुरञ्जनः /
राष्ट्रम् उत्तर-पञ्चालं याति श्रुतधरान्वितः (४॥२५॥५१)

devahūr nāma puryā dvā
uttareṇa purañjanaḥ /
rāṣṭram uttara-pañcālaṃ
yāti śrutadharānvitaḥ (4.25.51)

devahūr = devahūḥ = Deity Ritual, nāma – was named, puryā – of the city, dvā = dvāḥ = gate, uttareṇa – on the left side, purañjanaḥ - City Person, rāṣṭram – district, Uttara – higher, pañcālaṃ - name Religious Text. yāti – went, śrutadharānvitaḥ = śrutadhara (named Hearing Container) + anvitaḥ (escorted by)

Deity Ritual (Devahū) was on the left side. Through it, Purañjana went to the district known as Higher Religious Text (Uttara Pañcālaṃ). He was escorted there by his friend named Hearing Container (Śrutadhara). (4.25.51)

Detail

Hearing Container (Śrutadhara) operated through two gates, one on the left which specialized in ancestral affairs here and hereafter, and one on the right which was concerned with Deity Ritual (Devahū). These were two distinct accounting methods which credited ritual and factual actions, either to benefit ancestors and their current family members, or to benefit the individual self by causing promotion to higher environments hereafter.

Purañjan was dependent on Hearing Container (Śrutadhara) for accessing higher religion. These literatures were aural or literal.

This means that the coreSelf lacks realization about its situation hereafter. It could however get information from scriptures. Of special interest was the information which the left ear acquired. That concerned Deity Ritual (Devahū), and the map about the higher worlds where deities exist.

आसुरी नाम पश्चाद् द्वास् तया याति पुरञ्जनः /
ग्रामकं नाम विषयं दुर्मदेन समन्वितः (४॥२५॥५२)

āsurī nāma paścād dvās s
tayā yāti purañjanaḥ /
grāmakaṃ nāma viṣayaṃ
durmadena samanvitaḥ (4.25.52)

āsurī – Depraved Organ, nāma – known as, paścād = paścād = basement, dvās – gate, tayā – by which, yāti – went, purañjanaḥ - City Person, grāmakaṃ - Complex Pleasure, nāma – so named, viṣayaṃ - sensual energies, durmadena – by being Sexually Depraved, samanvitaḥ - along with

In the basement was a gate known as Depraved Organ (Āsurī). Through it, the City Person went to the district of Complex Pleasure (Grāmaka). He was accompanied by Sexually Depraved (Durmadena) and the Sensual Energies (Viṣaya). (4.25.52)

Detail

In the lowest part of the city, there was a special gateway. It was known as Depraved Organ (Āsurī). This was the genitals. In the female body, this is designed in one way. In the male forms, it is designed in another. The biological technology of Nature is such that in the males, the spigot is used both for urination and semen expulsion. This is convenient in one way and detrimental in another.

If the male contracts a disease in the sexual apparatus, it spreads to the urinary system because of the common tubing. In the females the tubing for urination is different to the one for sexual expression.

One can surmise that Nature and/or God produced these complex mechanisms, not just as physical machinery, but as psychic apparatus as well.

Purañjan for his part, and the beautiful well-served and accommodating queen, had no idea about the construction and complication of either themselves nor the Excitement City. If one does not understand the construction and intending purpose of a tool, how will one use it efficiently?

In the lowest part of the body, there is an opening known as the sexual organ. Through it, the coreSelf goes to the district of Complex Pleasure (Grāmaka). However, the self cannot utilize this place unless it is attentive to the sexual organ and the sensual energies which electrify the area.

From this we get the understanding that, just as Purañjan was dependent on the beautiful queen, the coreSelf is reliant on its intellect. That core had only its adventurous profile to offer. It came to the city with nothing, not even one single companion, except for an invisible person named Not-Recognized (Avijñāta). Even though escorted by this friend, Purañjan took no advice from him. Instead, Purañjan found the beautiful facilitating young woman.

It should be noted that Purañjan did not see his original friend Not-Recognized (Avijñāta). This begins an inquiry into why Purañjan could not recognize this person. Was this friend too subtle to be perceived?

निर्ऋतिर् नाम पश्चाद् द्वास् तया याति पुरञ्जनः /
वैशसं नाम विषयं लुब्धकेन समन्वितः (४॥२५॥५३)

nirṛtir nāma paścād dvās
tayā yāti purañjanaḥ /
vaiśasaṃ nāma viṣayaṃ
lubdhakena samanvitaḥ (4.25.53)

nirṛtir – Anus, nāma – so named, paścād = paścāt = in the basement, dvās = dvāḥ = gate, tayā – by which, yāti – went, purañjanaḥ - City Person, vaiśasaṃ = Death Locale, nāma –

so called, viṣayaṃ - sensual energies, lubdhakena - by Excretion, samanvitaḥ- along with

In the basement, there is another gate known as Putrefaction (Nirṛti). Through it, Purañjana went to the country known as Decay (Vaiśasa). He was accompanied by Excretory Function (Lubdhaka) and Evacuation Power (Viṣaya). (4.25.53)

Detail

There was a second gate in the basement of city. That was Putrefaction (Nirṛti). It is known otherwise as the anus of the enclosure which is the physical body. This is a very important gate but it is abhorred. This gate is concerned with excretion of waste matter which was not consumed in the intestinal track. People resent this opening because of its foul odor and unwanted excretions.

Whatever comes to this gate from within the body is in a state of decay. This is a foul gate. However, if this gate malfunctions, it must be fixed immediately, otherwise it ruins the body with the threat of death.

In one sense this is the best gate in the body, in that if it functions properly, one may assume that the body is healthy.

Once the coreSelf realized itself with a physical form, which is a skin-enclosed something, which is regarded as a person, that core is in an alliance with adjuncts. The main one is the intellect, which Nārad presented as a well-staffed and well-equipped queen.

The astonishing detail is that while it wandered over the earth, at least until it chanced to meet the intellect, the core felt incomplete. It was irresistibly attracted to this beautiful capable appliance which was skilled in domestic affairs and managed sensual interplay. The core was irresistibly attracted to it.

The intellect too, for its part, was attracted to the core. Both were thrilled to encounter the other. Both felt that their meeting was fated. Both had intuition which indicated that they were complimentary.

अन्धाव् अमीषां पौराणां निर्वाक्-पेशस्कृताव् उभौ /
अक्षण्वताम् अधिपतिस् ताभ्यां याति करोति च (४॥२५॥५४)

andhāv amīṣāṃ paurāṇāṃ
nirvāk-peśaskṛtāv ubhau /
akṣaṇvatām adhipatis
tābhyāṃ yāti karoti ca (4.25.54)

andhāv = andhāu = two blind persons, amīṣāṃ - among them, paurāṇāṃ - of people, nirvāk – speechless, peśaskṛtāv = peśaskṛtāu = accomplished, ubhau – both, akṣaṇvatām – of those with eyes, adhipatis – leader, tābhyāṃ - with them, yāti – travelled, karoti – he went, ca - and

Of those people, there were two blind persons named Speechless (Nirvāk) and Accomplished (Peśaskṛtāu). Though being the leader of people with sight, Purañjana travelled with the help of those blind fellows. (4.25.54)

Detail

Of the assistants of the queen, there were two blind persons, namely the limbs and the hands. These were for mobility and activity, but they could not see directly. They took information from the eyes, ears, nose, mouth, and sense of touch. Because they afforded movement, Purañjan appreciated these attendants.

स यर्ह्य् अन्तःपुर-गतो विषूचीन-समन्वितः /
मोहं प्रसादं हर्षं वा याति जायात्मजोद्भवम् (४॥२५॥५५)

sa yarhy antaḥpura-gato
viṣūcīna-samanvitaḥ /
mohaṃ prasādaṃ harṣaṃ
vā yāti jāyātmajodbhavam (4.25.55)

sa = saḥ = he, yarhy = yarhi = however, antaḥpura – bedroom, gato = gataḥ = would go, viṣūcīna – dispersing, samanvitaḥ - accompanying, mohaṃ - bewildering, prasādaṃ - satisfaction, harṣaṃ - happiness, vā – or, yāti – went, jāyātmajodbhavam = jāyā (wife) + ātmaja (children of self) + udbhavam (produced by them)

However, he would go to his bedroom with someone named Dispersing (Viṣūcīna). There bewilderment, satisfaction and happiness were produced from his wife and children. (4.25.55)

Detail

When all is said and done, when the body is tired, and the mind exerted itself enough, someone must retire for the day. Purañjan had a routine. After being served, he went to his bedroom to retire from social activities.

He did so with his mind, which is denoted by a dispersing quality, (Viṣūcīna). On some days, he assumed a state of bewilderment. Sometimes, he felt satisfied. At other times, he was extremely happy.

The concerns of the queen's staff were tended by the serpent who provided the security for the city. Still, Purañjan took it to himself to tend the queen and their children. In this way his immediate family got his attention.

It does happen that the coreSelf consults the mind and puts it to order just before the physical body rests. This consultation may cause bewilderment, satisfaction, or happiness. It may be that each mood is present simultaneously and in different combinations.

एवं कर्मसु संसक्तः कामात्मा वञ्चितोऽबुधः /
महिषी यद् यद् ईहेत तत् तद् एवान्ववर्तत (४॥२५॥५६)

evaṃ karmasu saṃsaktaḥ
kāmātmā vañcito 'budhaḥ /
mahiṣī yad yad īheta
tat tad evānvavartata (4.25.56)

evaṃ - thus, karmasu – in cultural activity, saṃsaktaḥ - completely involved, kāmātmā – self-absorbed for sexual love, vañcito = vañcitaḥ = deceived, 'budhaḥ = abudhaḥ = not intelligent, mahiṣī = Mistress, yad yad = yat yat = whatever, īheta – desire, tat tad = all that, evānvavartata = eva (as is) + anvavartata (he fulfilled)

Thus, Purañjana was completely involved, being deceived and being self-absorbed for sexual love, such that whatever his Mistress desired, all of it, he fulfilled. (4.25.56)

Detail

The relationship between the adventurer and the queen was as tight as could possibly be. It seemed that the hero gave more of his attention and love than he received collectively from the Mistress and her staff.

Purañjana was so in need of the beautiful capable woman, her staff, and facilities, that he indiscriminately gave himself over. He submitted to the social and environmental circumstance which he found in Excitement City.

One may recall that the security chief, the snake, was dedicated to the lady primarily, not to the staff, not to the city and certainly not to the man of her heart whom she met by chance.

This meant that the adventurer did not get every bit of information which related to the discrepancies in the city. For sure, the queen was informed by the snake, but being ignorant of the details, Purañjana could not participate in the security.

Being the mayor of the city, its governor, a person who depended on a woman for companionship, staff, and security, does not mean that one should be unaware of the affairs which transpired daily. Wanting to simply enjoy services, accept honors and be in a secured location, where one would not know what should be done to prevent a sad termination, is sure catastrophe.

Thus, a coreSelf which relies so heavily on the intellect and its accessories, is completely involved, being deceived. It was self-absorbed for sexual love, such that whatever the intellect desired, most of it was permitted. The core had neither the resistance nor the discrimination, to object to most of what the intellect hinted.

Caught in a web of emotional attraction, the core consented to whatever the intellect illustrated.

क्वचित् पिबन्त्यां पिबति मदिरां मद-विह्वलः /
अश्नन्त्यां क्वचिद् अश्नाति जक्षत्यां सह जक्षिति (४॥२५॥५७)

kvacit pibantyāṃ pibati
madirāṃ mada-vihvalaḥ /
aśnantyāṃ kvacid aśnāti
jakṣatyāṃ saha jakṣiti (4.25.57)

kvacit – on occasion, pibantyāṃ - while drinking, pibati – he indulged, madirāṃ - liquor, mada-vihvalaḥ = intoxicated, aśnantyāṃ - dining, kvacid = kvacit = then again, aśnāti – he ate, jakṣatyāṃ - chewing, saha – with her, jakṣiti – he chewed

On occasion while the Mistress drank liquor, he drank with her and became intoxicated. And again, when she dined, he ate with her. Just the same when she chewed anything, he chomped as well. (4.25.57)

Detail

It is amazing how the adventurer, a man who was enterprising by nature, toured the world except for a small area in the southern Himalayas. He was a world class traveler. Somehow, he got to that area where there was a posh place named Bhogavatī, the Excitement City.

Prior to that he did not submit to anyone. Suddenly without knowing even the background and ethnicity of a woman whom he met, he submitted entirely.

His lifestyle was adjusted to accommodate her schedule. When she drank liquor, he did the same. When she dined, he ate as well.

This means that the coreSelf makes adjustments to its preferences so that there is congruency between it and the intellect. At first, the core does not rate itself as being directive to the intellect. In fact, there is a curiosity which the core has about the intellect and the other adjuncts. This curiosity is a type of self-hypnosis which causes the core to be subordinate to those psychic accessories.

One may think that a great adventurer like Purañjan would be directive to a beautiful woman like the queen of the city. However, Purañjan never had a chance to take command. He wandered through the earth and came to Excitement City with nothing of his own, no property, no staff, nothing but his desire for a capable woman and luxurious accommodations.

The city of Bhogavatī Excitement Zone was not his property. It belonged to a woman who had a loyal security official, who protected the place from any possible abuse by anyone.

Purañjan could either keep wandering or he could submit conditionally to the woman. She was the queen. He could be king on the basis of an alliance with her. Only by her command, would the attendants serve him.

Considering that this story is a parallel version about the coreSelf and its adjuncts, one may realize, that because of its needs, the core is in an awkward position. Posting it as an infallible principle, does not clarify why the core became allied with an intellect and other assisting psychic operands.

A yogi has to investigate the alliance between his core and its adjuncts. Can the core ever rule the psyche? Can the core become independent where it does not require the services of the accessories?

क्वचिद् गायति गायन्त्यां रुदत्यां रुदति क्वचित् /
क्वचिद् धसन्त्यां हसति जल्पन्त्याम् अनु जल्पति (४॥२५॥५८)

kvacid gāyati gāyantyāṃ
rudatyāṃ rudati kvacit /
kvacid dhasantyāṃ hasati
jalpantyām anu jalpati (4.25.58)

kvacid – and then, gāyati – he sang, gāyantyāṃ - singing, rudatyāṃ - crying, rudati – he weeped, kvacit – sometimes, kvacid – and then, dhasantyāṃ = hasantyāṃ = laughing, hasati – he laughed, jalpantyām – speaking insensibly, anu – following her, jalpati – he spoke for speech's sake

When the Mistress sang, he sang. When she wept, he cried. When she laughed, he enjoyed. When she spoke insensibly, he, following her, did so as well. (4.25.58)

Detail

The adventurer stood alone in his travels over the earth, but when he met the queen of Excitement City, he lost his position as an observing tourist. He became a subordinate of the woman. As a shadow follows its object, as a pet animal follows it owner, so Purañjan helplessly mimicked the queen.

Since the protective power, the snake, secured the lady on all sides, she was conditioned by the reptile, such that what she did was in accordance with the suggestions of the snake. Hence indirectly, Purañjan became subordinate to the situations which were suggested and facilitated by the creature.

The meaning is that in the psyche, the kundalini lifeForce Power Central, compels each part of the body to act in a certain way. For their part, the intellect and the coreSelf mimic the fluctuations of the sensual apparatus. The majority of the actions and responses are involuntarily performed, with the core acting as a compelled consenting factor, which approves whatever is suggested.

As explained by Nārad, when the Mistress sang, the adventurer sang just the same. When she wept, he cried. When she laughed, he enjoyed. When she spoke insensibly, he, following her, did so as well.

क्वचिद् धावति धावन्त्यां तिष्ठन्त्याम् अनु तिष्ठति /
अनु शेते शयानायाम् अन्वास्ते क्वचिद् आसतीम् (४॥२५॥५९)

kvacid dhāvati dhāvantyāṃ
tiṣṭhantyām anu tiṣṭhati /
anu śete śayānāyām
anvāste kvacid āsatīm (4.25.59)

kvacid – and then, dhāvati – he walks, dhāvantyāṃ - while walking, tiṣṭhantyām – while standing, anu – following, tiṣṭhati – he stood, anu – following, śete – he reclined, śayānāyām – while reclining, anvāste = anu (following) + āste (he sat), kvacid – then, āsatīm – while she sat

When the Mistress walked, the City Person, stepped. While she stood, he did likewise. When she reclined, he did the same. When she sat, he reposed himself. (4.25.59)

Detail

Purañjan came to the Bhogavatī, Excitement City, looking for some convenience and companionship. He had no idea if his needs would be fulfilled. Since he already combed through most of earth in his quest, he was at the end of his tether.

Luckily, he met an attractive, sexually mature single woman who was a maiden with no sexual experience. Fortunately, the intuition of the young lady favored him. Thus, with little conversation, they realized that they were mutually in love with each other.

However, Purañjan was bewildered. The young woman was ignorant of her ancestry and could name neither her father nor mother. She admitted that she was oblivious as to how she came into existence, but naturally she had a capable security officer and sufficient servants to cater to her needs.

Purañjan for his part was happy for this circumstance. To him, this was a strange and agreeable fate. With no effort on his part, with not even one act to make him worthy of such an opportunity, he got what he desired, which was a capable woman, her security force, a royal staff, and a well-fitted city.

Due to that, when the Mistress walked, Purañjan strolled. While she stood, he did likewise. When she reclined, he did the same. When she sat, he reposed himself. Whatever purpose he had prior to meeting the woman was now either cancelled or suspended. He was converted to her lifestyle. His sense of self shifted.

This presentation explains the situation of the coreSelf's relationship with its adjunct, the intellect. The core is influenced. The intellect is an ongoing, moment by moment, streaming psychological force. It is mental but it has an emotional component which is just as effective as physical force.

Initially when they first met, the core had no chance to refuse the offer of the intellect. Since the rationality was protected on all sides, Purañjan had no way to deeply penetrate it. The queen was influenced heavily by her security officer. She was reciprocally influenced by the staff as well.

This may be diagrammed with a queen ruling a city, to which there are suburbs and parks just outside the walls of the buttressed construction. Besides the queen, there was a security officer who had full control of the gates to the city. This officer was a snake with five heads. The queen did not have a commanding relationship with the snake. It independently controlled the area. It did whatever it felt was in the interest of the zone.

The facilities of the place were available to the queen except when the snake closed an access. The snake was the engineer of the city. It maintained the place.

The queen trusted the serpent fully. It, in turn, lived up to the expectation that it was knowledgeable and would maintain and protect the locale, the queen, and her staff.

क्वचिच् छृणोति शृण्वन्त्यां पश्यन्त्याम् अनु पश्यति /
क्वचिज् जिघ्रति जिघ्रन्त्यां स्पृशन्त्यां स्पृशति क्वचित् (४॥२५॥६०)

kvacic chṛṇoti śṛṇvantyāṃ
paśyantyām anu paśyati /
kvacij jighrati jighrantyāṃ
spṛśantyāṃ spṛśati kvacit (4.25.60)

kvacic = kvacit = at the time, chṛṇoti = śṛṇoti = he heard, śṛṇvantyāṃ - listening, paśyantyām – seeing, anu – following her, paśyati – he looked, kvacij = kvacit = then when, jighrati – he smelt, jighrantyāṃ - while smelling, spṛśantyāṃ - while touching, spṛśati – he contacted something, kvacit – just when

When the Mistress heard something, Purañjan listened to the same. When the woman saw something, he looked as well. When she smelt an odor, he experienced it too. When the Mistress touched anything, he felt that object. (4.25.60)

Detail

The queen's senses were on high alert to discover what the psyche craved, detested, or was neutrally attracted to. She was the center of attention of her environment, her staff, and the security officer. If something was sensed which was detested, it was removed from the vicinity, or the queen was relocated immediately. If some other item produced a neutral interest, it was tolerated or switched to a remote location. If it was desirable, it was put within reach, or the queen was relocated to its vicinity.

The adventurer was never the center of attention unless he positioned himself to be with the queen. If he did that, he enjoyed her privileges. When the Mistress heard something, he listened to the same. When she saw something, he looked as well. When she smelt an odor, he experienced it too. When the Mistress touched anything, he contacted that object. That is how Purañjan enjoyed in the woman's association.

The position of the coreSelf is such that the intellect is the junction of procurement for sensual exchanges, such that when the kundalini lifeForce Power Central dispenses feelings through the senses, there is pursuit for objects of enjoyment.

If the intellect is removed, the core has no way of procuring feelings. It is not equipped to detect and react to the objects of this world. Just as Purañjan needed the queen with her security officer and staff, so a coreSelf needs an intellect, a lifeForce and a range of sensual services to detect the objects in this world.

The quest of the coreSelf is experience but it does not have a way to acquire unless it accepts service from the adjuncts.

क्वचिच् च शोचतीं जायाम् अनु शोचति दीनवत् /
अनु हृष्यति हृष्यन्त्यां मुदिताम् अनु मोदते (४॥२५॥६१)

kvacic ca śocatīṃ jāyām
anu śocati dīnavat /
anu hṛṣyati hṛṣyantyāṃ
muditām anu modate (4.25.61)

kvacic = kvacit = then, ca – and, śocatīṃ = grieving, jāyām – Mistress, anu – followed, śocati – he grieved, dīnavat – like someone in distress, anu – following, hṛṣyati – he was pleasured, hṛṣyantyāṃ - while she enjoyed, muditām – while being happy, anu – followed, modate- he enjoyed

When the lady grieved, he lamented like someone in distress. If she enjoyed, he was pleasured too. When she felt happiness, he was blissed all the same. (4.25.61)

Detail

The wanderer who traversed the earth, and luckily met the beautiful virgin queen, faced a new fortune of fulfillment when he cohabited with the woman in her bejeweled city. His quest for pleasure terminated by mimicking whatever she did. In pleasure and displeasure, he experienced whatever she felt. Nārad described that when the lady grieved, Purañjan lamented like someone in distress. If the woman enjoyed, he was pleasured too. When she felt happiness, he enjoyed as well.

This was a complete identification with her moods. If the lady was rained on, the adventurer experienced that. They were like twins except that he trailed whatever she initiated. If she did not like a preparation, Purañjan did not eat it. If her body was afflicted somehow, he felt inconvenienced too.

The application of this to the coreSelf and its intellect, is that the core does not relish anything first. It does so after the intellect checks a sense object. The opinion of the intellect carries the decisive energy, from which the core draws a conclusion, and executes actions.

The core is the puppet, for it is not equipped to touch any of the senses which probe the objects. The sequence of events is that the senses check. They report to the intellect. It analyses and decides. It advances reports to the core, which may consent or raise objections according to how it is influenced.

If the core resists the report of the intellect, the intellect will petition the memory for assistance in reinforcing those views. This will further weaken the resolve of the core, which will usually consent to the proposals.

When the intellect grieves, the core laments like someone in distress. If the intellect enjoys, the core is pleasured too. When intellect feels happiness, the core indulges all the same.

विप्रलब्धो महिष्यैवं सर्व-प्रकृति-वञ्चितः /
नेच्छन्न् अनुकरोत्य् अज्ञः क्लैब्यात् क्रीडा-मृगो यथा (४॥२५॥६२)

vipralabdho mahiṣyaivaṃ
sarva-prakṛti-vañcitaḥ /
necchann anukaroty ajñaḥ
klaibyāt krīḍā-mṛgo yathā (4.25.62)

vipralabdho = vipralabdhaḥ = psychologically occupied, mahiṣyaivaṃ - by the queen of the city, sarva – all, prakṛti – Nature, vañcitaḥ - deprived, cheated, necchann = na icchan = not wanting, anukaroty = anukaroti = he followed, ajñaḥ - uninformed person, klaibyāt – powerless, krīḍā – plaything, mṛgo = mṛgaḥ = animal, yathā – as

Being psychologically occupied by the queen of the city, deluded by all of Nature, even though he did not want to be conditioned like this, he, like an uninformed person, powerlessly followed the Mistress just as a pet animal tails its owner. (4.25.62)

Detail

Unknown to the wanderer, was the fact, that the queen was merely a function of Nature. She was not a reality which was positioned to itself. She was not a full-blown person like the wanderer.

The situation, the queen, her protector snake, her staff, her fortress, and the gates to the place, were a massive conspiracy posing as a natural event.

There was no intention for the wanderer to enjoy anything. In fact, the operation of the place was such that the wanderer served just as a focus for deriving energy to enliven the situation.

However, since the wanderer had no idea about the workings of Nature, he was comforted by the queen's antics, and by the services rendered by her protector and employees.

Being psychologically occupied by the woman, who charmed him, being deluded by Nature which bombarded him, even though he did not desire to be influenced, he, like an uninformed person, powerlessly followed the Mistress just as a pet animal follows its owner.

Even though the coreSelf lacks the objectivity to know of its original attraction to an intellect, still that core should investigate the origins. It contacts the intellect at every moment. It can study how this relationship is serviced.

Besides a coreSelf and an intellect, what are the other instruments or agencies?

Nārad reported that the wanderer did not desire to be subordinate to the queen of the city. Why then was he influenced to such an extent that he was like a pet animal which is sensitive to its owner?

Chapter 2
Purañjan escapes the Influence

नारद उवाच
स एकदा महेष्वासो रथं पञ्चाश्वम् आशु-गम् /
द्वीषं द्वि-चक्रम् एकाक्षं त्रि-वेणुं पञ्च-बन्धुरम् (४॥२६॥१)

nārada uvāca
sa ekadā maheṣvāso
ratham pañcāśvam āśu-gam /
dvīṣaṃ dvi-cakram ekākṣaṃ
tri-veṇuṃ pañca-bandhuram (4.26.1)

nārada – Nārada, uvāca – said, sa = saḥ = he, ekadā – once it happened, maheṣvāso = maheṣvāsaḥ = great archer, rathaṃ - chariot, pañcāśvam = pañca (five) + aśvam (horses), āśu – swiftly, gam - moving, dvīṣaṃ = dvi (two) + īṣaṃ (arrows), dvi – two, cakram – wheels, ekākṣaṃ = eka (one) + akṣaṃ (axle), tri – three, veṇuṃ - flags, pañca – five, bandhuram – operations

Nārada continued.
Once it happened that he, Purañjan, the great archer, mounted a chariot which was carried swiftly by five horses. He took two arrows. The chariot had two wheels, one axle, three flags and five operations. (4.26.1)

Detail

Somehow, the pressure to be social with the queen, was relaxed. The wanderer resumed his adventurous activities. He mounted a conveyance. This was an effort to resume his wandering self. It was like filling for formal separation from the queen. We must remember that he had a verbal agreement to remain within the city and its environs for one hundred years. If he breached that, there were consequences. Any plan to enjoy or experience without her initiating it, was a violation. However, the adventurer was not concerned. He felt his spirit for adventure again.

After he met the queen, Purañjan assumed a new attitude to life. By instinct alone, he left aside his normal composure and adapted the moods and lifestyle of the beautiful woman. He agreed to be serviced by her and her staff for one hundred years.

Somehow, this collapsed, where he found himself being an independent wanderer again. He remembered himself as being an adventurer who went here and there, a master in his own right.

Once it happened that some subconscious urges surfaced in his mind. He resumed himself as a great archer. He ceased mimicking whatever the queen did.

Purañjan was suddenly overcome by subliminal tendencies. These were different to those of the queen. He mounted a chariot which was carried by five swift horses. He took two arrows. The chariot had two wheels, one axle, three flags and five operations.

Purañjan exhibited interest which breached the contract he had with the queen. This analogy is interesting. It means that the coreSelf could on occasion breach the authority of the intellect. The core can be independent. It can make decisions which run contrary. But there arises the question of whether there would be unfavorable reactions for the core.

It is sad however, to think that the core may act without discrimination, and that would be to its detriment. Even though the intellect, like the queen, had whimsical desire, she never was interested in violent activities. The indication is that the core by itself lacks the discrimination of the intellect.

The core can make decisions on its own but it lacks a way to gage whether an act is criminal or approved. Of all the actions that could be committed by Purañjan, he selected to indulge in the use of weapons.

Purañjan was a great archer, a person of tremendous focus, an exceptional achiever. With the queen, he was not free to travel, doing as he pleased. She acted as serviced by her staff. When she made herself available for the servants, he did likewise. She always was restricted as requested by her security officer. Purañjan too was confined in that way.

Purañjan got the urge to be himself again. He mounted a chariot which was carried by five swift horses. He took two arrows. The chariot had two wheels, one axle, three flags and five operations.

Hearing of Purañjan, one may ask about his activities before he met the queen. What was the coreSelf doing before it became fused with an intellect which had accessory powers and services?

Purañjan has some equipment of his own. It is just that once he met the queen, his accessories disappeared. The queen had no interest in his behavior except his ability to mimic whatever she did in either giving commands to her staff or in receiving their services.

As for the core's focusing ability, it was in use by the queen but only in being attentive to what she wanted and in focusing on what she did, so as to perfectly mimic her responses and moods.

By himself however, once the magical influence of the queen was relaxed, Purañjan, focused on being a great archer, being capable of wounding any swift animal. He wanted to do this in challenging circumstances, as for instance even from a swiftly moving chariot, one that was carried by five nimble horses.

एक-रश्म्य् एक-दमनम् एक-नीडं द्वि-कूबरम् /
पञ्च-प्रहरणं सप्त- वरूथं पञ्च-विक्रमम् (४॥२६॥२)

eka-raśmy eka-damanam
eka-nīḍaṃ dvi-kūbaram /
pañca-praharaṇaṃ sapta-
varūthaṃ pañca-vikramam (4.26.2)

eka – one, raśmy = raśmi = rein, eka – one, damanam – charioteer, eka – one, nīḍaṃ - seat, dvi – two, kūbaram – yokes, pañca – five, praharaṇaṃ - weapons, sapta – seven, varūthaṃ - fenders, pañca – five, vikramam - maneuvers

It had one rein, one charioteer, one seat, two yokes, five weapons, seven fenders and five maneuvers. (4.26.2)

Detail

At first one got the opinion, that Purañjan was a lone wanderer, who travelled through the earth, but was unable to find a suitable spouse and citadel, where he could establish himself as king. In that view he had no possessions except for his body and desires. There was a friend who accompanied him, except that Purañjan was unaware of this person.

Now, we hear that he has one rein, one charioteer, one seat, two yokes, five weapons, seven fenders and five maneuvers. He even has a charioteer.

What happened to his attendant and equipment just before he met the beautiful woman, the honored queen of Excitement City?

Who made the decision for him to repossess his equipment?

Why was he naturally violent, being a specialist in weaponry?

Does the coreSelf have other adjuncts which may be disconnected or connected on occasion?

हैमोपस्करम् आरुह्य स्वर्ण-वर्माक्षयेषुधिः /
एकादश-चमू-नाथः पञ्च-प्रस्थम् अगाद् वनम् (४॥२६॥३)

haimopaskaram āruhya
svarṇa-varmākṣayeṣudhiḥ /
ekādaśa-camū-nāthaḥ
pañca-prastham agād vanam (4.26.3)

haimopaskaram = haima (golden) + upaskaram (embellishments), āruhya - riding, svarṇa – golden, varmākṣayeṣudhiḥ = varmā (armor) + akṣaya (endless) + iṣudhiḥ (quiver), ekādaśa – eleven, camū-nāthaḥ = commander of armed forces, pañca-prastham = five objectives, agād = agāt = went, vanam – forest

With golden embellishments riding with golden armor, having a quiver with endless arrows, accompanied by the eleventh military commander, Purañjan went to the forest known as the Five Objectives. (4.26.3)

Detail

Purañjan was penniless initially. He had no servant. There was no security official accompanying him. There was only his observational capacity. Wherefrom was there weaponry, a charioteer, and a military commander?

Before, whatever the queen needed and was catered for, became the instant need and fulfillment of Purañjan. Then, he was on his own with his desire to venture to the forest known as the Five Objectives.

This is direct enjoyment instead of mimicking what the queen initiated. Suddenly he had a desire to acquire and fulfill himself? What will the queen think? This was not part of their agreement.

Purañjan had luxury items, even his military gear and accoutrements were expensive equipment. These were not provided by the queen.

He had golden armor with golden embellishments. His armament, with a quiver of endless arrows, was matchless. He had military staff, a commander.

चचार मृगयां तत्र दृप्त आत्तेषु-कार्मुकः /
विहाय जायाम् अतद्-र्हां मृग-व्यसन-लालसः (४॥२६॥४)

cacāra mṛgayāṃ tatra
dṛpta āttesu-kārmukaḥ /
vihāya jāyā atad-arhāṃ
mṛga-vyasana-lālasaḥ (4.26.4)

cacāra – stalked, mṛgayāṃ - wild animals, tatra – there, dṛpta – being arrogant, āttesu = ātta (acquired) + iṣu (arrows), kārmukaḥ - bow, vihāya – not considering, jāyām

– the Mistress, atad-arhāṃ = irrational, mṛga – wild animal, vyasana – violating proper conduct, lālasaḥ - craving

There in the forest, he stalked wild animals. Being arrogant he took arrows and a bow. He did not consider his Mistress. Due to some craving, he irrationally killed animals, thus violating proper conduct. (4.26.4)

Detail

We must remember that Purañjan was an adventuring wanderer. The exception was that he had a need to be entertained. In his exploration of the earth, he found nothing which perfectly suited his needs. When he met the beautiful young woman, he was enchanted.

Before he could make some proposal, the lady informed that he could stay with her for one hundred years. That included royal services by her attendants and security protection by her guard, the five-headed serpent.

Somehow as he was charmed, his previous lifestyle disappeared. He lost track of himself to such an extent that his tendencies went into dormancy. He became occupied doing whatever the lady did and being catered in exactly the way her servants outlaid.

Suddenly there was a change. His former adventuring chauvinistic behavior became prominent. He forgot the queen.

This gives insight into the situations of the coreSelf, where by itself it acts in one way. When it is influenced by an intellect, it may perform to the contrary.

There was no incidence of killing animals when Purañjan was with the queen. Generally, women are not fond of killing other creatures. Men, however may not hesitate to do so. When he did what the queen did, there was no possibility of obvious violence.

The coreSelf is restrained by the intellect, so that the core gets no suggestion about violent acts. This does not mean that the potential for violence is not present with the queen. It simply indicates that generally, physical violence is not possible for the female of the human beings.

When he was alone with nothing to do but kill animals in the forest, Purañjan did not consider his Mistress. Due to some craving, he irrationally killed animals, thus violating proper conduct.

The application of this, is that the coreSelf gains a sense of discrimination about what is cruel and what is kind, from the intellect. If the intellect is silenced, the core cannot properly judge what is approved or disapproved social behavior. The intellect is responsive to social discourse but the core is oblivious of that, when it is deprived of the intellect's conclusions.

Without considering the social impact of this activity, Purañjan enjoyed killing other lifeforms. He did not have the analytical ability of the intellect. He could not calculate the reactions which would come.

When he explained the analogy in terms of its representation of King Barhi's life, Nārad will expound on this hunting incidence of Puranjan. It means that during the life of the physical body, the coreSelf conducts at least two lifestyles. One is the life of the physical world, where the person performs socially acceptable activities. This life is tailored by the inhibitions which are developed in the childhood of the body, when one is directed in what is approved, and what is condemned, during social interaction.

The other lifestyle is the one in dreams, where the developed intellect may not surface, such that one does not have a limiter which from within the mind or from people in the environment, causes one to be restricted by morality.

When he was with the queen Puranjan did whatever the catering woman performed. But on the astral side of existence, in his dream, she was not present and had no jurisdiction. He found himself to be equipped with weapons. He killed animals mercilessly. There was no censorship and no rule to follow. In dreams he did whatever he could. His person was not limited to the queen's selection, to what was reasonable and acceptable to civilized people.

This reveals more. Puranjan dreamt during his wanderings. When he met the queen, his dreams ceased for a time. He became synchronized into the physical world where the queen existed. Then he lost contact with his prior self. He was completely oblivious to it. Then suddenly, his mind switched to the astral existence for just enough time for him to kill some animals so as to transit to an astral environment in which he was an expert archer.

आसुरीं वृत्तिम् आश्रित्य घोरात्मा निरनुग्रहः /
न्यहनन् निशितैर् बाणैर् वनेषु वन-गोचरान् (४॥२६॥५)

āsurīṃ vṛttim āśritya
ghorātmā niranugrahaḥ /

nyahanan niśitair bāṇair
vaneṣu vana-gocarān (4.26.5)

āsurīṃ - criminal person, vṛttim – activity, āśritya – relying on, ghorātmā = ghora (horrible) + ātmā (self, tendency) niranugrahaḥ - without compassion, nyahanan – brutally killed, niśitair – by sharp, bāṇair – by arrows, vaneṣu – in the forest, vana-gocarān – grazing animals in the forest

Like a criminal with corresponding activities, being reliant on horrible tendencies, with no compassion, Purañjan, with sharp arrows, brutally killed grazing animals in the forest. (4.26.5)

Detail

Purañjan the roving adventurer resumed activities which he enacted before he met the queen. What was he doing? Enjoying himself! Playing God unrestrictedly! He had no conscience. He behaved like a criminal. His tendencies to do what came to mind without considering the consequences on other beings, surfaced when he was not mimicking the queen.

The indication is that without the queen, the wanderer could not determine what was approved and what was incorrect.

Considering this in terms of the psyche, a yogi should introspect and meditate deeply, to get insight into what would happen, if as the coreSelf, it was divested of an intellect. It would exist with no viable discrimination. It would have no way to judge what was faulty, and what was supportive of reality.

This is demonstrated in dream experiences, where a person finds the self to be without the moral values, which it developed during the life of the physical body. In some experiences, one recalls doing things which one would not commit, if one had the inhibitions from the physical side of life. This brings to mind some questions.

Can the core function rationally when it cannot access the analytical skill of the intellect?

For no sensible reason, the wanderer, that hero, brutally killed grazing animals in the forest. What were his feelings? Why did he act like a heartless butcher? Was he, like an innocent child, who has no idea about the harm involved in such butchery?

तीर्थेषु प्रतिदृष्टेषु राजा मेध्यान् पशून् वने /
यावद्-र्थम् अलं लुब्धो हन्याद् इति नियम्यते (४॥२६॥६)

tīrtheṣu pratidṛṣṭeṣu
rājā medhyān paśūn vane /
yāvad-artham alaṃ lubdho
hanyād iti niyamyate (4.26.6)

tīrtheṣu – of religious shrine, pratidṛṣṭeṣu – become known, is regarded, rājā – king, medhyān – for sacrificial ceremony, paśūn – animals, vane – in forest, yāvad – by point, artham – value, alaṃ - just enough, lubdho = lubdhaḥ = urged, hanyād = hanyāt = to kill, iti – thus, niyamyate – scripturally approved

At a religious shrine, a king may have a sacrificial ceremony to reverentially process animal carcasses. The point is that if one is eager to kill game, just enough may be done. One may do so in a scripturally suggested way. (4.26.6)

Detail

Nārad confronted King Barhi. After getting deep into the tale of Purañjan, Nārad switched to the habit of some kings of the time. These were cruel people, members of the ruling caste. They killed indiscriminately. Some ignored the stipulations in the scripture of the time. Others bridled their violent tendencies and killed only as allowed in the texts.

The contention between mankind and animal is there for two reasons.

- competing for food resources
- considering the bodies of each other as a food source.

Human beings will simply not tolerate animals who kill humans. Humans feel justified in eliminating any animal which attacks or eats a human.

But there is the factor of killing animals when they are competitive for other food; like for instance, when a fierce animal kills a vegetarian animal which a human being considers to be a food source.

Human also kill vegetarian animals who eat plants which the human considered as diet. Before modern time, this contention between humans and the animals was widespread.

Nārad addressed the motivation of the humans in committing this violence. He wanted to stir the conscience of Barhi, who had a history of needless killing.

Killing was to be kept to a minimum. The scripture of the time did not advocate animal destruction. It did however provide a way to restrict and reduce such killing. The kings could kill legally only as stipulated in the scriptural text. The intention was to restrict and discourage slaughter.

य एवं कर्म नियतं विद्वान् कुर्वीत मानवः /
कर्मणा तेन राजेन्द्र ज्ञानेन न स लिप्यते (४॥२६॥७)

ya evaṃ karma niyataṃ
vidvān kurvīta mānavaḥ /
karmaṇā tena rājendra
jñānena na sa lipyate (4.26.7)

ya = yaḥ = whosoever, evaṃ - thus, karma – social activity, niyataṃ - moral principle, vidvān – informed person, kurvīta – should do, mānavaḥ - person, karmaṇā – by what is done, tena – by this, rājendra – O King, jñānena – by knowing, na – not, sa = saḥ = he, lipyate – degraded

Whosoever does his social activity by moral principles is an informed person who does what should be done. O King, by that he is not degraded. (4.26.7)

Detail

Nārad is concerned to reform the social behavior of Barhi, even the king's considerations about the value of animal life. Nārad verbally targeted the king. The monarch introspected to consider if any of his activities of killing animals would bear terrible consequences.

Hiding under the cover of doing religious rites, feeling confident in killing predatory animals, and shooting grazing ones, may be done to a minimum. This is because Nature gives opportunities to every species it created. A king does not have the right to kill any other species indiscriminately.

From Nature, one acquired the tendency to kill but that feature of behavior should be tempered. It is present to be monitored and restricted.

अन्यथा कर्म कुर्वाणो मानारूढो निबध्यते /
गुण-प्रवाह-पतितो नष्ट-प्रज्ञो व्रजत्य् अधः (४॥२६॥८)

anyathā karma kurvāṇo
mānārūḍho nibadhyate /
guṇa-pravāha-patito naṣṭa-
prajño vrajaty adhaḥ (4.26.8)

anyathā – conversely, karma – lifestyle, kurvāṇo = kurvāṇaḥ = while acting, mānārūḍho = mānārūḍhaḥ = supported by pride, nibadhyate – entrapped, guṇa – Nature, pravāha – influence, patito = patitaḥ - degraded, naṣṭa – deprived of, prajño = prajñaḥ = insight, vrajaty = vrajati = he goes, adhaḥ - lower

Conversely, if the lifestyle is supported by pride, one becomes entrapped by the influence of Nature, and is degraded. Being deprived of insight, that person is lowered. (4.26.8)

Detail

Guna, or the mood of Nature, is a big event in someone's life. One may be upgraded or degraded according to which influence one absorbs. Who can resist Nature? For instance, we heard in this tale that Purañjan met an attractive young lady on the outskirts of Bhogavatī Excitement City.

He was so captivated and lured, that he forgot himself. Under her influence, his lifestyle altered. This happened in a jiffy. He did not understand how he was influenced.

Who can become objective or opposed to Nature's influence? Who can know when it is in one's interest to absorb Nature's suggestions?

Nārad declared that if a person's lifestyle is supported by pride, that someone becomes entrapped, and is degraded.

But King Barhi always committed unnecessary and whimsical killing of animals, and he did not suffer for it. That means that Nature delayed the reactions. One should not think that if one is not punished, there will be no consequence. The backlash is sure to come, as Nārad assured Barhi.

In the mind too, something done, or a lack of action even, may bring anguish to a self. In as much as Nature has the upper hand in term of producing the history of the world, there is also an intuitive force which will be sure to subject a specific self to psychological discomfort.

When the lifestyle is supported by pride (*mānārūḍho*), one gets the feeling that there will be no accounting, or that if there is, it will be in one's favor. This is incorrect both in the external world where physical morality is enforced, and in the internal psyche where the actions of the coreSelf, or any of its adjuncts, causes changes in the psychological energies.

Purañjan had to be considerate of the queen, her security officer, and her staff. When he is rated as a coreSelf, with the queen being his intellect, he had to consider her advice. Initially, he made a verbal agreement to accept her decisions and catering, for one hundred years. If she made an incorrect decision, he had to comply. If she did something advantageous, he benefited from it.

Suddenly, we heard of his deviation, when he got the urge to mount an expensive war machine. He did so, killing just for the heck of it.

तत्र निर्भिन्न-गात्राणां चित्र-वाजैः शिलीमुखैः /
विप्लवो ऽभूद् दुःखितानां दुःसहः करुणात्मनाम् (४॥२६॥९)

tatra nirbhinna-gātrāṇāṃ
citra-vājaiḥ śilīmukhaiḥ /
viplavo 'bhūd duḥkhitānāṃ
duḥsahaḥ karuṇātmanām (4.26.9)

tatra – there, nirbhinna – wounded, gātrāṇāṃ - of bodies, citra – varied, vājaiḥ - by feathers, śilīmukhaiḥ - by arrows, viplavo = viplavaḥ = devastation, 'bhūd = abhūt = unprecedented, duḥkhitānāṃ - most grievous, duḥsahaḥ - intolerable, karuṇātmanām – for kind people

There were wounded bodies of various types. Some were pierced by feathered arrows. The devastation was unprecedented. It was grievous and intolerable for kind people. (4.26.9)

Detail

Nārad described Purañjan's precise killings. No limited being is free to do as it pleases. There is censorship of Nature and of God.

Because the reactions do not come instantly, a limited being may misunderstand and think that what he or she does, is approved.

Purañjan was marked because his killing of the animals was something that was grievous and intolerable for kind people. Their feelings and opinions in this regard would carry reactions even if they were not present as physical witnesses.

शशान् वराहान् महिषान् गवयान् रुरु-शल्यकान् /
मेध्यान् अन्यांश् च विविधान् विनिघ्नन् श्रमम् अध्यगात् (४॥२६॥१०)

śaśān varāhān mahiṣān
gavayān ruru-śalyakān /
medhyān anyāṃś ca vividhān
vinighnan śramam adhyagāt (4.26.10)

śaśān – rabbits, varāhān – boars, mahiṣān – buffaloes, gavayān – bison, ruru – black deer, śalyakān – porcupines, medhyān – animals permitted as victims in a religious sacrifice, anyāṃś = anyān = others, ca – and, vividhān – various, vinighnan – slaughter, śramam – exhausted, adhyagāt – he was

Rabbits, boars, buffaloes, bison, black deer, and porcupines, as well as animals permitted as victims in a religious sacrifice, were part of the slaughter. Then, Purañjan became exhausted. (4.26.10)

Detail

This was Purañjan's first opportunity to be himself. The queen was absent. Her social pressure which caused him to mimic her and not to act independently, had no effect on him. He did what came to mind.

He acted with excess, killing whatever excited his fancy. After some time, he was exhausted. In this, Purañjan was not alone. He was staffed for the killing spree but none of the attendants were the queen's employees.

The question now concerns the appearance of a fully equipped chariot with a military staff. How was this manifested? When he met the queen, the adventurer was a sole wanderer. Did he hide his military commander, soldiers, and machinery?

ततः क्षुत्-तृट्-परिश्रान्तो निवृत्तो गृहम् एयिवान् /
कृत-स्नानोचिताहारः संविवेश गत-क्लमः (४॥२६॥११)

tataḥ kṣut-tṛṭ-pariśrānto
nivṛtto gṛham eyivān /
kṛta-snānocitāhāraḥ
saṃviveśa gata-klamaḥ (4.26.11)

tataḥ - thus, kṣut-tṛṭ = by hunger and thirst, pariśrānto = pariśrāntaḥ = being fatigued, nivṛtto = nivṛttaḥ = no energy, gṛham – home, eyivān - reached, kṛta – acted to, snānocitāhāraḥ = snāna (bath) + ucita (suitable) + āhāraḥ (procuring food), saṃviveśa – reclined, gata – relieved, klamaḥ- fatigue

Thus, afflicted by hunger and thirst, being fatigued and with no energy, he reached his home. He bathed and procured sufficient food. Then he reclined and was relieved of the fatigue. (4.26.11)

Detail

Wherever that wanderer went, into which ever magical place, where his accoutrements were manifest, that place was set for masculine sports but it did not render endless energy. He was fatigued.

Afflicted by hunger and thirst, with little vitality, he returned to his quarters in the Excitement City. He bathed and procured sufficient food. Then he reclined and was relieved.

For relief of the horrors of a dream, one awakens to the physical side of life. Conversely, to be removed from physical reality, a person slips into dreams.

आत्मानम् अर्हयां चक्रे धूपालेप-स्रग्-ादिभिः /
साध्व्-लङ्कृत-सर्वाङ्गो महिष्याम् आदधे मनः (४॥२६॥१२)

ātmānam arhayāṃ cakre
dhūpālepa-srag-ādibhiḥ /
sādhv-alaṅkṛta-sarvāṅgo
mahiṣyām ādadhe manaḥ (4.26.12)

ātmānam – self, arhayāṃ - respectably dressed, cakre – performed, dhūpālepa = dhūpa (incense) +ālepa (smearing the body with ungruents), srag-ādibhiḥ = with garlands and other auspicious things, sādhv = sādhu = excellent, alaṅkṛta - decorated, sarvāṅgo = sarvāṅgaḥ= all limbs, mahiṣyām – to the queen, ādadhe – he submitted, manaḥ - mentally

He was respectably dressed. He used incense and smeared ungruents. He wore garlands and other auspicious things which were excellent. He decorated his limbs and mentally submitted himself to the queen. (4.26.12)

Detail

Gradually, as if shifting from a dimension, Purañjan was respectably dressed. It is not that he was a helpless male who depended on his wife for attire. After all, we were informed that this wanderer was a capable hero. His body was built for adventure.

Now that he forgot the queen and shifted from being dependent on her for services and conveniences, he resumed his independent behavior. He used incense and smeared ungruents. He wore garlands and other auspicious things which were excellent. He decorated his limbs. By a shift of mentality, he submitted to the queen.

This happened spontaneously with no deliberation on his part. This adventurer again fell under the influence of the queen except that she was not present in his quarters. He did not realize that he acted independent of the capable woman.

Using references from memory and instinct, the wanderer respectably dressed. He used incense and smeared ungruents. He wore garlands and other auspicious things which were excellent. He decorated his limbs. When he first met the queen, he was dressed in a way that suited her fancy. That was all by chance. Now however, he carefully attired himself for her satisfaction. He felt a bit uneasy about the sportive violence against the animals, but he was confident that he could submitted himself to his woman.

Regardless of how one was attired in a dream, one rectifies oneself when one switches to the physical side.

तृप्तो हृष्टः सुदृप्तश् च कन्दर्पाकृष्ट-मानसः /
न व्यचष्ट वरारोहां गृहिणीं गृह-मेधिनीम् (४॥२६॥१३)

trpto hrṣṭaḥ sudṛptaś ca
kandarpākṛṣṭa-mānasaḥ /
na vyacaṣṭa varārohāṃ
gṛhiṇīṃ gṛha-medhinīm (4.26.13)

trpto = tṛptaḥ = satisfied, hṛṣṭaḥ - happiness, sudṛptaś = sudṛptaḥ = very proud, ca – and, kandarpākṛṣṭa = Kandarpa (deity of infatuation) + ākṛṣṭa (influenced by), mānasaḥ - mind, na – not, vyacaṣṭa – not perceptive, varārohāṃ - spiritually elevated, gṛhiṇīṃ - the Mistress, gṛha-medhinīm – woman who is skillful at facilitating domestic pleasures

Feeling satisfied, happy, and very proud, being influenced by Kandarpa, the deity of infatuation, his mind was not perceptive, nor spiritually elevated. Instead, he thought of the lady, a woman who was skilled at facilitating domestic pleasures. (4.26.13)

Detail

There was no objectivity on the part of Purañjan. There were two mental dimensions so far. One was his adventurer self. The other was the person who mimicked whatever the queen did, such that if she ate, he did likewise. If she laughed, he giggled as well.

After slipping from being the sporting hunter, he experienced himself as the serviced companion of the queen. Even though she was not present in his chamber, he felt satisfied, happy, and proud.

In that way Purañjan moved seamlessly from being a sportsman to being a married man who indulged in his woman's fancy. He did not consider that after breaching their agreement, it would be awkward to be in her company. This was the first time he deviated from her routine, but he felt that his sportive hunt was a natural event which she would appreciate.

This is interesting when it is applied to the psyche, where the coreSelf deviated from its romantic relationship with the intellect. The core decided to act by itself with no consultation with the intellect.

The problem is that just as the beautiful woman had skills, servants, a proficient security officer and aristocratic accommodations, which the wanderer needed but did not have, so the coreSelf lacked certain aspects where when it acted independently, its lack of these features caused it to commit actions which brought to it costly liabilities.

When Purañjan prepared himself to be with the queen, he felt satisfied, happy, and proud. He lacked the insight to know that she was disenchanted.

अन्तःपुर-स्त्रियोऽपृच्छद् विमना इव वेदिषत् /
अपि वः कुशलं रामाः सेश्वरीणां यथा पुरा (४॥२६॥१४)

antaḥpura-striyo 'pṛc
chad vimanā iva vediṣat /
api vaḥ kuśalaṃ rāmāḥ
seśvarīṇāṃ yathā purā (4.26.14)

antaḥpura – bedroom, striyo = striyaḥ = women, 'pṛcchad =apṛcchat = he questioned. vimanā – feeling nervous, iva – like, vediṣat – King Barhi, known for being at the Vedi sacrificial altar, api – also, vaḥ - your, kuśalaṃ - well-being, rāmāḥ - sweet woman, seśvarīṇāṃ - with the Mistress, yathā – as, purā – as before

In the bedroom, he questioned the women. He was nervous O King Barhi, person who is known as Vediṣat, the one who is constantly at the sacrificial altar. He inquired of their well-being and of the sweet woman, their Mistress, as to if it was as before. (4.26.14)

Detail

Nārad hinted that the famous and confident King Barhi, who had a reputation as Vediṣat, the one who is constantly at the sacrificial altar, had an uncertain future which was the result of his whimsical and inconsiderate actions in killing animals under religious pretensions.

As Purañjan departed from reason and followed his blind instincts to heroically kill animals while he pretended that the motivations were related to religious rituals, so King Barhi left aside good advice about religious procedures, which stipulate what violence one could enact with minimal consequences.

Purañjan that great adventurer, discovered to his dismay that his queen was not present in her chambers. In their bedroom, he questioned the attendant women about her situation.

Why the sudden change? Why was he not greeted affectionately as before? Who was responsible for the queen's absence?

The coreSelf lacked the intuition to know what displeasured and what enthused its intellect. When the core acts without coordination with the intellect, a rift occurs in the mind where the intellect retracts itself, and does not allow the core to access information, which would allow the core to make informed decisions.

न तथैतर्हि रोचन्ते गृहेषु गृह-सम्पदः /
यदि न स्याद् गृहे माता पत्नी वा पति-देवता /
व्यङ्गे रथ इव प्राज्ञः को नामासीत दीनवत् (४॥२६॥१५)

na tathaitarhi rocante
gṛheṣu gṛha-sampadaḥ /
yadi na syād gṛhe mātā
patnī vā pati-devatā /
vyaṅge ratha iva prājñaḥ
ko nāmāsīta dīnavat (4.26.15)

na – not, tathaitarhi = tathā (as it was) + etarhi (now), rocante – be pleasing, gṛheṣu – in the home, gṛha-sampadaḥ = household items, yadi – if, na – not, syād = syāt = there is, gṛhe – at home, mātā – mother, patnī – wife, vā – or, pati-devatā = woman who regards her husband as a god, vyaṅge – without wheels, ratha = rathe = in a chariot, iva – as if, prājñaḥ - informed person, ko = kaḥ = who, nāmāsīta = nāma (name) + āsīta (sit), dīnavat – like a helpless person

He inquired.
"In this home, the items are not pleasing as before. In a residence, if there is no wife, a woman who regards the husband as a god, that is like a chariot without wheels. Which informed person would remain there? Name a fool who would? (4.26.15)

Detail

Purañjan faced reality. He understood the consequence of being deprived of the association of the queen. With the lady of the city out of reach, he found himself to be like a homeless someone, a person undone, abandoned, miserable and unsettled. He was forced to cease his happiness and broad outlook. His jovial mood diminished.

In terms of the psyche as the residence of the coreSelf, that core found itself alone in the mind, where it could not access the information and decisions of the intellect.

The psyche felt unresponsive and lonesome. The presence of the core with no communication of the intellect, did not set things to order. The adventurer, the hero, the charming man who was kingly, became uncertain and insecure. This happens to the coreSelf when its relationship with the intellect is ruptured, by an act of the core which was done with no consultation from the intellect.

This situation is disruptive and should be reviewed carefully by the core, so that it could better understand its limitations when it is deprived of intellectual considerations.

Since the intellect's accessories and its sensual accounting, was available only when it is in a positive relationship with the core, that coreSelf should take that into consideration before it decides to be independent of the intellect. Instead of acting impulsively, where it commits acts which the intellect did not review, it should first consult the intellect which has access to related past incidences and current information about the liabilities involved.

The core should consider that in a psyche, where the adjuncts are not pleasing as before, it is a hellish mental and emotional place, just as when there is no wife in a home. Where the core is not catered as if it is a god, it would be like a chariot with no wheels.

क्व वर्तते सा ललना मज्जन्तं व्यसनार्णवे /
या माम् उद्धरते प्रज्ञां दीपयन्ती पदे पदे (४॥२६॥१६)

kva vartate sā lalanā
majjantaṃ vyasanārṇave /
yā mām uddharate prajñāṃ
dīpayantī pade pade (4.26.16)

kva – where, vartate – residing, sā – she, lalanā – lady, majjantaṃ - drowning, vyasanārṇave = vyasana (misfortune) + ārṇave (in the ocean), yā – who, mām – me, uddharate – extricates, prajñāṃ - wise counsel, dīpayantī – enlighten, pade pade = step by step

"Where is she, that lady, who when I am in the ocean of misfortune, extricates me by enlightening, step by step, with wise counsel?" (4.26.16)

Detail

In one way, this allegory about Purañjan is pathetic. If this is the condition of the coreSelf, one is left to wonder about the nature and ability of that core. What are its skills? What does it lack? How dependent on an intellect is it?

Purañjan was forced to come to his senses. His independent actions proved to be costly. The capable woman disappeared. Prior to this, Purañjan had no idea that he was this dependent on the woman for happiness and wellbeing. This was a jolt to his carefree lifestyle, one in which everything, almost everything he needed, was supplied.

He did not have to protect himself from enemies, as other kings did. There was a five headed snake which did that. He did not have to acquire anything because the queen' servants facilitated. He was honored as their king. The incidence of his going to the forest to kill animals, caused him to realize that he was not complete by himself. He needed the beautiful woman. Her presence was assuring. It was underscored by social security and service, which he could not provide.

In the future, Purañjan would take that into account. Prior to this, he stayed close to the queen and mimicked her as a matter of course. Now he would deliberately do it, for his wellbeing. He could not afford to lose her discrimination.

A coreSelf has to realize that if it is deprived of the intellect, there may be circumstances, where it may find itself to be in misfortune. The discriminating ability of the intellect would be absent. Decisions made may be faulty. Thus, the core will be deprived of analytical insight.

A core must consider if it can access memories, current information, and conclusions, when the intellect is decommissioned.

रामा ऊचुः
नर-नाथ न जानीमस् त्वत्-प्रिया यद् व्यवस्यति /
भूतले निरवस्तारे शयानां पश्य शत्रु-हन् (४॥२६॥१७)

rāmā ūcuḥ
nara-nātha na jānīmas
tvat-priyā yad vyavasyati /

bhūtale niravastāre śayānāṃ
paśya śatru-han (4.26.17)

rāmā – women, ūcuḥ - replied, nara-nātha = governor of men, na – not, jānīmas = jānīmaḥ = we known, tvat – your, priyā – dear one, yad = yat = why, vyavasyati – exertion, bhūtale – on the ground, niravastāre – without bedding, śayānāṃ - reclining, paśya – observe, śatru-han = killer of enemies

The women replied, "O governor of men, we do not know why your dear one, exerted herself in this way. She reclined to the ground with no bedding. Observe, O killer of enemies!" (4.26.17)

Detail

It is startling that the adventurer could not access his queen. Instead, he communicated with her attendants. Why is it that the core cannot instantly access the intellect whenever it needs to communicate with that adjunct?

When it wants to be seen by the core, the intellect will display its operations. Usually, it does not display itself directly. The core perceives it by seeing its thinking, recalling, and imagining. Otherwise, the intellect is unseen?

Nārad gave more information by stating that the adventurer was unable to access the queen. Some of her assistants were responsive, however.

This is negative for the core. In Purañjan's case, he had access to some servants of the queen. They were sympathetic to his condition. But there was no sight of the queen nor the security official. This meant that when the core is segregated from the intellect, that core becomes handicapped and misinformed because of no access to the intelligence of the intellect.

When Purañjan questioned some servants about the whereabouts of the queen, they informed that governor of men, that they had no idea why she was absent. They stated that she was reclined with no bedding. They pointed and said, “Observe, this, your mistress, O killer of enemies!”

Indirectly, the servants blamed Purañjan, for the situation. Stated plainly, they said, “Here is the result of your independent actions. You ruined the beautiful queen.” For the coreSelf, the ruination of the intellect, for any reason, is devastating.

The queen reclined with no bedding, which meant that the intellect was in a state of disarray. It was not functional. The action of a coreSelf, to not regard the intellect, could result in chaos of the intellect, such that when the core again requires the services of the intellect, that core would find the intellect in disarray.

नारद उवाच
पुरञ्जनः स्व-महिषीं निरीक्ष्यावधुतां भुवि /
तत्-सङ्गोन्मथित-ज्ञानो वैक्लव्यं परमं ययौ (४॥२६॥१८)

nārada uvāca
purañjanaḥ sva-mahiṣīṃ
nirīkṣyāvadhutāṃ bhuvi /
tat-saṅgonmathita-jñāno
vaiklavyaṃ paramaṃ yayau (4.26.18)

nārada – Nārada, uvāca – said, purañjanaḥ - Purañjan, the City Person, sva – his, mahiṣīṃ - queen, nirīkṣyāvadhutāṃ = nirīkṣya (observing) + avadhutāṃ (lone ascetic yogi), bhuvi – on the ground, tat - her, saṅgonmathita = saṅga (associate) + unmathita (feeling undone), jñāno = jñānaḥ = wise man, vaiklavyaṃ - bewildered, paramaṃ - totally, yayau – went

Nārada said.
“Purañjan observed his queen who was lying on the ground. She was like a lone ascetic yogi. Feeling undone, he went to associate with her. Though a wise man, he was totally bewildered. (4.26.18)

Detail

For all he was, great hero, adventurer, handsome and remarkable individual, still for understanding women, Purañjan was lacking. He did not have the intuition to know what actions of his would cause the alienation of the young woman, who was the love of his life.

There are two forms of education. One is formal or academic. The other is experiential which is intuitive. In reference to his understanding of women, Purañjan had neither. The experience of the queen’s absence from her chamber and her being in disarray on the ground, was distressing to him.

Feeling undone, he went to associate with the lady. Though a wise man, he was bewildered because her response was unexpected. He had no idea she would react in that way.

It is interesting that if the coreSelf finds itself without the services of the intellect, that core may be in for a rude awakening, because of the equipment in the psyche not being available to it.

Some servants of the queen were assigned to assist Purañjan when he was alone and needed help, but these attendants were the queen’s employees. None of them would help the adventurer with anything which he independently wanted.

Their tendency was limited to helping Purañjan, when he needed to rectify himself, but only in terms of making himself responsive to the queen. They facilitated whatever was necessary for him to get himself in a condition which was suited to his being complimentary to the lady.

सान्त्वयन् श्लक्ष्णया वाचा हृदयेन विदूयता /
प्रेयस्याः स्नेह-संरम्भ- लिङ्गम् आत्मनि नाभ्यगात् (४॥२६॥१९)

sāntvayan ślakṣṇayā
vācā hṛdayena vidūyatā /
preyasyāḥ sneha-saṃrambha-
liṅgam ātmani nābhyagāt (4.26.19)

sāntvayan – pacifying, ślakṣṇayā – pleasant, vācā – speech, hṛdayena - heartfelt, vidūyatā – regretting, preyasyāḥ - of his beloved, sneha – from affection, saṃrambha – intense anger, liṅgam – indication, ātmani – in herself, nābhyagāt = na (not) + abhyagāt (aggravate)

"Pacifying her with pleasant speech, which was heartfelt, regretting what happened, he did nothing to aggravate the intense anger which converted from her affection. (4.26.19)

Detail

Purañjan was sure to pacify the queen. She was estranged enough. He could tolerate no increase in her rejection. Being afraid of the alienation, he wanted the lady to shower her graces again.

His idea of independence vanished. That was a distant memory. The only mental occupation he had was to change the situation to what it was before.

The first salve he applied was pleasant speech which was heartfelt. He stated that he regretted his absence and wanted to appease her distress.

He explained that he could not sensibly explain what possessed him to get on a chariot which was not provided by the queen. He wanted to be forgiven for the irrational conduct and heartless selfish decisions.

The relationship with the intellect is such that the core does not have full autonomy. This is so because it did not produce the intellect. If one did not produce a psychic equipment, one cannot control it absolutely. Whoever or whatever produced the intellect has the root control of it. This is why the core's effort to manhandle the intellect may fail for most entities.

If the intellect becomes alienated to the coreSelf, that core will lose some intellectual services. This will cause the core to make uninformed decisions. As Purañjan was brought to his knees in his effort to pacify the queen, so the coreSelf may submit to the intellect on occasion, when the core acts in a way which causes the intellect to deprive the core of analytical operations.

At that time, the core may pacify the intellect. The core may regret actions done without consultation. It will avoid acting in a way to further alienate the intellect.

It is experienced that when a decision is made to drink liquor, the intellect may become hostile to the core, which will regret having indulged in the alcohol. The anguish of this may last for hours until the alcohol's effects cease in the physical and subtle bodies.

The suggestion to use alcohol is first mentioned by the kundalini Power Central. The intellect rejects the suggestion but the coreSelf may favor the kundalini and permit the use of the liquor. The intellect will be negative towards this and will distance itself from the core. That results in a crisis.

अनुनिन्ये ऽथ शनकैर् वीरो ऽनुनय-कोविदः /
पस्पर्श पाद-युगलम् आह चोत्सङ्ग-लालिताम् (४॥२६॥२०)

anuninye 'tha śanakair
vīro 'nunaya-kovidaḥ /
pasparśa pāda-yugalam
āha cotsaṅga-lālitām (4.26.20)

anuninye – agreeable, 'tha = atha = even so, śanakair = śanakaiḥ = gradually, vīro = viraḥ = hero (City Person), 'nunaya = anunaya = appeasing, kovidaḥ - sweet speaker, pasparśa – touched, pāda-yugalam = both feet, āha – he said, cotsaṅga = ca (and) + utsaṅga (on the lap), lālitām – lovingly embraced

"Gradually over time, being agreeable, that heroic man, with sweet speech, appeased his Mistress. He touched her feet, spoke to her, put her on his lap, and embraced lovingly." (4.26.20)

Detail

Purañjan, the adventurer, the one who suddenly decided to make his own decisions, to be sportive and detached while killing animals, found himself in a fix, when he could not access his wife. Once the woman became disagreeable, whatever he did by his own selection, lost meaning.

He was so humble that he touched her feet. He spoke lovingly with submission. He put her on his lap. He embraced her lovingly, giving the most attention that he could share with anyone. He realized forthwith that if he lost access to the lady and her staff, he would be depressed.

पुरञ्जन उवाच
नूनं त्व् अकृत-पुण्यास् ते भृत्या येष्व् ईश्वराः शुभे /
कृतागःस्व् आत्मसात् कृत्वा शिक्षा-दण्डं न युञ्जते (४॥२६॥२१)

purañjana uvāca
nūnaṃ tv akṛta-puṇyās te
bhṛtyā yeṣv īśvarāḥ śubhe /
kṛtāgaḥsv ātmasāt kṛtvā
śikṣā-daṇḍaṃ na yuñjate (4.26.21)

purañjana – City Person, uvāca – said, nūnaṃ - definite, tv = tu = but, akṛta – not acting, puṇyās = puṇyā = responsible behavior, te – that, bhṛtyā = bhṛtyāḥ = servants, yeṣv = yeṣu = to whom, īśvarā = īśvarāḥ = masters, śubhe – honored self, kṛtāgaḥsv = kṛtāgaḥsu = done an offense, ātmasāt - one's own, kṛtvā – doing, śikṣā – instruction, direction, daṇḍaṃ - punishment, na – not, yuñjate – given

Purañjan, the City Person, said.
"It is definite, O honored self, that when acting in an irresponsible way, servants who regard themselves as masters, and who do an offense, are unfortunate if they are not punished. (4.26.21)

Detail

Here we are informed by none other than the great hero and adventurer, Purañjan, that the relationship between the queen and himself is such, that if he is faulted through committing an independent action, he should be harshly punished, and should appreciate any, even the tiniest attention which he gets from the mistress. He addressed her as the honored self. He condemned himself as an offensive servant.

In terms of the psyche, this is an illustration of the relationship between the coreSelf and the intellect, whereby the intellect has the upper hand, and the core is nothing but a doting slave.

By itself, as the adventurer, the heroic wanderer, the core acted as a proficient hunter, sporting in the forest killing animals, using weapons with expertise. But when he was with the queen, he did no violence. That was not her habit.

The core, if it remains linked to the intellect, finds itself consenting or dissenting to the activities of that adjunct. Sometimes the core is influenced to do as suggested, but at other times, it may resist and refuse to authorize the conclusions of that adjunct.

How much should a coreSelf rely on its intellect? How would a core know when the intellect draws the wrong conclusions or when it consents because it is under the influence of the senses?

The core may regard the intellect as a superior. This is because of the services rendered, functions which the core cannot perform as proficiently as the intellect would.

This is a technical arrangement which the core should study, so that it can change the situation where it could be dominant and informed, without having to kowtow to the intellect.

In a dream, when Purañjan transited to a forest where he hunted animals, he had no developed discrimination. That was left behind in the physical existence. That was the Queen. The coreSelf should study its situation to realize that when it transfers to some other dimension, it may lack its analytical faculty in that other place.

परमो ऽनुग्रहो दण्डो भृत्येषु प्रभुणार्पितः /
बालो न वेद तत् तन्वि बन्धु-कृत्यम् अमर्षणः (४॥२६॥२२)

paramo 'nugraho daṇḍo
bhṛtyeṣu prabhuṇārpitaḥ /
bālo na veda tat tanvi
bandhu-kṛtyam amarṣaṇaḥ (4.26.22)

paramo = paramaḥ = best, 'nugraho = anugrahaḥ = favor, daṇḍo = daṇḍaḥ = penalty, bhṛtyeṣu – to servants, prabhuṇārpitaḥ = prabhuṇā (by the master) + arpitaḥ (assigned), bālo = bālaḥ = childish, na – not, veda – know, tat – that, tanvi – slender woman, bandhu – friend, kṛtyam – duty, amarṣaṇaḥ - hasty

"It is the best favor for servants when a master assigns a penalty, but childish attendants do not know this, O slender woman. They are hasty and do not appreciate the duty of a friend. (4.26.22)

Detail

In this statement, Purañjan appealed to the sexual attraction between himself and the queen. Both were irresistibly drawn to the other. He hoped that the queen was just as afflicted as he was. By addressing her as *Tanvi*, the sexually alluring woman, he draws her attention to their sexual needs.

Condemning himself further, he showed humility and submission. He begged to be pardoned. How could he live happily when the queen was aggravated by his behavior.

It seems that the coreSelf, who was represented in the tale as Purañjan, would say anything or do anything, to be in the graces of the intellect. The core becomes morose when it finds that the intellect does not have a plan, and is divorced from it, not rendering opinions, and barring the senses and the vital energy from rendering service.

With the intellect disabled, the core enjoys no royal privileges. It becomes dissatisfied and nervous. It disliked being kept at a distance from the intellect.

सा त्वं मुखं सुदति सुभ्रव् अनुराग-भार-
व्रीडा-विलम्ब-विलसद्-धसितावलोकम् /
नीलालकालिभिर् उपस्कृतम् उन्नसं नः
स्वानां प्रदर्शय मनस्विनि वल्गु-वाक्यम् (४॥२६॥२३)

sā tvaṃ mukhaṃ sudati
subhrv anurāga-bhāra-
vrīḍā-vilamba-vilasad-dhasitāvalokam /
nīlālakālibhir upaskṛtam unnasaṃ naḥ
svānāṃ pradarśaya manasvini valgu-vākyam
(4.26.23)

sā – specific female, tvaṃ - you, mukhaṃ - face, sudati – woman with beautiful teeth, subhrv = subhru – with attractive eyebrows, anurāga – sweet attachment, bhāra – carrying, vrīḍā – playfulness, vilamba – dropping, vilasad = vilasat = glittering, dhasitāvalokam = hasitāvalokam = hasita (smiling) + avalokam (glancing), nīlālakālibhir = nīla (blue) + alaka (with hair) + alibhir (bee-like), upaskṛtam – perfected beauty, unnasaṃ - raised nose, naḥ - us, ?, svānāṃ - owned by you, pradarśaya – display, manasvini – genius of a woman, valgu – sweet, vākyam - speech

"O! See your specific face with beautiful teeth, attractive eyebrows, expressing sweet attachment, carrying playfulness, radiating, and glittering with smiling and glancing, with blue beelike hair, having perfect beauty and a raised nose. I am owned by you. Please display your sweet speech, O genius of a woman. (4.26.23)

Detail

Nārad revealed to humanity, the usual relationship between the coreSelf and the intellect, with the intellect being in the superior position. Is this what it is? Why were we told otherwise by other teachers? What are the limits of the autonomy of the core over its adjuncts?

Purañjan that swashbuckling adventurer, is revealed as a slave of the young woman whom he met while wandering over the earth. For all he is, as a marksman with deadly arrows, he was nothing but a mimicking companion of a queen.

To bring himself into the favor of the lady, he showered her with a description of her beautiful figure and alluring facial profile. He declared that he was owned by her, and could not be happy unless she uttered sweet speech. He declared her as a genius.

Purañjan was allured by the queen's face with beautiful teeth, attractive eyebrows, sweet attachment, playfulness, radiating, and glittering with smiling and glancing, with blue beelike hair, having perfect beauty, and a raised nose. Without the use of a weapon, with not even one single arrow, she owned him.

The core finds itself in a lowly position under the authority of the intellect, which gets the cooperation of the sensual energies and memories. Wanting the services of the intellect and its accessory powers, the core sells itself to get information from the senses but the senses do not take orders directly from the core. Disregarding the core, the senses ignore its suggestions, and instead, do as directed by the intellect. Such is the power struggle except that in most cases, the intellect wins control. It makes the core endorse conclusions.

The senses are the information and video collection agency but they do so, as directed by the intellect and the kundalini Power Central. Any order from the core is executed by the senses only with the permission of the intellect. Even the access for storage of and retrieval of memory, is controlled by the intellect.

There is a conspiracy. The intellect, the memory, the senses, and the sensual energies (kundalini) are in cahoots in contrast to the core.

तस्मिन् दधे दमम् अहं तव वीर-पत्नि
यो ऽन्यत्र भूसुर-कुलात् कृत-किल्बिषस् तम् /
पश्ये न वीत-भयम् उन्मुदितं त्रि-लोक्याम्
अन्यत्र वै मुर-रिपोर् इतरत्र दासात् (४॥२६॥२४)

tasmin dadhe damam ahaṃ tava vīra-patni
yo 'nyatra bhūsura-kulāt kṛta-kilbiṣas tam /
paśye na vīta-bhayam unmuditaṃ tri-lokyām
anyatra vai mura-ripor itaratra dāsāt (4.26.24)

tasmin – to him, an offender, dadhe – give, damam - punishment, ahaṃ - I, tava – on your behalf, vīra-patni = wife of a hero, yo = yaḥ = who, 'nyatra = anyatra = elsewhere, another, bhūsura = bhū sura = god on the earth, kulāt – from the group, kṛta – done, kilbiṣas = kilbiṣaḥ = offense, tam – him, paśye – I see, na - no, vīta – without, bhayam – fear, unmuditaṃ - without anxiety, tri-lokyām – three realms, anyatra – any other, vai – indeed, mura-ripor = mura-ripoḥ= of Krishna, of the enemy of Mura, itaratra – conversely, dāsāt – than the servant

"On your behalf, I will give punishment to any offender, O wife of a hero, unless that person is a god on the earth. With the exception of a servant

of Krishna, the enemy of Mura, have no fear or anxiety of anyone in the three realms, if that someone commits a breach against you. (4.26.24)

Detail

In the time of Nārad, Krishna was known as the Supreme Person. He killed an evil sorcerer known as Mura. Due to that reputation, it was believed that if one molested a servant of Krishna, one would be ruined. Except for a devotee of Krishna, Purañjan said that he would curb anyone who offended the queen.

Purañjan can be credited with recognizing the queen's value. When this is applied to the psyche, it means that the coreSelf must be wise enough to estimate the intellect. Even though that adjunct has limitation, it is useful. It is necessary for the self when making informed decisions.

This is applied to the situation of a psyche, which has an observing element, the coreSelf, and adjuncts. For full operation that core must be conscious. But it requires the cooperation of the adjuncts, with the intellect being an essential one. It is so indispensable, that if it turns its face away from the core and deprives the core of its conclusions, that core will be uninformed. Hence the core may submit itself for full cooperation, and even increase its submission, just as Purañjan surrendered to the queen.

With the queen in an unhappy state, with her ignoring him, depriving him of her pleasing moods, the hero was crippled. He had to offer himself in full submission. He promised not to act independently again.

वक्त्रं न ते वितिलकं मलिनं विहर्षं
संरम्भ-भीमम् अविमृष्टम् अपेत-रागम् /
पश्ये स्तनाव् अपि शुचोपहतौ सुजातौ
बिम्बाधरं विगत-कुङ्कुम-पङ्क-रागम् (४॥२६॥२५)

vaktraṃ na te vitilakaṃ malinaṃ viharṣaṃ
saṃrambha-bhīmam avimṛṣṭam apeta-rāgam /
paśye stanāv api śucopahatau sujātau
bimbādharaṃ vigata-kuṅkuma-paṅka-rāgam
(4.26.25)

vaktraṃ - face, na – never, te – your, vitilakaṃ - with no makeup, malinaṃ - without bathing, viharṣaṃ - sour-faced, saṃrambha – with anger, bhīmam – fierce-looking, avimṛṣṭam – not-attractive, apeta-rāgam = without affection, paśye – I saw, stanāv = stanău = breasts, api – also, śucopahatau = śucā (distressed) + upahatau (smeared), sujātau – welcoming, bimbādharaṃ - red lips, vigata – without, kuṅkuma – saffron paste, paṅka – clay, rāgam – color

"I never saw your face without makeup, without bath, sour-faced, with an angry appearance, fierce-looking, non-attractive, and with no affection. Your nice breasts are distressed and smeared. Your welcoming lips are without the red hue. There is no saffron paste and colorful clay. (4.26.25)

Detail

The services provided by the queen were one attraction. Besides that, she was attractive in all respects. Purañjan noticed her beauty. That alone was sufficiently valuable as a trade for his independence.

He wanted her to reinstate her mood, her good looks, her sexy challenging form, everything. He was miserable without that. To state it directly.

The core is sexually attracted to the intellect, and likes to be in a position to appreciate the intellect's beauty.

This happens in the mind, where one adjunct may have an emotional relationship with the coreSelf. It could be the core and the intellect, or the core and the kundalini lifeForce Power Central, or the core and a specific sense organ. It could be the core and its need for a memory.

We experience the attractive power of the adjuncts from moment to moment. The majority of coreSelves who use physical bodies, either as humans or otherwise, are primarily under the influence of the adjuncts.

Purañjan was not the leader in the Excitement City. He was the loyal and obedient slave. Once, when he expressed independence and branched out on his own, he was checkmated by the disagreeable moods of the queen. When he discovered that the queen disapproved of his independent behavior, his happy mood collapse. He compromised. The changes required to normalize their lifestyle were made by him.

In the dream existence Purañjan had weapons. He was a first-class bowman. But his armaments and expertise there were no match for the unpleasant moods of the queen on the physical side.

As he could not take his eyes away from the queen, even though she did not gaze on him, so the coreSelf is usually compelled to look at the intellect. If that adjunct is in a disagreeable mood, the core becomes distressed as well.

तन् मे प्रसीद सुहृदः कृत-किल्बिषस्य
स्वैरं गतस्य मृगयां व्यसनातुरस्य /
का देवरं वश-गतं कुसुमास्त्र-वेग-
विस्रस्त-पौंस्नम् उशती न भजेत कृत्ये (४॥२६॥२६)

tan me prasīda suhṛdaḥ kṛta-kilbiṣasya
svairaṃ gatasya mṛgayāṃ vyasanāturasya /
kā devaraṃ vaśa-gataṃ kusumāstra-vega-
visrasta-pauṃsnam uśatī na bhajeta kṛtye (4.26.26)

tan = tat = that, me – to me, prasīda – be compassionate, suhṛdaḥ - dear friend, kṛta – did, kilbiṣasya – committing injury, svairaṃ - strong-willed, gatasya – gone, mṛgayāṃ - hunting, vyasana - violation, āturasya – of sickness, kā – what lady, devaraṃ - husband, vaśa-gataṃ = influenced by, kusumāstra – flower-arrow of sexual arousal, vega – rapid, - visrasta – reject, pauṃsnam – manly, uśatī – hurtful words, na – no, bhajeta – embrace, kṛtye – what is appropriate

"For that my dear friend, be compassionate to me for committing injury and being strong willed, by going hunting and violating the relationship. Which lady would reject her husband, who was influenced by the rapid flower-arrow of sexual arousal? Which woman would say hurtful words and would not embrace him and do what is appropriate?" (4.26.26)

Detail

From the onset, from the time Purañjan met the queen, the agreement they reached for staying in each other's company, was biased towards the queen. It was a contract under her definition, where her assistants and security officer would provide royal services to both the queen and Purañjan, with the queen's needs dictating the format and rendering of what was provided.

Hence, we heard that when she ate, he did likewise. When she became happy, he enjoyed as well. Whatever she experienced to whatever degree, he felt the same excitement.

Purañjan however, did not consider the details. He was so occupied with the events, that he did not examine what he did, as to his mimicking actions, which were a repeat of the queen's behavior.

From the onset of the relationship with its intellect, the core did not carefully examine how the alliance with that adjunct would reduce the core's controlling powers. The core committed itself to an agreement which was in its interest, only some of the time.

If Purañjan acted independently, his doing so, resulted in him being deprived, of the services of the queen and her staff. The core did not have the proficiency to provide those functions for itself. This summarized the core as being a dependent of the intellect.

Chapter 3
Purañjan is intimidated

नारद उवाच
इत्थं पुरञ्जनं सध्र्यग् वशमानीय विभ्रमैः /
पुरञ्जनी महाराज रेमे रमयती पतिम् (४॥२७॥१)

nārada uvāca
itthaṃ purañjanaṃ sadhryag
vaśamānīya vibhramaiḥ /
purañjanī mahārāja reme ramayatī patim (4.27.1)

nārada – Nārada. uvāca – said, itthaṃ - thus, purañjanaṃ - Puranjan, the City Person, sadhryag = sadhryat = united, vaśamānīya – subduing, vibhramaiḥ - by charms, purañjanī – Puranjani, the City Person's woman, mahārāja – O King, reme - eagerly, ramayatī - she enjoyed, patim – her man

Nārada said: Thus, Puranjan was charmed and subdued. He was united with his woman. Then, O king, she eagerly enjoyed her man. (4.27.1)

Detail

This is the verse which magnifies the relationship between the coreSelf and the intellect. It is a romantic affair, happening in the psyche from moment to moment.

In this one verse, Nārada exposed the pitiful condition of the core, where it is enjoyed by its intellect, but where the core mimics the behavior of the intellect, and fools itself into considering that it experiences the circumstances of life directly. The intellect uses the energy of the coreSelf.

When Puranjan acted independently, he left aside the queen. He did not inform her and did not get her consent. Acting on his own, he considered neither the reactions of his acts nor the queen's opinion.

This means that the core did not have a way of gaging what consequence would be derived from an activity. The discriminating faculty, which is represented in the allegory as the queen of the city, is necessary as an adjunct of the core. With it, the core is informed. Otherwise, like Purañjan, the coreSelf will use the physical body to commit acts for which it will regret.

In a dream dimension, Purañjan went hunting for animals. He did not include the queen in this activity. In fact, prior to this, whatever he did after he made the pact to live with the woman, was done after she initiated the action. He was not a free agent. His function was to mimic her experiences.

After hunting, he wanted to approach the queen. He was disappointed however because she isolated herself. Being love-struck, he became miserable due to having no access to her person.

When Purañjan assumed the profile of a vicious skilled hunter, he had no discrimination of his own. The result was excessive animal slaughter. In the dream state, he as the coreSelf lacked moral guidance, which in the tale was present in the physical world as the queen.

The coreSelf is the highest principle in the psyche, and yet, if it acts whimsically and does not include the intellect in decisions, it is likely that the intellect will retract from the core.

When Purañjan returned to the Excitement City, he felt the need to bathe and make himself presentable. That he did. Feeling confident, his mind visualized his meeting with the lady of the city.

He noticed that there was a gloomy atmosphere in the rooms. He questioned some servants. They informed that the queen was in distress and was withdrawn. He went to her bedroom and discovered that she was disheveled and miserable.

He spoke to her. After some appealing, she agreed to forgive him and normalize the situation. He was charmed. They united. She eagerly enjoyed her man.

This indicates that the coreSelf is enjoyed by the intellect. But Nārad explained that the initiator of actions was the queen not the wandering adventurer. Primarily, it was the intellect which enjoyed. It was the coreSelf which mimicked whatever the intellect did.

This may sound absurd. It depends on one's assessment of enjoyment. Regarding if it is a type of energy movement or something else.

स राजा महिषीं राजन् सुस्नातां रुचिराननाम् /
कृत-स्वस्त्ययनां तृप्ताम् अभ्यनन्दद् उपागताम् (४॥२७॥२)

sa rājā mahiṣīṃ rājan
susnātāṃ rucirānanām /
kṛta-svastyayanāṃ tṛptām
abhyanandad upāgatām (4.27.2)

sa = saḥ = he, that, rājā – King, mahiṣīṃ - queen, rājan – O Monarch, susnātāṃ - well-bathe, rucirānanām – attractive face, kṛta-svastyayanāṃ = having dressed irresistibly, tṛptām – filled with plesure, abhyanandad – going to, upāgatām – went to

That king saw the queen, O Monarch. She was well-bathe, and with her attractive face, having dressed irresistibly, he was filled with pleasure. He went to greet her. (4.27.2)

Detail

It seems that Purañjan enjoyed the greatest pleasure when the queen was favorably disposed to him. When she absorbed his attention and allowed him to see her sexually attractive body, his feelings excelled. He was filled with pleasure, and was irresistibly pulled to her influence.

Even though somehow, he broke the spell of her influence, and sported, killing animals, once that spree was over, he resumed her association and was happy to be in her spell.

This information gives more insight into the relationship between the coreSelf (Purañjan) and the intellect (queen). The core derived happiness from being entertained by the intellect. This was such that when the intellect resisted the core, that core became distressed and felt the need to do whatever was necessary to befriend the intellect.

तयोपगूढः परिरब्ध-कन्धरो रहो ऽनुमन्त्रैर् अपकृष्ट-चेतनः /
न काल-रंहो बुबुधे दुरत्ययं दिवा निशेति प्रमदा-परिग्रहः (४॥२७॥३)

tayopagūḍhaḥ parirabdha-kandharo
raho 'numantrair apakṛṣṭa-cetanaḥ /
na kāla-raṃho bubudhe duratyayaṃ
divā niśeti pramadā-parigrahaḥ (4.27.3)

tayopagūḍhaḥ = tayā (by her) + upagūḍhaḥ (embraced), parirabdha – hugged from every side, kandharo = kandharaḥ = neck, raho = rahaḥ = privacy, 'numantrair = anumantraiḥ = agreeable speech, apakṛṣṭa – degraded, lowered, cetanaḥ - frame of mind, na – not, kāla – time, raṃho = raṃhaḥ = rapidity of, bubudhe – perceive, duratyayaṃ - cannot be regulated, divā – day, niśeti = niśā (night) + iti (hence), pramadā – by the attractive woman, parigrahaḥ - influenced in every way.

He was embraced by her. He hugged her from every side and especially her neck. In privacy, they exchanged agreeable speech. Thus, the king was in a degraded frame of mind. He did not perceive the passing of time in the form of days and nights which no one can regulate. He was influenced in every way by that attractive woman. (4.27.3)

Detail

Nārad reported that Purañjan was degraded. His elation from being in the good favors of the queen, was not to his credit. Instead, it put him under her influence.

From one angle, Purañjan did well to reestablish a loving relationship with the woman. From another, that reconciliation put him under a deeper influence. It was degrading because it did not allow his mental and emotional development. He was again in full dependence. He would again only do what was initiated by her, where if she ate, he swallowed just the same. When she laughed, he became jovial.

In considering the coreSelf and its adjuncts, the core was in a fix in both situations; when it acted independently, and when it confirmed to the intellect in every way. The need for the core for discrimination is a telling feature. Initially, it did not have the analytic powers and had to attached itself to an intellect, which facilitated it with a psyche, which was like a well-fortified city, which had a royal staff and a sleepless security officer.

The initial mistake made by Purañjan when he met that queen, was that Purañjan did not negotiate the contract. He allowed the queen to draft a statement which dictated that he would be catered for one hundred years. This arrangement was not to his advantage.

Of course, he enjoyed. She provided luxurious accommodation and security. She made the decisions about their activities. He had no direct control over the royal servants. He did not communicate directly with the security officer.

Due to fascination with his good luck in meeting the agreeable lady, Purañjan signed on for the services without considering the consequences. He set himself for failure and disappointment.

The marriage contract between Purañjan and the queen was drafted by her, where she limited it to one hundred years. Purañjan did not analyze the agreement. He did not determine if any of it would lead to embarrassment. He never said to himself, "Why only one hundred years? If this is a good agreement, why not commit this for all time?"

He had such a good time, that he did not perceive the passing of time in the form of days and nights which no one can rate. Except for when he hunted animals, he was influenced in every way by that attractive woman.

He never thought that the relationship would soon terminate. Would the queen and her staff be vacated from the place? What would he do then? Move from Bhogavatī, the Excitement City? Hence being distracted, Purañjan was unconcerned with the advance of time.

शयान उन्नद्ध-मदो महा-मना
महार्ह-तल्पे महिषी-भुजोपधिः /
ताम् एव वीरो मनुते परं यतस्
तमो-ऽभिभूतो न निजं परं च यत् (४॥२७॥४)

śayāna unnaddha-mado mahā-manā
mahārha-talpe mahiṣī-bhujopadhiḥ /
tām eva vīro manute paraṃ yatas
tamo-'bhibhūto na nijaṃ paraṃ ca yat (4.27.4)

śayāna – reclining, unnaddha – increasing, mado = madaḥ = bewildered, mahā – great, manā = manāḥ = mind, mahārha – valuable, talpe – on bed, mahiṣī – of the queen, bhujopadhiḥ = bhuja (arms) + upadhiḥ (pillow), tām – her, eva – sure, vīro = vīraḥ = hero, manute – thought, paraṃ - best, yatas = yataḥ = from which, tamo = tamaḥ = by confusion, 'bhibhūto = abhibhūtaḥ = overwhelmed, na – not, nijaṃ - self, paraṃ - best, ca – and, yat – what

Being increasingly bewildered, while reclining on a most valuable bed, with his queen's arm as the pillow, the great minded man, that hero, thought of her as the best. By confusion, he was overwhelmed not serving the best interest of his self. (4.27.4)

Detail

The reliance of the coreSelf on its intellect is such that Nārad contrasted it with a king who reposes comfortably and satisfyingly on the arm of a queen. As a newborn infant is comforted on the breast of its mother, so Purañjan was relieved of anxiety, when he had the queen in proxmity where she did the needful to provide him with every convenience.

And yet, Nārad was critical of this dependence of Purañjan. Crossing to the situation of the psyche, where the coreSelf relies on the intellect, that core discovers itself being fully dependent on its intellect. It relies so much on that adjunct, that the relationship may be compared to a dignified man who gives himself in every way to an attractive woman, where the woman serves even as the discrimination of the man, where he does not check her decisions, and allows her to dictate their lifestyle.

Nārad suggested that when this happens, the coreSelf is in a state of confusion and cannot serve its best interest. Handing over its decision-making ability to the intellect, the core does not free itself from the liabilities. It still has to experience the good or bad consequences.

How should the core solve this? What should it do since it cannot on its own derive the information needed to make decisions? To be informed it has to rely on the intellect, but it should not be lazy. It should use the sensual information to make decisions. It should not enjoy itself to such a degree that it cannot spare the time to monitor the intellect's conclusions.

Purañjan's mistake was that he relaxed his discrimination. This happened because he did not have the complete equipment for making decisions. He lacked the sensual equipment in the form of smelling, tasting, seeing, touching, and hearing. He had the attention sense which is the master sense which can operate the five procuring senses. That equipment was present naturally with the queen in the form of her staff and the five-headed security officer.

Purañjan's agreement with the queen was detrimental to his interest. It was to last for one hundred years which was a reasonable amount of time. That was sufficient for him to be informed about the situation of living in the Excitement City. But Purañjan lazily allowed the queen to make decisions regarding how they should live together.

She made the decisions from day to day. He merely consented. This saved him the mental process and anxiety but it was at the cost of not knowing the outcomes of the decisions made by the beautiful queen.

The coreSelf wanted an easy life, enjoying itself in various sensual ways. Hence when it was coupled with its intellect, it felt happy to be a consenting force, not a decisive one which must gather sensual data and make decisions. That way of thinking is unacceptable because some decisions made are not in the interest of the self.

Initially the queen admitted that she had no idea about her parentage. She had no information or experience about how she was created, nor about who built the city. Her intuition assured that the snake and servants would continue facilitating whatever desire came to her creative mind.

She knew that the occasion of life with Purañjan would last for one hundred years. She guaranteed that but how it would end, she did not describe. Purañjan should have spent some of his time researching that, to make a plan for transfer to some other place.

Each coreSelf considers its intellect to be handy. There is so much arrogance in the psyche, that even persons with a faulty intellect, which was proven to be error-prone, feel that the intellect is perfect in the way it shuffles information and draws conclusion.

This happens because the core is reluctant to interrogate the intellect. The core prefers to relax and rely solely on the intellect, so that the core can use the intellect to shuffle information from the senses and make decisions.

While enjoying itself, not being attentive to sensual information, being increasingly bewildered in the sense of not checking the decisions made by the intellect, being assured that the situations will be comfortable and beneficial, that great self, the core of the psyche, considers the intellect to be admirable and rational. Being fooled like this, it is overwhelmed and does not serve its best interest.

तयैवं रममाणस्य काम-कश्मल-चेतसः /
क्षणार्धम् इव राजेन्द्र व्यतिक्रान्तं नवं वयः (४॥२७॥५)

tayaivaṃ ramamāṇasya
kāma-kaśmala-cetasaḥ /
kṣaṇārdham iva rājendra
vyatikrāntaṃ navaṃ vayaḥ (4.27.5)

tayaivaṃ = tayā (with her) + evam (thus), ramamāṇasya - having a good time, kāma – sexual exchanges, kaśmala – self-destructive act, cetasaḥ - emotion, kṣaṇārdham – split second, iva – certainly, rājendra – O King of men, vyatikrāntaṃ - coming to an end, navaṃ - youth, vayaḥ - lifespan

Thus, while having a good time with her in sexual exchanges which were self-destructive, and emotionally degrading acts, everything happened in a split second. Thus, O King of men, he had no idea that his youth and lifespan would end. (4.27.5)

Detail

The zenith of the relationship between Purañjan and the queen was their sexual union. That was the peak of their mutual pleasure. Every other sensual activity which they indulged, pivoted to sexual indulgence. Even when Purañjan struct out on his own, and hunted, even then he was dissatisfied when he could not find the queen for sexual union.

This means that there is a love affair between the two. They are irresistibly attracted. Even though the core is the superior principle, still the attractive force between it and its intellect is such, that the superiority of the core is neutralized during their participation. Because the core does not have the appropriate sensual tools to scout the environment for adventures, it conveys itself to the intellect.

When Purañjan left Excitement City, for a hunting expedition, he had with him the collective of the mind, the eleventh military commander. He had munitions for hunting. But even then, he had no queen. Due to needing her attention, and due to needing to give her his attention, he returned, bathe, and dressed himself, to meet her for sexual union. When he discovered that she was annoyed, he humbly begged for forgiveness.

He got her pardon. Then they resumed their relationship and indulged their sensual needs. The highlight of that was sexual intercourse.

Apart from the fact that Purañjan did not monitor the queen's decisions, he overlooked something important which was the time factor. It proceeded on its infallible course, without alerting him to its accounting.

Initially, he was informed by the beautiful woman, that the time of their habitation would be one hundred years. He did not think of getting an extension. He did not think about where he would go once that time was exhausted. He did not think about the services of the queen's staff, ending after that period. Living like a child, with not a care in the world, he was negligent of his interest.

The lady did inform him about what she knew for sure, which was that there was no information about her origin or about the cause of anyone else in her retinue. Still Purañjan made no effort to investigate. He was focused on one thing which was pleasure.

Once a coreSelf discovers itself as a physical body, it becomes anxious for its survival in that physical format. When it secures itself in an agreeable social circumstance, it seeks enjoyments. The threat against it is time. That advances from moment to moment. However, if the self is sensually occupied, it does not rate time. It does not gage that other persons are being dismantled. Hence a self does not confront itself with the idea that it cannot continue forever. As it mysteriously came into existence, as the queen admitted, so the self may assume that it will mysteriously disappear.

Instead of considering that, the self avoids the threat. Alternately, it focuses on sensual challenges. While having a good time with the intellect, by consuming its proposals, imagination, memory displays, and emotionally degrading acts, the coreSelf does not realize that it all happens in about a split second. The core does not rate the continuum which terminates the situations.

तस्याम् अजनयत् पुत्रान् पुरञ्जन्यां पुरञ्जनः /
शतान्य् एकादश विराड् आयुषो ऽर्धम् अथात्यगात् (४॥२७॥६)

tasyām ajanayat putrān
purañjanyāṃ purañjanaḥ /
śatāny ekādaśa virāḍ
āyuṣo 'rdham athātyagāt (4.27.6)

tasyām – with her, ajanayat – produced, putrān – sons, purañjanyāṃ - wife of Puranjan, the City Person, purañjanaḥ - Puranjan, śatāny = śatāni = hundreds, ekādaśa – eleven, virāḍ = virāt = O father of people, āyuṣo = āyuṣaḥ = life, 'rdham = ardham = half, athātyagāt = atha (what happened) + atyagāt (he used)

With her, his wife, Puranjan produced eleven hundred sons. O father of the people, as it happened, he used half of his life in that way. (4.27.6)

Detail

By the time one reaches middle-age, one may have indulged and produce children. This happens rapidly with the self not clocking the events, not knowing that the time spend cannot be reclaimed.

In the mind, many ideas, memories, and analytical operations, take place. These occupy the core to such an extent that it remains unaware of the time consumed. The core, like Purañjan, does not tally the involvement. Instead, without rating the durations, it switches from incidence to event.

दुहितॄर् दशोत्तर-शतं पितृ-मातृ-यशस्करीः /
शीलौदार्य-गुणोपेताः पौरञ्जन्यः प्रजा-पते (४॥२७॥७)

duhitṝr daśottara-śataṃ
pitṛ-mātṛ-yaśaskarīḥ /

śīlaudārya-guṇopetāḥ
paurañjanyaḥ prajā-pate (4.27.7)

duhitṝr = duhitṝḥ = daughter, daśottara – more than ten, śataṃ - hundred, pitṛ - father, mātṛ - mother, yaśaskarī – being appreciated, śīlaudārya = śīla (disposition) + audārya (generous), guṇopetāḥ = guṇa (character) + upetāḥ (exceptional), paurañjanyaḥ - daughters of Puranjan the City Person, prajā-pate = king of people

He had more than one hundred and ten daughters, whom their father and mother appreciated, due to the girls' generous dispositions and exceptional characters. So it was, O King of the people. (4.27.7)

Detail

One aspect Purañjan could not increase was the one-hundred-year limit for residence in Excitement City. And yet, he never paused to consider this. He was so preoccupied enjoying the other variables that he did not consider what he should do to offset the residency limit.

No matter what a man achieves, his lifespan cannot be increased. It is set in the biological limitations of the cells of his body. The only thing he can adjust is his focus so that he can view what would happen, as to where he may go when the physical body no longer lives.

He may query himself: To which favorable place, could I transit, when my body is no longer viable as a residence?

स पञ्चाल-पतिः पुत्रान् पितृ-वंश-विवर्धनान् /
दारैः संयोजयाम् आस दुहितृः सदृशैर् वरैः (४॥२७॥८)

sa pañcāla-patiḥ putrān
pitṛ-vaṃśa-vivardhanān /
dāraiḥ saṃyojayām āsa
duhitṝḥ sadṛśair varaiḥ (4.27.8)

sa = saḥ = that one, pañcāla-patiḥ = the governor of Pañcāla Five Region Country, putrān - sons, pitṛ-vaṃśa = descendants of his father, vivardhanān – increasing, dāraiḥ - with wives, saṃyojayām āsa = married, duhitṝḥ - daughters, sadṛśair = sadṛśaiḥ = matching, varaiḥ - with husbands

To increase the descendants of his father, that governor of Pañcāla Five Regions Country, had his sons married to spouses, and his daughters wedded to matching husbands. (4.27.8)

Detail

The tendency to propagate one's body is so entrenched, that even though Purañjan had no idea about his father, nor about the lineage of the queen, still he acted with confidence that he had forefathers, to whom he was instinctually obligated. It did not matter if he or the queen lacked ancestors. What was primal was that the urge to propagate be fulfilled by reproducing sons and daughters, who were capable folks, and who in turn would be matched to spouses to continue the lineages.

The significance of this in terms of what happens in the psyche, is that the coreSelf has a relationship with the intellect, which is similar to that between an adventuring man and a beautiful woman whom he loved. As they would consummate their relationship by coitus, so the coreSelf indulges with the intellect, resulting in the expansive activities of the intellect and the kundalini Power Central.

Together that self and its adjuncts are involved in numerous psychic activities who are precursors for physical history.

Purañjan was the governor of Pañcāla Five Regions Country, but only in the superficial sense. The actual director was the queen. Many philosophers presented the notion that in the psyche, the coreSelf is the primal factor, the ruler. On a close inspection, it is found that in most psyches, the administrator is the intellect.

- Is the core higher or lower than the intellect?

That question is answered when one considers that something may be higher and still be under a lower influence. Because Purañjan needed a capable woman with a staff, security service, and aristocratic accommodations, he bargained his autonomy for those aspects. Thus, he lowered himself to benefit from the service of the beautiful lady.

This runs parallel to the coreSelf which discovered itself existing but without a discriminatory and creative faculty, with no senses nor sensual energy. To acquire those services, it had to submit to an intellect.

पुत्राणां चाभवन् पुत्रा एकैकस्य शतं शतम् /
यैर् वै पौरञ्जनो वंशः पञ्चालेषु समेधितः (४॥२७॥९)

putrāṇāṃ cābhavan putrā
ekaikasya śataṃ śatam /
yair vai paurañjano vaṃśaḥ
pañcāleṣu samedhitaḥ (4.27.9)

putrāṇāṃ - of sons, cābhavan = ca (and) + abhavam (were produced), putrā = putrāḥ (sons) ekaikasya = eka (one) +

ekasya (of one), śataṃ - hundred, śatam – hundred, yair = yaiḥ = by whom, vai – indeed, paurañjano = paurañjanaḥ = concerning Purañjan the City Person, vaṃśaḥ - family, pañcāleṣu – of the Pañcāla Five Region country, samedhitaḥ - fully occupied

Of the sons, other sons were produced, such that there were hundreds from one son who produced hundreds more. Indeed, Purañjan's family fully occupied the Pañcāla Five Regions Country. (4.27.9)

Detail

Purañjan's descendants multiplied sufficiently. They occupied the Pañcāla Five Regions Country. This relates to the existential situation of the psyche, where the coreSelf and the intellect, proliferate in activities which cause rapid expansion in terms of sensual quest, fulfillment, and frustration.

After finding itself with an opportunity-suppling adjunct, its intellect, the coreSelf indulged in whatever the intellect provided. It assumed that the convenient conditions would never end. By ignoring the advancing time factor, the core protected itself from thinking about the end in one hundred years. The queen, who is represented as the intellect, clearly stated that the king could share in her royal accommodations and enjoy her company for one century.

The proliferation of the five sensual activities and of accompanying physical actions, served to distract Purañjan from thinking of the deadline. The queen for her part never considered that inevitable limit. She was too busy processing fresh desires and regurgitating memories. Her staff was focused on providing pleasure. The five-hooded serpent, the security officer, was too concerned with the protection of the city, to be involved directly in anything else. He provided energy to run the five sensual operations of hearing, touching, seeing, tasting, and smelling.

The snake was the one which made repairs to the walls and the inner parts of the city. He alone did this because the many servants of the queen, were occupied in preparing pleasure occasions for the couple.

Purañjan and the queen needed more entertainment. As such their staff increased exponentially as did their offspring. These events consumed their mental and emotional energy, which advanced the deterioration of their bodies.

तेषु तद्-रिक्थ-हारेषु गृह-कोशानुजीविषु /
निरूढेन ममत्वेन विषयेष्व् अन्वबध्यत (४॥२७॥१०)

teṣu tad-riktha-hāreṣu
gṛha-kośānujīviṣu /
nirūḍhena mamatvena
viṣayeṣv anvabadhyata (4.27.10)

teṣu – by them, tad = tat = that, riktha - assets, hāreṣu – of what was enjoyed, gṛha – residence, kośānujīviṣu = kośa (finances) + anujīviṣu (to dependents), nirūḍhena – by the regular, mamatvena – by a strong sense of possession, viṣayeṣv = viṣayeṣu = to attractive objects, anvabadhyata – was captivated

He enjoyed his assets, residences, finances, and dependents. He had a strong sense of possession and was captivated by the attractive objects. (4.27.10)

Detail

For his part, Purañjan focused on enjoyment. He had no time to think about the situation. He did not consider that the contract for residence would soon be void. What would he do? Would he move with the queen, their relatives, the staff, and the security officer? Which other city would they inhabit?

In the psyche of the individual entity, the coreSelf and its adjuncts are involved in one activity, which is *experience*. In some there are pleasures. In others they are displeasures. In yet some others, there is a kaleidoscope of either. The entire psyche is involved in consuming and sampling psychological and physical events.

There is a strong sense of possession throughout the psyche. Even the cells are attracted to specific gratifications which render health or illness to the body and psyche.

ईजे च क्रतुभिर् घोरैर् दीक्षितः पशु-मारकैः /
देवान् पितॄन् भूत-पतीन् नाना-कामो यथा भवान् (४॥२७॥११)

īje ca kratubhir ghorair
dīkṣitaḥ paśu-mārakaiḥ /
devān pitṝn bhūta-patīn
nānā-kāmo yathā bhavān (4.27.11)

īje – he worshipped, ca – and, kratubhir = kratubhiḥ = by a sacrifice, ghorair = ghoraiḥ = by horrible, dīkṣitaḥ - conductor of a sacrifice, paśu-mārakaiḥ = by killing animals, devān – deities, pitṝn – departed ancestors, bhūta-patīn = rulers of human beings, nānā – types, kāmo = kāmaḥ = deires, yathā – as, bhavan – yourself

As the conductor who killed animals, he worshipped in horrible sacrifices. This was addressed to deities, departed ancestors and rulers of human beings. He did various types according to his desires, just as yourself. (4.27.11)

Detail

Nārad directly criticized King Barhi. First Nārad spoke about the legendary but fictitious Purañjan, the City Person, the adventurer who wooed the beautiful queen of Excitement City. Suddenly Nārad brought King Barhi to relevance by stressing the independent activity of Purañjan who ventured away from Excitement City to indulge in the sport of killing animals in horrible sacrifices.

To make those activities acceptable, Purañjan, invoked deities, departed ancestors and members of royal families. This was similar to what King Barhi did during his lifetime.

Nārad disapproved. He alerted the king that those sportive acts of killing animals could not be absolved by offering the carcasses of the animals in religious ceremonies. There would be a time of reconning for that unholy violence. Nārad wanted Barhi to realize this.

युक्तेष्व् एवं प्रमत्तस्य कुटुम्बासक्त-चेतसः /
आससाद स वै कालो यो ऽप्रियः प्रिय-योषिताम् (४।।२७।।१२)

yukteṣv evaṃ pramattasya
kuṭumbāsakta-cetasaḥ /
āsasāda sa vai kālo
yo 'priyaḥ priya-yoṣitām (4.27.12)

yukteṣv = yukteṣu = to social activities, evaṃ - thus, pramattasya – being overconfident, kuṭumbāsakta =

kuṭumba (family) + āsakta (influenced), cetasaḥ - thinking, āsasāda – reached the point, sa – that. vai – definitely, kālo = kālaḥ = time, yo = yaḥ = which, 'priyaḥ = apriyaḥ = disliking, priya-yoṣitām = men who are fond of women

Thus, being regularly involved with social activities, being overconfident, influenced by his family, thinking like that, he reached the point in time which is disliked by those who are fond of women. (4.27.12)

Detail

For men who regard sexual intercourse as the greatest pleasure, old age is unwanted. This is due to malfunction of the genitals, the reproductive apparatus.

A woman's body has special value because it is designed with a birth canal, which is a passage for the introduction of semen and the expulsion of a fetus. A new body is created by ejaculation of sexual fluids into the birth canal. Later, after these fluids produce a viable fetus, the embryo is pushed from the womb. It is routed through the same passage used for introduction of the sexual fluids.

However, as the male body gets older, its semen producing capacity is reduced. Its erectile organ, the penis, may become unresponsive. That means that it will no longer become firm. As a flabby, dangling instrument it is unable to penetrate a woman's vagina.

Though being regularly involved with social activities, being confident, being influenced by his family, though thinking of them constantly, Purañjan reached the point in time which is disliked by those men who focus on sexual intercourse. His body suffered from the afflictions of old age. He could no longer enjoy every aspect of life which was facilitated by the queen.

From a psychological viewpoint, this meant that the five-hooded serpent, the industrious security official, had difficulty maintaining the psyche. Things deteriorated as they do with the passage of time. The core was helpless. The intellect too was unhappy about it. Its services of providing events were curtailed. Even with the serpent exerting itself to the fullest, there were many malfunctions which no one would correct.

Initially, the core had the feeling that its involvement with the intellect and the kundalini Power Central, was enough participation for the health of the psyche. Being that the core was confronted by a willing intellect which was equipped with senses and a Power Central, that core felt that only its participation in permitting and supporting the intellect was necessary. This attitude, though intuitive, was flawed.

The kundalini Power Central can maintain the body when it is youthful but in the adult stage and later in the elderly years, the psyche needs more attention from the core. By then however, the core developes the habit of neglect and finds it difficult to assist the kundalini.

Other parts of the body even the complex glands, act like Purañjan's children and grandchildren. They only live to enjoy the facilities. But they should help the kundalini lifeForce to protect the psyche from deterioration which is within and without the psychic chamber which it knows itself to be.

चण्डवेग इति ख्यातो गन्धर्वाधिपतिर् नृप /
गन्धर्वास् तस्य बलिनः षष्ट्यु्-त्तर-शत-त्रयम् (४॥२७॥१३)

caṇḍavega iti khyāto
gandharvādhipatir nṛpa /
gandharvās tasya balinaḥ
ṣaṣṭy-uttara-śata-trayam (4.27.13)

caṇḍavega – Caṇḍavega = Corrosive-Force, iti – thus, khyāto = khyātaḥ = famous, gandharvādhipatir = gandharva (psychic agents) + (adhipatir) (adhipatiḥ) (lord of), nṛpa (O ruler of men), gandharvās = gandharvāḥ = celestial musicians, tasya – his, balinaḥ - powerful, ṣaṣṭy - ṣaṣṭi – sixty, uttara – the most, śata – hundred, trayam – three

Caṇḍavega, Rapid Corrosive-Force, is the famous lord of the psychic agents, O ruler of men. His powerful group are three hundred and sixty powerful males. (4.27.13)

Detail

The meeting between Purañjan and the queen, took place within the purview of the queen's staff and her security officer. No other limited person was present to witness their initial conversation.

There was no discussion about rapid corrosive agents operating in the vicinity. There was a hint though. This was given by the queen as the limit of the contract which was one hundred years.

Did the lady know that there were invisible forces which would demolish the Excitement City? If she was aware, why did she omit the information when making the agreement with the wanderer?

Nārad informed King Barhi that suddenly, there was a military assault on the city. It was directed by the famous lord of the psychic agents, a general named Caṇḍavega Corrosive-Force. He had three hundred and sixty powerful males at his disposal. Their actions deteriorated everything in the city.

Initially their presence was not felt but after some time, after Purañjan got children and then grandchildren, he noticed the damage. By then there was nothing he could do to prevent it. It was when he had sexual dysfunction, that he was forced to acknowledge that the city was crumbling.

Caṇḍavega, the Rapid Corrosive-Force, was a psychic energy which had physical effects, except that when it first bombarded the city, those effects were not obvious. By the time someone could notice it, the problems which arose were irreversible.

In terms of the city of the physical body, its deterioration begins at the onset when it is first created as a sperm particle and when that sperm is embedded in an ovum. This is because of the massive influence of change which is intrinsic in every part of the biological apparatus that is the body. At every stage, there is deterioration but in the youthful stage, the person becomes preoccupied enjoying the body.

Later in the elderly years, one still craves the pleasures of youth, but Nature insists that one should be subjected to the ravages of old age. It is this shift in focus that causes one to realize that some forces attack to ruin the body. The assault began even before the birth of the body. How so? In the parents' forms, the demolition forces operate. Even there, they establish tactics with intention to ruin the reproductive fluids.

In the parental bodies, there is the plan for full ravishing of their forms. This same phalanx of forces proliferates and takes down whatever progeny is reproduced successfully.

It is not that Purañjan could defeat the Rapid Corrosive-Force. But that does not mean he was correct to ignore it. It was hinted to him, that it would not demolish the place until one hundred years transpired. What he could do was to maintain some of the situations in the city so as to decrease the number of years his family would suffer under the military assault. But that would mean spending less time enjoying the pleasures the queen provided.

गन्धर्व्यस् तादृशीर् अस्य मैथुन्यश् च सितासिताः /
परिवृत्त्या विलुम्पन्ति सर्व-काम-विनिर्मिताम् (४॥२७॥१४)

gandharvyas tādṛśīr asya
maithunyaś ca sitāsitāḥ /
parivṛttyā vilumpanti
sarva-kāma-vinirmitām (4.27.14)

gandharvyas = gandharvyaḥ = female celestial musicians, tādṛśīr = tādṛśīḥ = complimentary, asya – of Rapid Corrosive-Force, maithunyaś = maithunyaḥ = people occupied with coitus, ca – and, sitāsitāḥ = sita (white) + asitāḥ (black), parivṛttyā – working from every angle, vilumpanti – they destroyed, sarva – all, kāma – what is pleasurable, vinirmitām – provided

In compliment, there were female agents of the same Caṇḍavega Rapid Corrosive-Force. They were occupied with coitus. Some were white, some black. Working from every angle, they destroyed all provided pleasure. (4.27.14)

Detail

The systematic destruction of the body occurred during the day and night, with male militants operating in daylight and female ones hacking at night. There was no pause in the attack. Still, Purañjan was for the most part unaware of it. This was due to his lack of focus on the condition of the city. He was so enthralled enjoying whatever services the queen provided, that he was unconcerned, even when there were alerts about anything being damaged somewhere.

Nārad mentioned that the female corrosive agents were occupied with coitus, sexual intercourse. How so? We know that when Purañjan sported by hunting in the forest, he soon became exhausted. When he got back to the city, he rested, bathe and was attired to meet his woman for sexual entries.

The highlight of the services provided by the queen was sexual pleasure. Now we hear that the female agents of Caṇḍavega Rapid Corrosive-Force had sexual intercourse as a primary focus. This meant that their destructive capacity was specifically applied to the genitals which are the means for the sexual functions.

It was not until his body became older, that Purañjan realized that something was amiss. By then he lost the power to wean himself from seeking erotic pleasure. He continued ignoring the destructive advances of aging cells in the body.

His sexual potency decreased. That affected his chauvinistic tendency, which in turn affected his sexual prowess. His genitals did not respond promptly to sexual overtures from the queen. She noticed his reluctance to indulge. She was concerned that he would become a crippled impotent somebody.

Caṇḍavega Rapid Corrosive-Force operated both day and night. There was no reprieve. While

Purañjan was busy during daylight, they worked. While he relaxed at night, they continue the dismantling assignments. Some of their force sabotaged the sex indulgence apparatus.

ते चण्डवेगानुचराः पुरञ्जन-पुरं यदा /
हर्तुम् आरेभिरे तत्र प्रत्यषेधत् प्रजागरः (४॥२७॥१५)

te caṇḍavegānucarāḥ
purañjana-puraṃ yadā /
hartum ārebhire tatra
pratyaṣedhat prajāgaraḥ (4.27.15)

te – they, caṇḍavegānucarāḥ = caṇḍavega (Massive Reaction) + anucarāḥ (followers), purañjana – City Person, puraṃ - city, yadā – when, hartum – to plunder, ārebhire – promptly, tatra – there, pratyaṣedhat – defended, prajāgaraḥ - Ever-Conscious serpent

When Caṇḍavega Rapid Corrosive-Force and his followers plundered the city, the Ever-Conscious serpent promptly defended the place. (4.27.15)

Detail

Despite the negligence of Purañjan, there was someone who was concerned to protect the Excitement City. That was the five-hooded snake. Even before Purañjan met the queen, this creature was keen to protect her, the staff, and the buildings. Puranjan for his part was an adventurer with no concern about maintaining a residence. Previously he moved from place to place in search of excitement.

His primary interest, other than sexual indulgence was sporting activities, even violent ones like hunting and killing animals. He was not the maintenance type. Luckily, he met an aristocratic woman who had a maintenance official. She only needed a man who would share in her pastimes and pleasures.

This was ideal for Purañjan but it put him at a disadvantage. It prevented him from rating the time factor under which he lived, according to the contract allowed by the queen.

Under the pressure of time, and by the reactive power of the materials in the city, Purañjan and the queen realized that their city deteriorated. It happened slowly. They ignored the destruction. The sleepless serpent felt dutybound to counteract the demolition. This creature defended the place as best as it could. It did so singlehandedly.

स सप्तभिः शतैर् एको विंशत्या च शतं समाः /
पुरञ्जन-पुराध्यक्षो गन्धर्वैर् युयुधे बली (४॥२७॥१६)

sa saptabhiḥ śatair eko
viṃśatyā ca śataṃ samāḥ /
purañjana-purādhyakṣo
gandharvair yuyudhe balī (4.27.16)

sa = saḥ = that someone, saptabhiḥ - with seven, śatair = śataiḥ = with hundred, eko = ekaḥ = alone, viṃśatyā – with twenty, ca – and, śataṃ - hundred, samāḥ - years, purañjana – City Person, purādhyakṣo = pura (city) + adhyakṣaḥ (primary protector), gandharvair = gandharvaiḥ = with skilled psychic agents, yuyudhe – did combat, balīḥ - powerful people

For one hundred years, that serpent alone fought seven hundred and twenty combatants. He was the primary protector of the city. He did combat against the skilled psychic agents. (4.27.16)

Detail

The serpent was a force to contend with. It felt that it was capable to protect the city. It knew the city inside out. Sometimes it had a victory where it injured one of the seven hundred and twenty combatants. However, these were skilled psychic agents. Even though the serpent was itself a mystic, still it could not eliminate the enemy.

The serpent did not ask for help from Purañjan or from any of the males in the queen's staff. The creature was proud. It was confident that it would rid the city of the enemy forces.

Going here, going there, applying defensive procedures, and repairing damaged areas, that serpent endeavored day and night to save the situation. In time, it was overwhelmed.

The queen did not have the heart to alert Purañjan that he should assist the serpent. She was disinclined to instruct any member of her staff to do so. This was because she was attached to pleasuring and facilitating Purañjan.

Wanting to keep her man by her side, the queen felt that the serpent would eventually bring the enemies under subjugation.

It is evident that the coreSelf in its relationship with the intellect, is hardly concerned about the security issues for the psyche.

The core relied on the kundalini Power Central to repair any malfunction and to secure the openings of the psyche as necessary. Everyone's role was established as designed by whosoever created the queen, her staff, the security officer, and the secured residences. To put it in psychological terms, the coreSelf came into a situation where it was permitted to do certain things only. It could not rearrange anything. The contract it made with its intellect was preset for a specific role, where the core was entertained and chaperoned in specific ways.

क्षीयमाणे स्व-सम्बन्धे एकस्मिन् बहुभिर् युधा /
चिन्तां परां जगामार्तः स-राष्ट्र-पुर-बान्धवः (४॥२७॥१७)

kṣīyamāṇe sva-sambandhe
ekasmin bahubhir yudhā /
cintāṃ parāṃ jagāmārtaḥ
sa-rāṣṭra-pura-bāndhavaḥ (4.27.17)

kṣīyamāṇe - deteriorating, sva-sambandhe = his dear friend, ekasmin – one only, bahubhir – with many, yudhā – battle, cintāṃ - thinking, considering, parāṃ - best, jagāmārtaḥ = jagāma (felt) + ārtaḥ (painful, aggrieved), sa – with, rāṣṭra – of the country, pura – of the city, bāndhavaḥ - relatives, friends

When Purañjan noticed the deterioration of his dear friend, the one and only person who fought many enemies in that battle, he, the relatives, and friends, considered the situation of the country. They were aggrieved. (4.27.17)

Detail

Even though the attack on the city began even before Purañjan discovered it, he did not realize the extent of the destruction. This was due to being occupied with the enjoyments and excitements which the queen's staff provided.

Purañjan was faced with the effects when he noticed that the sleepless serpent could not do its duties as before. This means that the psyche's deterioration is not realized directly by the core. When the intellect explains to the core about the danger which transpires, then the core realizes the situation.

At that time, the core, along with the sensual energies and senses, become aggrieved. The core sensed that the situation was dangerous for one and all.

Despite being healthy and vibrant early on, the subtle and physical bodies may suddenly show their inability to counteract the time factor. This causes despondency.

When in the elderly years, the physical body begins to show rapid deterioration, the coreSelf questions itself in regards to what it should do to reverse the flow of time.

Considering one's parents' ill-health or death, one accepts that time is inexorable. No limited being can supersede it. It ruins everything.

After years of enjoying the facilities in the body and the world which is exterior to it, the coreSelf notices that many functions do not work efficiently. This causes ill-health. When this is first noticed, the core ignores it, feeling that its kundalini Power Central will rectify the situation. When this does not happen after days, weeks, months or years, the core is forced to address the situation.

Realizing that the Power Central exerted itself to the maximum but could not repair the damage, the core and its adjuncts become disheartened. With their enthusiasm for enjoying sapped, they assume a depression. The psyche sinks into gloom.

Purañjan reconsiders his life, to find events which he neglected. He grasped shadows of many memories. He could not focus properly. This caused his mind to descend into more negativity. Observing his wife and relatives, he realized that everyone was in distress. They were helpless.

स एव पुर्यां मधु-भुक् पञ्चालेषु स्व-पार्षदैः /
उपनीतं बलिं गृह्णन् स्त्री-जितो नाविदद् भयम् (४॥२७॥१८)

sa eva puryāṃ madhu-bhuk
pañcāleṣu sva-pārṣadaiḥ /
upanītaṃ baliṃ gṛhṇan
strī-jito nāvidad bhayam (4.27.18)

sa – that person, eva – also, puryāṃ - within the city, madhu-bhuk = enjoying wine, pañcāleṣu - in Five-Regions Country, sva-pārṣadaiḥ = his dependents and servants, upanītaṃ - brought near, baliṃ - taxes. gṛhṇan – taking, strī-jito = strī-jitaḥ = charmed by women, nāvidad = na (not) + avidat (consider), bhayam – fear of death

In the city, that person, Purañjan, with his dependents and servants, enjoyed wine in Pañcāla Five-Regions Country. He collected taxes but he was charmed by the women. He did not consider the fear of death. (4.27.18)

Detail

To escape from seeing the deteriorating conditions and the reduction of services given by the queen's staff, Purañjan used the simply solution, which was to enjoy fermented beverages.

Over the years since he first met the queen outside the city, he mimicked her liquor consumption. It was a habit which required no reinforcing. It was embedded in his psyche and in that of the queen and their adult children.

The alcohol adjusted the state of mind, removing the perception of the destruction of the body. It even cancelled the depression of mind. Purañjan continued enjoying his body and the queen's accommodations.

Instead of becoming depressed further, he ignored the sacking of the city and the exhaustion of the five-hooded snake. He ignored the pressure of the time factor, which at every moment reduced the time he could stay at that place.

In terms of the psychology, the coreSelf with its adjuncts, senses, and sensual energy, found itself deprived of certain facilities. This is due to the advance of time where the services become reduced and are of a lower quality. This is noticed by the intellect and the core, except that the core bears the larger liability.

But the core has a tendency to avoid considering this. Instead of engaging the intellect, the core indulges the intellect further for sensual enjoyment through the five senses, which though they become weaker as the days go by, still, they exert themselves to procure the experiences.

The coreSelf makes a mistake in that instead of applying the intellect and the other adjuncts to conserve energy by reducing the enjoyments, it increases sense consumption. That is like an unreasonable tax applied to poor citizens by a greedy government.

कालस्य दुहिता काचित् त्रि-लोकीं वरम् इच्छती /
पर्यटन्ती न बर्हिष्मन् प्रत्यनन्दत कश्चन (४॥२७॥१९)

kālasya duhitā kācit
tri-lokīṃ varam icchatī /
paryaṭantī na barhiṣman
pratyanandata kaścana (4.27.19)

kālasya – of time, duhitā – daughter, kācit – someone, trilokīṃ - three realms, varam – husband, icchatī – she wishes, paryaṭantī –travelled everywhere, na – not, barhiṣman – O King Barhi, pratyanandata – wanted, kaścana – anyone

Time's daughter travelled everywhere in the three realms. She wished for a husband. But O King Barhi, no man wanted her. (4.27.19)

Detail

The creep of time through the body is realized as old age. It surfaces as a wrinkled face, failing memory, grey thinning hairs, baldness, and many ailments in the body. As a man begets a child, so time produces the elderly condition of the body.

Perhaps, the most dangerous encroachment is the effects of time. It is unrelenting. It chokes everyone. It acts before it is visible. It continues even after it is observed.

And yet, that which follows the delivery of time, is unseen. It is deterioration itself. It is known as old-age. It encroaches on a person or material. Suddenly, someone or something does not function as it should.

Nārad alerted King Barhi, that time's daughter, the most dangerous woman in the world, travels everywhere in these existential realms. She did have a need, which was for a most loving husband. But somehow the men detested her. No one thought she was sexy. Not a man welcomed her.

It is not that anyone stood against her or rejected her outright. Pretty much, no one dared to ridicule her. Everyone was fearful of being grasped or selected by her. They had ways of avoiding her.

Because her father is the inscrutable time factor, no ordinary entity could escape her grip. Subsequently, every man was grasped by her. This happened sooner or later, where everyone was invaded by her dilapidating powers.

Existentially, time's daughter is a relative problem. It does not apply directly to the coreSelf, which is a perpetual factor which transcends the transits. However, in so far as the core is allied to adjuncts and bodies, it is affected when those accessories are afflicted.

Since time's daughter is not fulfilled because no man loves her sufficiently, she has a sour attitude and travels with a corrosive power. Even if one does not like her, she clings. In time one realizes that one is chained to her.

There were many ascetics who boasted of being transcendent to time. Still, it cuts everyone down regardless. The most an ascetic could do is to wait for time to complete the destruction of the physical body. One cannot make peace with the daughter of time, except to accept the fact that she has the power to kill. No one can stop her advances.

So long as one is in the physical existence or is connected to it in some way, one will be assailed by her. That is the constant. Nārad alerted King Barhi of this deadly despicable woman by stating the identity of her father, who is Time personified. Some men mishandle and subordinate women but this one reverses the equation and puts men under subordination.

In terms of the psyche, where the supposed governor of it, the coreSelf, gains experiences through its intellect, which the core married; that core was propositioned by another woman, who was the daughter of time.

That new woman, a flare of time, wanted the coreSelf to be her man but the core could not appreciate her looks which signified old-age. No part of the psyche wanted to be fond of the daughter of time, of deterioration.

दौर्भाग्येनात्मनो लोके विश्रुता दुर्भगेति सा /
या तुष्टा राजर्षये तु वृतादात् पूरवे वरम् (४॥२७॥२०)

daurbhāgyenātmano
loke viśrutā durbhageti sā /
yā tuṣṭā rājarṣaye tu
vṛtādāt pūrave varam (4.27.20)

daurbhāgyenātmano = daurbhāgyena (by bad luck) + ātmanaḥ (of self), loke – in the world, viśrutā – known, durbhageti = durbhagā (Unlucky) + iti (thus), sā – she, yā – who, tuṣṭā – pleased, rājarṣaye – to the enlightened king, tu – in turn, vṛtādāt = vṛtā (complied with) + adāt (gave), pūrave - to King Puru, varam - a blessing

Hampered by bad luck in this world, she was known as Durbhagā Unlucky. Once she became pleased with the enlightened King Puru, who complied with her. In appreciation she gave him a blessing. (4.27.20)

Detail

Usually, people fear that bad luck will be followed by more misfortune. This however does not occur in every case. Some instances of bad luck produce favorable events as a consequence.

Nārad wanted to inform King Barhi of at least one historic incidence, where someone, a king named Puru, took the daughter of time, the personification of old-age, and benefited by accepting her marriage proposal.

Puru did his afflicted father a favor by giving youth and health to the old man. This was for a thousand years, after which the father, King Yayati, compensated the favor and crowned Puru as king, even though Puru was the youngest of the sons of Yayati.

The daughter of time is known as Durbhagā, the Unlucky One. Humans misunderstand her and feel that her approach is the reduction of the enjoying ability of the physical body. They do not see a benefit in becoming her lover.

Remaining youthful forever in a physical body would be a misfortune. This is because in an eternal physical body, one would not be challenged to seek liberation. Old-age however is likely to induce thinking about the impact of time. Still, humans are disinclined to old-age.

कदाचिद् अटमाना सा ब्रह्म-लोकान् महीं गतम् /
वव्रे बृहद्-व्रतं मां तु जानती काम-मोहिता (४॥२७॥२१)

kadācid aṭamānā sā
brahma-lokān mahīṃ gatam /
vavre bṛhad-vrataṃ māṃ tu
jānatī kāma-mohitā (4.27.21)

kadācid – it so happened, aṭamānā - touring, sā – she, brahma-lokān = brahma-lokāt = from the creatorGod's world, mahīṃ - earth, gatam – went, vavre – proposed, bṛhad-vrataṃ = one who took a vow of perpetual celibacy, māṃ - to me, tu – then, jānatī – knows, kāma – sexual desire, mohitā – influenced by

It so happened, that while touring she met me when once I wandered from the creatorGod's

world to this earth. She proposed to me, even though it was known that I took a vow of perpetual celibacy. She was urged by sexual desire. (4.27.21)

Detail

The daughter of Time, Durbhagā Unlucky, is no ordinary being. She is supernatural. Rejecting her could be costly. It has penalty. Accepting her and not being discriminative about it, not figuring some way of constructively using her, is silly. Except for Nārad no one could reject her without dire consequences.

Of all the beings who wander from dimension to dimension, assuming different body formats, Nārad was successful with a vow of celibacy. Durbhagā, the Unlucky, was attracted to him for the very reason of his youthful body which appears to be in the prime of its sexual maturity.

From the psychological view, the coreSelf has to contend with its perishable body. Eventually it becomes evident that the body is in a downward spiral towards death. Its sexual desire is greatly reduced, being replaced by impotence and a depressed mood.

This has a double effect. The desire to enjoy sexual indulgence remains, but conversely there is a feeling that one should curtail sex. Thus, the person is afflicted.

मयि संरभ्य विपुल- मदाच् छापं सुदुःसहम् /
स्थातुम् अर्हसि नैकत्र मद्-याच्ञा-विमुखो मुने (४॥२७॥२२)

mayi saṃrabhya vipula-
madāc chāpaṃ suduḥsaham /

sthātum arhasi naikatra
mad-yācñā-vimukho mune (4.27.22)

mayi – to me, saṃrabhya – being totally angered, vipula – excessive, madāc = madāt = irrational, chāpaṃ = śāpaṃ = curse, suduḥsaham - terrible, sthātum – to stay, arhasi – you can, naikatra = na (not) + ekatra (one place), mad = mat = my, yācñā – request, vimukho = vimuktaḥ = refused, mune – O wiseman

To me, she was totally angered. Being excessively irrational, she pronounced a terrible curse. She said, "You cannot stay in any place for any time." O wiseman, this was due to refusing her request. (4.27.22)

Detail

To Nārad, Durbhagā, the unlucky but supernatural woman, was unwanted. He had the power to reject her but to Puru she was willingly accepted when Puru's father, Yayati, was forced to accept her early on in his life. During his youth, Yayati was cursed by his father-in-law.

Puru's father, King Yayati, had children by two women. One was his official wife, while the other was his mistress who was a friend of his wife.

When his wife, a woman name Devayani, discovered that Yayati had sexual relations with her friend, a woman name Sharmistha, Devayani reported the incidence to her father, Shukracharya. He cursed Yayati to lose sexual virility. This happened. With Shukracharya's permission, Yayati temporarily exchanged his abrupt impotency for the sexual virility of his youngest son who was Puru.

Since Puru willingly without hesitation took his father's premature elderly condition and did not censor Durbhagā Unlucky, she who was a supernatural being, was pleased with him, making his adoption of unfavorable energy to be temporary. It lasted for only a thousand years. After that he resumed his youth. His father Yayati resumed the elderly condition.

Conversely, Nārad without hesitation rejected Durbhagā the Unlucky One. She pronounced a terrible curse barring him from staying at any place for any length of time. Because she was a supernatural being who was empowered by what is fated to happen, her wishes in this regard were effective.

Nārad told King Barhi, that Durbhagā, the Unlucky one, was irrational. She is set in her ways and cannot make adjustments. Once she overpowers someone, he must accept her. She influences the course of the person's life so that old-age and senility takes effect.

Purañjan had no chance to reject or divert her. By the time he realized that she was part of the destructive force which assailed him, the damage was beyond repair. His efforts to help his wife, the staff and children was to no avail.

In the psyche there are unfavorable changes taking place. These are ushered into the being by time itself which is a cosmic pressure which no limited person can prevent. One must consider how Nārad became an exception, where time was unable to enforce its decaying hand in the form of its agent, the supernatural seemingly feminine force, Durbhagā the Unlucky one. How did Nārad escape her influence?

In his psyche she was unable to create the havoc of the elderly years, while he had to shift from place to place. His relationship, as a coreSelf to its adjuncts, remained in the clarifying energy, giving him supernatural insight.

ततो विहत-सङ्कल्पा कन्यका यवनेश्वरम् /
मयोपदिष्टम् आसाद्य वव्रे नाम्ना भयं पतिम् (४॥२७॥२३)

tato vihata-saṅkalpā
kanyakā yavaneśvaram /
mayopadiṣṭam āsādya
vavre nāmnā bhayaṃ patim (4.27.23)

tato = tataḥ = then, vihata – withdrawal, saṅkalpā - idea, kanyakā – daughter of time, yavaneśvaram – king of the barbarians, mayopadiṣṭam = mayā (by me) + upadiṣṭam (advised), āsādya – approached, vavre – proposed, nāmnā – known as, bhayaṃ - fear, patim - husband

Then withdrawing the idea of a marriage with me, that daughter of time, as advised by me, approached the king of the barbarians, who was known as Fear Personified. She petitioned him to be her husband. (4.27.23)

Detail

Even though Nārad rejected the offer for marriage with Durbhagā the Unlucky one, he felt that he should recommended a husband. He befriended her and suggested that she should petition the king of the barbarians, who was known as Fear Personified.

Purañjan had no idea of the psychic activities which transpired. He took clues from the condition of the physical system. Whatever negative aspect he noticed there, he avoided.

He had no idea that enemies moved into the subtle body which was the important dimension of the

Excitement City. He was unaware of Durbhagā the Unlucky one. The fact that Nārad evaded her and was affected by her curse for wandering with no homestead, was unknown to Purañjan.

The power of Durbhagā, the Unlucky One, is such that one cannot evade her. If, however, one resists her, one must accept that one will not locate a queen with a staff and protective agent. One will not be serviced with the pleasures of domestic life. One will be condemned to wander from place to place as Purañjan did before he met the queen.

This reveals a hint, which is that once a coreSelf meets an intellect, that core gains stability, but at a cost which is that the core must consent to and enjoy whatever the intellect designs. The free coreSelf, like Nārad, does not mimic every whim of the intellect, but it does not have the services of the intellect, nor the sensual energies, senses, and the security, which is provided by the kundalini Power Central.

Of course, not every person, not every aspiring ascetic, may resist the opportunity to have sexual intercourse with the queen of Excitement City. One may resist old-age when it approaches as Durbhagā the Unlucky One, but if she comes after one already accepted the queen of Excitement City, one cannot resist her. The acceptance of the queen destroys any resistance one may have to Durbhagā the Unlucky One.

ऋषभं यवनानां त्वां वृणे वीरेप्सितं पतिम् /
सङ्कल्पस् त्वयि भूतानां कृतः किल न रिष्यति (४॥२७॥२४)

ṛṣabhaṃ yavanānāṃ tvāṃ
vṛṇe vīrepsitaṃ patim /

saṅkalpas tvayi bhūtānāṃ
kṛtaḥ kila na riṣyati (4.27.24)

ṛṣabhaṃ - best, yavanānāṃ - of the uncivilized people, tvāṃ - you, vṛṇe – select, vīrepsitaṃ = vīra (hero) + īpsitaṃ (desired), patim – husband, saṅkalpas = saṅkalpaḥ = resolved to do, tvayi – to you, bhūtānāṃ - of the entities, kṛtaḥ - what was done, kila – certainly, na – not, riṣyati – hurt

(She said.)
"I selected you, who are the best of the uncivilized people. I desire you, O hero, to be my husband. I am resolved to be with you. No one is hurt, who is protected by you. (4.27.24)

Detail

There are many forces living within the psyche of a coreSelf. These are secondary factors which may overpower the core. It begins first of all by accepting the intellect which seems to be the perfect match for a core.

When Purañjan accepted the queen's proposition, he also accepted the services of her staff and security officer. However, there were other factors which were unknown to him, and which he was destined to fall under their spell.

If Fear Personified became her husband, Durbhagā the Unlucky one was assured that no limited being could obstruct her. When she possessed someone that person's body was doomed to decay and death.

There are many flaws in the psyche. These are supported by the fear of being inconvenienced. However, fear itself is a power in its own right. Everyone is frightened by it. Being shocked by fear, people avoid even the positive lifestyles which would shield them from many ailments. Instead, they proceed with self-destructive habits which increase their pains and anxieties.

द्वाव् इमाव् अनुशोचन्ति बालाव् असद्-वग्रहौ /
यल् लोक-शास्त्रोपनतं न राति न तद् इच्छति (४॥२७॥२५)

dvāv imāv anuśocanti
bālāv asad-avagrahau /
yal loka-śāstropanataṃ
na rāti na tad icchati (4.27.25)

dvāv = dvāu = two, imāv = imau = those, anuśocanti – they pity, bālāv = bālāu = childish, asad = asat – not practical, avagrahau – following, yal = yat = that, loka – by anyone, śāstropanataṃ = śāstra (written law) + upanataṃ (convention), na – not, rāti – give favor, na – not, tad = tat = that, icchati - wishes

"People pity those two, the childish and the impractical persons, who do not follow the decrees of law and convention, about what should be given, and what should be accepted as a favor. (4.27.25)

Detail

Over time, as the body ages, one should develop a philosophy which is based on realism. That is one benefit of old-age. Otherwise, if one is childish and impractical, one will trample the decrees of law and convention, regarding what should be given, and what should be accepted as a favor. This will result in social and judicial inconvenience.

अथो भजस्व मां भद्र भजन्तीं मे दयां कुरु /
एतावान् पौरुषो धर्मो यद् आर्तान् अनुकम्पते (४॥२७॥२६)

atho bhajasva māṃ bhadra
bhajantīṃ me dayāṃ kuru /
etāvān pauruṣo dharmo
yad ārtān anukampate (4.27.26)

atho – it is reasonable, bhajasva – fascilitating, māṃ - me, bhadra – O dear man, bhajantīṃ - serving, me – for me, dayāṃ - accommodating, kuru - do, etāvān – these, pauruṣo = pauruṣaḥ = for a worthy man, dharmo = dharmaḥ = righteous conduct, yad = yat = that which, ārtān – to one in need, anukampate – kindness

"It is reasonable that you should facilitate me, O dear man. I will serve and accommodate you. A worthy man of righteous conduct will render kindness to a person in need." (4.27.26)

Detail

Durbhagā the Unlucky one, and Fear Personified, king of the barbarians, were supernatural persons, and yet they had needs for companionship. The Unlucky One begged Fear to accept her. In turn, she pledged special services.

काल-कन्योदित-वचो निशम्य यवनेश्वरः /
चिकीर्षुर् देव-गुह्यं स सस्मितं ताम् अभाषत (४॥२७॥२७)

kāla-kanyodita-vaco
niśamya yavaneśvaraḥ /
cikīrṣur deva-guhyaṃ sa
sasmitaṃ tām abhāṣata (4.27.27)

kāla – time, kanyodita = kanya (daughter) + udita (was said), vaco = vacaḥ = speech, niśamya – hearing, yavaneśvaraḥ - leader of the uncivilized people, cikīrṣur = cikīrṣuḥ = wanting to do, deva – of God, guhyaṃ - mysterious work, sa – he, sasmitaṃ - smiling, tām – her, abhāṣata - spoke

Hearing the speech of the daughter of time, the leader of the uncivilized people, wanting to do the mysterious work of God, smiled and spoke to her. (4.27.27)

Detail

Though their presence resulted in negative effects for anyone they possessed, the Unlucky one, and Fear Personified, king of the barbarians, were empowered by God. They were supernatural beings who were agents of the time factor.

मया निरूपितस् तुभ्यं पतिर् आत्म-समाधिना /
नाभिनन्दति लोको ऽयं त्वाम् अभद्राम् असम्मताम् (४॥२७॥२८)

mayā nirūpitas tubhyaṃ
patir ātma-samādhinā /
nābhinandati loko 'yaṃ
tvām abhadrām asammatām (4.27.28)

mayā – by me, nirūpitas = nirūpitaḥ = selected, tubhyaṃ - for you, patir = patiḥ = husband, ātma – spiritual self, samādhinā – meditating, nābhinandati = na (not) + abhinandati (inclined), loko = lokaḥ = people, 'yaṃ = ayam = these, tvām – you, abhadrām – unfortunate, asammatām – unacceptable

He replied.
"After meditating on the spiritual self, a husband for you was selected by me. Never mind, that people are disinclined to have you because you are unfortunate and unacceptable. (4.27.28)

Detail

Fear Personified rejected the idea of taking Durbhagā as his wife. Still, he took responsibility for her as one would for a relative. Even though Fear had negative effects, he was an agent of God for corralling people in this creation. He informed Durbhagā that he meditated on the spiritual self, and knew of the person who would be her spouse.

त्वम् अव्यक्त-गतिर् भुङ्क्ष्व लोकं कर्म-विनिर्मितम् /
या हि मे पृतना-युक्ता प्रजा-नाशं प्रणेष्यसि (४॥२७॥२९)

tvam avyakta-gatir bhuṅkṣva
lokaṃ karma-vinirmitam /
yā hi me pṛtanā-yuktā
prajā-nāśaṃ praṇeṣyasi (4.27.29)

tvam – you, avyakta – impreceptible, gatir = gatiḥ = process, bhuṅkṣva – exploit, lokaṃ - world, karma – social interactions, vinirmitam – produced by, created, yā – one who, hi – hence, me – my, pṛtanā – army, yuktā – proficient, prajā – living beings, nāśaṃ - killing, praṇeṣyasi – you will consume

"Your process of exploiting is imperceptible. The world is produced by social interactions. Being assisted by my proficient army, you will consume the living beings. (4.27.29)

Detail

Fear Personified explained that Durbhagā's method of diminishing physical bodies was imperceptible. The limited beings cannot figure her movements. Since this world operates on the principle of social interactions, the living beings are constantly distracted by those involvements, making it near impossible for them to figure how to either curtail or cease the advance of old-age.

But Fear adds power to the assaults of Durbhagā. To be certain that she would consume all living beings, he granted her the assistance of his proficient army.

प्रज्वारो ऽयं मम भ्राता त्वं च मे भगिनी भव /
चराम्य् उभाभ्यां लोके ऽस्मिन्न् अव्यक्तो भीम-सैनिकः (४॥२७॥३०)

prajvāro 'yaṃ mama bhrātā
tvaṃ ca me bhaginī bhava /
carāmy ubhābhyāṃ loke 'sminn
avyakto bhīma-sainikaḥ (4.27.30)

prajvāro = prajvāraḥ = named prajvāra Pyrexia, 'yaṃ = ayam = this, mama - my, bhrātā – brother, tvaṃ - you, ca – and, me – my, bhaginī – dear sister-in-law, bhava – be, carāmy = carāmi = I will roam, ubhābhyāṃ - by the two of you, loke – in the world, 'sminn = asmin = this, avyakto = avyaktaḥ = not seen, bhīma – formidable, sainikaḥ - with the army

"Accept this one, who is called Prajvāra Pyrexia. He is my brother. You should be my dear sister-in-law. I will roam the world with the two of you and with my formidable army." (4.27.30)

Detail

As supervised by Fear Personified, Durbhagā and Fear's brother, who was known as Pyrexia, would wreak havoc in the lives of the limited beings. Again and again, they would kill creatures.

Chapter 4
Purañjan as a Princess

नारद उवाच
सैनिका भय-नाम्नो ये बर्हिष्मन् दिष्ट-कारिणः /
प्रज्वार-काल-कन्याभ्यां विचेरुर् अवनीम् इमाम् (४॥२८॥१)

nārada uvāca
sainikā bhaya-nāmno ye
barhiṣman diṣṭa-kāriṇaḥ /
prajvāra-kāla-kanyābhyāṃ
vicerur avanīm imām (4.28.1)

nārada – Nārad, uvāca – said, sainikā – army, bhaya – Fear, nāmno = nāmnaḥ = named, ye – them, barhiṣman – King Barhi, diṣṭa-kāriṇaḥ = doing as fated, prajvāra – with Pyrexia, kāla – with Time, kanyābhyāṃ - with Daughter, vicerur = viceruḥ= scorch, environment – world, imām – this

Nārad said, "O King Barhi, with his army, the one named Fear (Bhaya) did, as fated. He was with Pyrexia and Time's Daughter. They scorched the world." (4.28.1)

Detail

Initially, in the beginning when one assumes the format as an infant, that form is healthy. Usually, it takes some time for the body to develop a terminal disease. When Fear, Old-Age and Fever are established, when they coordinate their debilitating features, they damage the body.

Since Purañjan was not trained in how to protect Excitement City, he had no idea of how to counteract the enemy. He noticed some of their assaults but he was at a loss of how to challenge them.

As for the queen, she had full confident that the five-hooded serpent, would protect the place. She noticed some breaches, but she gave it no thought as she had no interest in security concerns.

This means that the intellect is disinclined to check with the kundalini Power Central about assisting in the protection of the physical and subtle bodies.

त एकदा तु रभसा पुरञ्जन-पुरीं नृप /
रुरुधुर् भौम-भोगाढ्यां जरत्-पन्नग-पालिताम् (४॥२८॥२)

ta ekadā tu rabhasā
purañjana-purīṃ nṛpa /
rurudhur bhauma-bhogāḍhyāṃ
jarat-pannaga-pālitām (4.28.2)

ta = te = they, ekadā – once it happened, tu – then, rabhasā – violate, purañjana – Purañjana the City Person, purīṃ - city, nṛpa – O King, rurudhur = rurudhuḥ = surrounding, bhauma – physical, bhogāḍhyāṃ - best excitements, jarat – old, pannaga – serpent, pālitām – secured

Once it so happened that Fear's army violated Purañjan's place. O King, they surrounded that city which had the best of the physical excitements and which was secured by the old serpent. (4.28.2)

Detail

It took some time, nearly one hundred years before the assault penetrated Excitement City. Eventually it reached the inner area where the queen's palace was situated. That place had the best of the physical excitements. It was secured by the old serpent, the skilled security officer.

In terms of the psyche, this palace of the queen was the brain of the physical body. It has special chemical barriers which are unique for protecting the cranium. However, those security features were breached in the combined assault by Fear, Old-Age, and Fever. Because the systems outside the head were compromised, these could not help to protect the brain from debilitating influences. Hence Purañjan, the queen, her staff, and even the snake, were at a loss for how to defend themselves.

At this point in the discourse, King Barhi was astonished. He was anxious to know if Purañjan, the queen and the others, either escaped from the ghastly conditions, or successfully buffered the assault.

काल-कन्यापि बुभुजे पुरञ्जन-पुरं बलात् /
ययाभिभूतः पुरुषः सद्यो निःसारताम् इयात् (४॥२८॥३)

kāla-kanyāpi bubhuje
purañjana-puraṃ balāt /
yayābhibhūtaḥ puruṣaḥ
sadyo niḥsāratām iyāt (4.28.3)

kāla-kanyāpi = kāla (Time) + kanya (Daughter) + api (also), bubhuje – consumed, purañjana-puraṃ = town of the City Person, balāt – by force, yayābhibhūtaḥ = yayā (by whom) + abhibhūtaḥ (influenced), puruṣaḥ - someone, sadyo = sadyaḥ = quickly, niḥsāratām – no power, iyāt – bcecame

Time's Daughter forcefully consumed that city. Anyone she influenced, quickly became powerless. (4.28.3)

Detail

It took some time, for Time's Daughter, Durbhagā, Old-Age, to consume Excitement City. Nevertheless, she was unstoppable because her father was Fate itself, the very time factor. In addition, she was adopted as a sister by Fear Personified. She was married to his younger brother, who was Pyrexia, Fever in person.

We recall that Purañjan agreed to live with the queen for one hundred years. Only on one occasion did he violate the plan. That was when he left the city in a military conveyance for sporting activity to whimsically kill animals.

Purañjan was carefree, eating when the queen did, laughing when he enjoyed incidences, having sexual intercourse when she felt to do it and mimicking whatever else she experienced.

He will be distressed as the queen will be. He will be fearful as she will feel. He will be concerned about violence being applied by the enemy, just as the queen would.

It appears that initially, when Purañjan met the queen with her assistants and security officer, the destructive features which were psychic authorities, were absent from the vicinity.

तयोपभुज्यमानां वै यवनाः सर्वतो-दिशम् /
द्वार्भिः प्रविश्य सुभृशं प्रार्दयन् सकलां पुरीम् (४॥२८॥४)

tayopabhujyamānāṃ vai
yavanāḥ sarvato-diśam /
dvārbhiḥ praviśya subhṛśaṃ
prārdayan sakalāṃ purīm (4.28.4)

tayopabhujyamānāṃ = tayā (by her) + upabhujyamānāṃ (confiscate), vai – indeed, yavanāḥ - barbarians, sarvato-diśam = all directions, dvārbhiḥ - by the doors, praviśya – entering, subhṛśaṃ - excessively, prārdayan – demolishing, sakalāṃ - around, purīm – city

Indeed, while the city was confiscated by her, the uncivilized people entered its doors from all directions. They excessively demolished it from all sides. (4.28.4)

Detail

When the body gets old, there are cell malfunctions in every part. The ill-health becomes a daily problem with an endless struggle which bombards the self with anxiety.

Purañjan was overwhelmed. He was the man for the queen but he was not her security officer. He was her companion for enjoyment but he did not command anything or anyone. He merely mimicked the woman.

Purañjan had no autonomy. Once when he escaped from the control of the queen, he regretted it. When he returned to her convenience, she spurned him. He had to beg her pardon to resume a pleasant relationship.

For all the queen was, as the aristocratic head of Excitement City, she did not establish the defense of the place. That was done by the five-hooded serpent who protected it.

Indeed, while the city was confiscated by Durbhagā the Unlucky one, who was the daughter of Time, which is an infallible supernatural force and by the soldiers of Durbhagā's brother-in-law, the queen could do nothing.

No one from the queen's staff and certainly not Purañjan, ever lifted a finger to help the serpent to protect the city, neither for its internal upkeep nor for its external enclosure. Now that the place was imperiled, no one could do anything to barricade the location. It was excessively demolished from every direction.

From the psychological angle, the coreSelf mimics its intellect to such a degree that the core cannot distinguish between itself and its analytical tool. When the intellect thinks, the core feels that as its action. When the intellect imagines an idea, the core feels that it created that view. When the intellect operates to illustrate a memory, the core is of the view that it did so. The core is entertained. It is not a creator of mental impressions.

When a particular sense does something to collect or reject an odor, flavor, color, surface or sound, the core assumes itself as the initiator and executor of that psychic and/or physical action. Thus, the coreSelf superimposes itself on such experiences and is misplaced in its considerations.

Because of not being attentive to its relationship to the adjuncts, because of the failure to differentiate itself from what is experiences, the core becomes more and more helpless, *and* becomes trapped where it has to experience the varying conditions of the body it assumed.

तस्यां प्रपीड्यमानायाम् अभिमानी पुरञ्जनः /
अवापोरु-विधांस् तापान् कुटुम्बी ममताकुलः (४॥२८॥५)

tasyāṃ prapīḍyamānāyām
abhimānī purañjanaḥ /
avāporu-vidhāṃs tāpān
kuṭumbī mamatākulaḥ (4.28.5)

tasyāṃ - that place, prapīḍyamānāyām – harassed, abhimānī – arrogant, purañjanaḥ - City Person, avāporu – endured much stress, vidhāṃs = vidhān = kinds, tāpān – tensions, kuṭumbī – head of a family, mamatākulaḥ =

mamatā (extended sense of possession) + ākulaḥ (overburdened with)

That place being harassed, the arrogant Purañjan endure much stress of various types. As a head of a family with an extended sense of possession, he was overburdened with various tensions. (4.28.5)

Detail

It may be expressed that Purañjan was not an arrogant person. He was submissive to the queen and agreed to her proposal of companionship for one hundred years. Only once did he breach the agreement but he sincerely apologized and was granted pardon. He was not a habitual offender.

However, from another view, he arrogantly signed on to be served by the staff of the queen and to be under the security shelter of her guardian, the five-hooded snake. Wherefrom did he get the idea that he deserved such facilities?

He did inquire about the queen's parents and her opulent surroundings. She had no memory of how her existence happened. After inquiring in that way, Purañjan arrogantly settled and enjoyed himself to the fullest. When he got the idea to act independently, when he went into the forest to kill animals, he came to his senses when the queen had a cold response.

That arrogance of his was in reference to his contract with the queen. He was also arrogant in the sense that he did not pry into her origin. He did not feel obligated to whosoever created the queen, her servants, the security officer and the city.

कन्योपगूढो नष्ट-श्रीः कृपणो विषयात्मकः /
नष्ट-प्रज्ञो हृतैश्वर्यो गन्धर्व-यवनैर् बलात् (४॥२८॥६)

kanyopagūḍho naṣṭa-śrīḥ
kṛpaṇo viṣayātmakaḥ /
naṣṭa-prajño hṛtaiśvaryo
gandharva-yavanair balāt (4.28.6)

kanyopagūḍho = kanyā (daughter) + upagūḍhaḥ (embraced), naṣṭa – deprived, śrīḥ - beauty, kṛpaṇo = kṛpaṇaḥ = small-minded, viṣayātmakaḥ = self-absorption on sensuality, naṣṭa – without, prajño = prajñaḥ = discrimination, hṛtaiśvaryo = hṛta (lost) + aiśvaryaḥ (authority). gandharva – supernatural being, yavanair – with uncivilized enemies, balāt – using force

Being embraced by the Unlucky One, the Daughter of Time, Purañjan was deprived of beauty. Being small-minded, and absorbed in sensuality, he was without discrimination. His authority was forcibly confiscated by supernatural beings and uncivilized enemies. (4.28.6)

Detail

Because he was not respectful of the time factor, that adventurer who met with fortune on the southern side of the Himalayan mountains, came to misfortune. He did not keep an account of the one-hundred-year limit for his stay in Excitement City. His keen interest was to enjoy life at the queen's expense. He had little idea that from moment to moment the surroundings deteriorated.

Even though there were enemies inside and outside the city, he went to a forest outside the city to sportingly kill animals. The real enemies which were time, time's daughter, and pyrexia (fever), were sheltered by him because he ignored their advances.

This indicates that when one enters a dream state one steps into another dimension. There one forgets the condition of the physical body. Becoming absorbed with the astral situation, one gives no thought to the physical conditions one transited from.

On the physical side of existence, with little knowledge about the implications of associating with the daughter of time, Purañjan embraced her for the benefit of being respected by his children and grandchildren. She gave him seniority as a benefit for his being deprived of bodily beauty.

Initially when Purañjan met the queen, he was desperate for sexual access. The queen herself was in need of a heroic adventurer. They were fascinated with each other.

From the tale one can deduce that Purañjan lacked a skilled intellect, which was something the queen embodied. She was expert in sensuality, especially in sexual enjoyment. Before meeting Purañjan she was sexual inexperienced. Yet, she instinctively knew how to satisfy a man during sexual participation.

Whatever autonomy Purañjan had before he met the queen, was suspended as part of their agreement, for enjoyment of domestic life, for one hundred years. There was one exception, when independently he went to hunt animals. On the psychic side, this meant that he escaped from the physical reality by slipping into astral reality in dreams.

The first woman to embrace Purañjan was the queen of Excitement City. It was a conditional embrace because it signified that he was to be controlled by the queen. It was a restriction. He was not to initiate any activity, only to comply with what the queen did, and to be at her disposal, to experience what she was involved with.

Later, he fell under the control of some supernatural beings and some uncivilized enemies, who were unfamiliar with civilized methods.

This suggest that the coreSelf in its reliance on the intellect, did in effect sell itself as a servile permitter, with the implications that the core would observe and render permissions, but would not object nor hamper any activity of the intellect. Later, the core also sold itself to time, to time's daughter, Old Age, and to Pyrexia. Whatever little independence the core had was confiscated either by the queen or by the enemies.

विशीर्णां स्व-पुरीं वीक्ष्य प्रतिकूलान् अनादृतान् /
पुत्रान् पौत्रानुगामात्यान् जायां च गत-सौहृदाम् (४॥२८॥७)

viśīrṇāṃ sva-purīṃ vīkṣya
pratikūlān anādṛtān /
putrān pautrānugāmātyān
jāyāṃ ca gata-sauhṛdām (4.28.7)

viśīrṇāṃ - destroyed, sva-purīṃ = his city, vīkṣya – seeing, pratikūlān – opposition, anādṛtān – disrespected, putrān – sons, pautrānugāmātyān = pautra (grandsons) + anuga (servants) + amātyān (officials), jāyāṃ - wife, ca – and, gata-sauhṛdām = lacking affection

He saw that his city was destroyed. He was opposed and disrespected by his sons, grandsons,

servants, and officials. His wife too lacked affection for him. (4.28.7)

Detail

Once Purañjan' body was riddled by old-age, its appearance was against him. The senses of his queen and family members got no satisfaction from his elderly body. Just to look at him was a problem. Something happened such that even his wife lacked affection for him.

It had much to do with Durbhagā the Unlucky one. She was none other than Old-Age personified. She forcibly embraced him. Her deadly hug is such that once she becomes espoused to someone, she does not release that person until the death of his body. More and more, the body of that person becomes incapacitated.

This was a painful circumstance for Purañjan. He was deprived of the pleasure of associating with the queen and their children. Now they were discomforting and disagreeable.

The relevance is that the physical body was being destroyed by disease and incapacitation. The coreSelf found that it could do nothing to reverse this. It pondered solutions but it discovered nothing which was effective.

To make matters worse, the core noticed its intellect was unable to analyze properly. The intellect emitted confusion instead. All related functions like sensual detection, and muscular movement, did not function as before. Sometimes when the core gave a command in compliance with the actions of the queen, it found that the order though relayed by the willpower, was not serviced anywhere in the psyche.

आत्मानं कन्यया ग्रस्तं पञ्चालान् अरि-दूषितान् /
दुरन्त-चिन्ताम् आपन्नो न लेभे तत्-प्रतिक्रियाम् (४॥२८॥८)

ātmānaṃ kanyayā grastaṃ
pañcālān ari-dūṣitān /
duranta-cintām āpanno
na lebhe tat-pratikriyām (4.28.8)

ātmānaṃ - finding the self, kanyayā – by the Daughter of Time, grastaṃ - incapacitated, pañcālān – Five-Region Country, ari – enemy, dūṣitān – demolished by, duranta – insurmountable, cintām – feelings, āpanno = āpannaḥ = troubled by, na – not, lebhe – found, tat – of that, pratikriyām – solution

Finding himself incapacitated by the Daughter of Time, with the Five-Region Country being demolished by the enemy, he was troubled by insurmountable feelings and found no solutions. (4.28.8)

Detail

By the time, Purañjan understood his dire situation, it was too late to either slow the onslaught or cease it entirely. On review, one can understand that he could not cease it, but he could have reduced its rapidity, and may have hatched a plan to escape before the one-hundred years expired.

Due however, to his quest for enjoyment and accommodation, he was absorbed enjoying with the queen and was not attentive to the negative features which ripped the city with its opulence residences.

The question which Purañjan should have consider from the onset, was the one about his situation after the one-hundred years expired. As far as we known from Nārad, that inquiry never crossed Purañjan's mind.

If it was that when he signed the agreement with the queen, he had one hundred years with no more nor less, then he was negligent, and failed to pursue his interest about where he could go, and whom he would be with.

In the psyche, the coreSelf discovered itself to be incapacitated by the Daughter of Time which surfaced before, only as a passive easement which was hardly noticed. It whittled away at the core's attention little by little.

Later however, when the time factor affected the core's sensual consumption, the psyche was troubled by insurmountable feelings. It found no solutions.

कामान् अभिलषन् दीनो यात-यामांश् च कन्यया /
विगतात्म-गति-स्नेहः पुत्र-दारांश् च लालयन् (४॥२८॥९)

kāmān abhilaṣan dīno
yāta-yāmāṃś ca kanyayā /
vigatātma-gati-snehaḥ
putra-dārāṃś ca lālayan (4.28.9)

kāmān – enjoyments, abhilaṣan – craving, dīno – pitiful fellow, yāta – gone, vacated, missing, yāmāṃś = yāmān = course, passage, ca – and, kanyayā - by the Daughter of Time, vigatātma – loss the estimation of self, gati – objective, snehaḥ - attachment, putra – sons, dārāṃś = dārān = wife, ca – and, lālayan – caring for

Still craving enjoyments, that pitiful fellow felt vacated by the course of life, made so by the Daughter of Time. He lost estimation of the self but still felt attachment and concern for his sons and wife. (4.28.9)

Detail

Purañjan had no idea of the psychological aspects of self. He was totally involved with his sons and wife, such that he lacked self-interest. For him, the priority was his children. He was so occupied that there was no investigation into what he would do when the one-hundred years expired.

He felt that something stole his life, and diminished his participation in the affairs of his children, and grandchildren. He was too busying tending social affairs to evaluate the rapidity of time.

Purañjan's attention was so diffused into the affairs of the queen and their dependents, that he could not collect and apply any interest to himself.

In terms of the psyche, this means that the coreSelf has so little interest in itself, that it is absorbed in its intellect, sensual energies, and lifeForce. It is fused into those adjuncts, with no understanding that it could divert attention to itself.

गन्धर्व-यवनाक्रान्तां काल-कन्योपमर्दिताम् /
हातुं प्रचक्रमे राजा तां पुरीम् अनिकामतः (४॥२८॥१०)

gandharva-yavanākrāntāṃ
kāla-kanyopamarditām /
hātuṃ pracakrame rājā
tāṃ purīm anikāmataḥ (4.28.10)

Gandharva – psychic people, yavanākrāntāṃ = yavana (uncivilized people) + ākrāntāṃ (trampled by), kāla – Time, kanyopamarditām = kanya (Daughter) + upamarditām (ruthlessly demolish), hātuṃ - to leave, pracakrame –

happened, rājā – King Purañjan, tāṃ - that, purīm – city, anikāmataḥ - unwilling

With psychic people and uncivilized ones having trampled the city, which was ruthlessly demolished by the Daughter of Time, that King Purañjan was forced to leave, even though he was unwilling. (4.28.10)

Detail

The contract for being with the queen and enjoying her prestige, privileges, and accommodations, was for one hundred years. This was clocked by time, the inscrutable power which initiates, sustains, and then shatters events. Time is the breaker. It is ruthless.

King Purañjan, the adventurous wanderer, ignored the time factor. He did so at his peril. He was caught off-guard. He was ill-prepared to shift somewhere else.

The psychic people who demolished the city and the uncivilized disordered ones who moved into it, frightened him. He could not challenge them. He even forgot that he made an agreement to live there for one hundred years, a time which was near completion.

Time is such that it may act in a logical way, but sometimes what it does, is unreasonable, where it produces chaos. In the psyche, time was terminating. The coreSelf would no longer have a physical body. Some demolition forces were physical. Some were psychic.

Since the core focused mainly on physical existence, it did not develop subtle perception. When the physical system is no longer available, the coreSelf must transit to some other existence, a subtle, or psychic place. From there, it may again develop a physical presence. But if it is not attentive to psychic activities, it may have no perception of subtle events.

A core may live in a physical body for up to one hundred years. Sooner or later, it will be deprived. There is no exception. Yet some cores ignore the advance of time as if to say that time will dare not upset their history.

With the psychic people and uncivilized ones having trampled the city, which was ruthlessly demolished by the Daughter of Time, that King Purañjan was forced to leave, even though he was unwilling.

भय-नाम्नो ऽग्रजो भ्राता प्रज्वारः प्रत्युपस्थितः /
ददाह तां पुरीं कृत्स्नां भ्रातुः प्रिय-चिकीर्षया (४॥२८॥११)

bhaya-nāmno 'grajo bhrātā
prajvāraḥ pratyupasthitaḥ /
dadāha tāṃ purīṃ kṛtsnāṃ
bhrātuḥ priya-cikīrṣayā (4.28.11)

bhaya-nāmno = bhaya-nāmnaḥ = known as Fear Itself, 'grajo = agrjaḥ = elder, bhrātā – brother, prajvāraḥ - Pyrexia, pratyupasthitaḥ was evident, dadāha – set fire, tāṃ - to that, purīṃ - city, kṛtsnāṃ - entire, bhrātuḥ - brother, Priya – dear to, cikīrṣayā – satisfying

Then the elder one known as Fear Itself (Bhaya) was evident, but with his brother, Pyrexia (Prajvāra), who set fire to the entire city completely, to please his dear brother. (4.28.11)

Detail

The physical demolition of Bhogavatī, Excitement City, was one challenge; the psychological damage was another. For his life prior, Purañjan enjoyed the services and aristocratic trappings provided by the staff of the queen. He never pondered disaster as the outcome.

As a fun-loving man he was the match for the honored queen, but when disaster struck, he was not prepared. He had no plan to defend either himself, the queen, or her servants. As for the security officer, that agent was fully occupied striking back to defeat the enemies. Purañjan never offered this person even one minute of assistance. That was because the contract with the queen did not include such participation.

Seeing the physical damage, some of which took years to show, Purañjan was anxious. He could think of no solution. He was attacked from within his mind and feelings by the psychological corrosive known as fear. This eats away at one's psyche. It stuns one, mentally and emotionally.

Fear was accompanied by its brother which is Pyrexia, a fevered state which is both physical and psychic. It is difficult to cure. During the elderly years, it overcomes the biological and psychological functions of the psyche.

The coreSelf, when it uses the conveniences provided by the intellect, may not consider that the services may one day come to an end. Instead of considering how it could develop less dependence on the intellect, the core relies more heavily on the intellect. That spells disaster.

Since a physical body will not last forever. Since that is factual. A self should prepare for being ejected in less than one-hundred years. The intellect is not infallible. It cannot buffer time forever. A self should be fearful from the onset, from the time it became allied to the intellect, where that self should develop detachment and psychic insight.

Instead of using its independence for sporting to kill animals or any other activity, the core should investigate the origins of itself and its adjuncts, especially the queen, her security officer, and the kundalini Power Central.

Near the time of death of the physical form, there would be the manifestation of fear, who is always accompanied by his brother Pyrexia, which is a psychic and physical fever. Since this happens repeatedly and is witnessed by the survivors of a dying body, there is no excuse for not preparing for it, either to be cured or to pass away physically with it.

Each self should have a transit plan to escape from that city of the psyche, which is the physical body.

तस्यां सन्दह्यमानायां सपौरः सपरिच्छदः /
कौटुम्बिकः कुटुम्बिन्या उपातप्यत सान्वयः (४॥२८॥१२)

Tasya sandahyamānāyāṃ
sapauraḥ saparicchadaḥ /
kauṭumbikaḥ kuṭumbinyā
upātapyata sānvayaḥ (4.28.12)

tasyāṃ - that place, sandahyamānāyāṃ - a conflagration, sapauraḥ - those people, saparicchadaḥ - servants and the others, kauṭumbikaḥ - clan of the City Person, kuṭumbinyā – wife of the City Person, upātapyata – affected emotionally, sānvayaḥ - other people associated

Due to the conflagration of that place, which affected those people, the servants, and others, the Purañjan's clan and his wife, were emotionally distressed. (4.28.12)

Detail

The final assault on Bhogavatī, the Excitement City, was unprecedented. In the life of a physical body, the death of it is a one-time occurrence. One may experience a tragic condition of the body. One may survive that. However eventually there is a final end for it. Such was the situation of the city with nine gates which Purañjan enjoyed through the one-hundred-year contract with the queen.

Some persons wish for destruction of the body, but most people want to avoid that. In either case no one has absolute control over death. Just as birth of a body happens without one being in full control, so death occurs as fated.

A being is limited in terms of its birth, its continuation and physical death. One may not understand the psychic side of life but that does not mean that there is no such parallel.

According to the theory of reincarnation, Purañjan will again be touring the world in search of an aristocratic companion who has luxurious accommodations. He will take another physical body.

The self will again have the fortune of gaining the services of an intellect. It will again be challenged to accept a contract for living one hundred years as a physical person.

Due to the conflagration in Excitement City, its inhabitants, the servants, the clan of Purañjan, his wife, and other people, were emotionally distressed. They were frightened. Sometimes, the subtle body continues on the psychic side with abnormalities and afflictions which it developed while it had its last physical form.

यवनोपरुद्धायतनो ग्रस्तायां काल-कन्यया /
पुर्यां प्रज्वार-संसृष्टः पुर-पालो ऽन्वतप्यत (४॥२८॥१३)

yavanoparuddhāyatano
grastāyāṃ kāla-kanyayā /
puryāṃ prajvāra-saṃsṛṣṭaḥ
pura-pālo 'nvatapyata (4.28.13)

yavanoparuddhāyatano = yavana (uncivilized people) + uparuddha (captured) + āyatanaḥ (place), grastāyāṃ - seized, kāla-kanyayā = by the Daughter of Time, puryāṃ - city, prajvāra – Pyrexia, saṃsṛṣṭaḥ - approached by, pura – city, pālo = pālaḥ = protector, 'nvatapyata = anvatapyata = was terrified

When the uncivilized people captured the place, it, being seized by the Daughter of Time, and by Pyrexia who approached, the protector of the city was terrified. (4.28.13)

Detail

The protector of Bhogavatī, Excitement City, was a terror in his own right. The only person in Purañjan's family who was not respectful of that snake was the queen herself. She was familiar with the reptile because it was endearing to her. Its purpose was to protect her from every side. Even when he deviated and went to the forest to sportingly kill animals, the snake never challenged Purañjan.

Despite the snake's power, it was terrified when the place was seized by the Daughter of Time and by Pyrexia. The heat emanating from Pyrexia tormented it and caused it to be fearful of death. Still the snake tried its best to keep defending the place. Its actions for this were heroic.

In the psyche, once the elderly years happen, the kundalini Power Central becomes filled with anxiety. Its methods of protecting the physical body from disease no longer cure the ailments. Then there is a scramble to try anything in the hope of reversing the ill health of the body.

Despite its reasoning, the intellect finds that its conclusions are useless. The senses become afflicted because cells in the organs malfunction. They render incorrect interpretations. Remedies which worked previously no longer are applicable. The entire system is riddled with decay and threat.

न शेके सोऽवितुं तत्र पुरु-कृच्छ्रोरु-वेपथुः /
गन्तुम् ऐच्छत् ततो वृक्ष- कोटराद् इव सानलात् (४॥२८॥१४)

na śeke so 'vituṃ tatra
puru-kṛcchroru-vepathuḥ /
gantum aicchat tato vṛkṣa-
koṭarād iva sānalāt (4.28.14)

na – not, śeke – was able, so = saḥ = he, 'vituṃ =avitum = to defend, tatra – there, puru – much, kṛcchroru = kṛcchra (difficult) + uru (great), vepathuḥ - trembling, gantum – to leave, aicchat – he wanted, tato = tataḥ = that place, vṛkṣa – tree, koṭarād = koṭarāt = from a burrow, iva – as, sānalāt – on fire

Not being able to defend that place any longer, the snake with great difficulty, trembled. Like a creature, which wished to leave its burrow, in a tree which was on fire, he wanted to leave that place. (4.28.14)

Detail

For the convenience of protecting the place on all sides, the snake arranged itself in the Excitement City. Just as a serpent selects a choice location for its burrow, so the snake lived in Excitement City for full security. It did however situate itself in a trap.

The city had nine gates. It failed to secure those entrances properly. In addition, it did not figure that an enemy would breach each of those gates simultaneously and would be in the city, giving the snake no entrance from which to escape.

The snake was arrogant as well. It did not train any of the queen's staff, or her sons, or grandsons, to assist in the protection of the city. The snake was confident that it could protect the place singlehandedly.

For his part, Purañjan was so involved mimicking the queen, that he did not help the snake to secure the city. Even when it was evident that the place was subjected to a siege, Purañjan offered no assistance.

Even though Purañjan was expert in weaponry, he was not trained in repelling a full-scale assault on their city. He never considered the possibility.

In the physical body, there is a lifeForce psychic mechanism which keeps the system working from moment to moment. This kundalini Power Central is anchored in the body. It energizes even the subtle body. This Power Central is in the sperm which is created in the father's body. When it is transferred to mother's form, it anchors to an egg that grips the mother's uterine wall. In that place it develops a nervous system for power distribution.

When the body reaches the elderly years, this lifeForce finds itself in a predicament. Due to the age of the body, many of its functions no longer respond to the willpower commands.

Due to the elderly condition, the lifeForce cannot defend the body. It becomes nervous and unreliable. It is afflicted with fear and uncertainty.

शिथिलावयवो यर्हि गन्धर्वैर् हृत-पौरुषः /
यवनैर् अरिभी राजन्न् उपरुद्धो रुरोद ह (४॥२८॥१५)

śithilāvayavo yarhi
gandharvair hṛta-pauruṣaḥ /
yavanair aribhī rājann
uparuddho ruroda ha (4.28.15)

śithilāvayavo = śithila (flabby) + avayavaḥ (muscles), yarhi – when, gandharvair – by psychic people, hṛta – subdued, pauruṣaḥ - bodily power, yavanair = yavanaiḥ = by uncivilized ones, aribhī = aribhīḥ = by enemies, rājann = rājan = O King Barhi, uparuddho = uparuddhaḥ = captive, ruroda – cried in distress, ha – as it happened

With flabby muscles, when he was subdued by the psychic people and the uncivilized ones, his enemies, O King, being held captive, he cried in distress. That is what happened. (4.28.15)

Detail

The one who was created to protect the queen and her concerns, the security chief who was relied on, was weakened by the assault on the city. At this time, the five-hooded snake began to think of the danger to itself.

In the psyche, the kundalini Power Central is vigilant day and night. To protect the physical body, it does this faithfully. If however, it malfunctions, its only recourse is to abandon other concerns and tend to its safety. Finally, the specter of death faces it head-on.

दुहितॄः पुत्र-पौत्रांश् च जामि-जामातृ-पार्षदान् /
स्वत्वावशिष्टं यत् किञ्चिद् गृह-कोश-परिच्छदम् (४॥२८॥१६)

duhitṝḥ putra-pautrāṃś
ca jāmi-jāmātṛ-pārṣadān /
svatvāvaśiṣṭaṃ yat kiñcid
gṛha-kośa-paricchadam (4.28.16)

duhitṝḥ - daughters, putra – sons, pautrāṃś = pautrān = grandsons, ca – and then, jāmi – daughters-in-law, jāmātṛ - sons in law, pārṣadān - attendants, svatvāvaśiṣṭaṃ = svatva (belongings) + āvaśiṣṭaṃ (remaining), yat kiñcid = yat kiñcit = what was there, gṛha – home. kośa – valuables, paricchadam – household items

Purañjan's daughters, sons, and grandsons, his daughters-in-law, sons-in-law, his attendants, and his remaining belongings, with whatever was there, his houses, valuables, and household items, (4.28.16)

Detail

Like every other living being, Purañjan had concerns, not just for his family but for the employees, property and whatever else they possessed. He thought of his houses, valuables, and household items. He found no reprieve. His mind could imagine no way out of the wrecked city.

There are parts and subparts in the physical body. Some organs are vital. Some have little value. Even though some parts can be removed and the body will keep living, still there comes a time, when even if the vital organs continue to operate, the body will be deceased.

There are extensive developments which are noted as an embryo, or as a swelling of a woman's abdomen. Actually, it begins with sexual urge, impregnation, and fetal development. From this there is a complex display which is recognized as a human body.

All of this which is facilitated by time, is later torn down by it. Each entity is supported by time and is stripped by it as well. Nails, horns, and hair on the outside, with bones and teeth on the inside, serve for reinforcing a form for a time. Eventually even that becomes unserviceable.

अहं ममेति स्वीकृत्य गृहेषु कुमतिर् गृही /
दध्यौ प्रमदया दीनो विप्रयोग उपस्थिते (४॥२८॥१७)

ahaṁ mameti svīkṛtya
gṛheṣu kumatir gṛhī /
dadhyau pramadayā
dīno viprayoga upasthite (4.28.17)

ahaṁ - I, mameti = mama (mine) + iti (thus), svīkṛtya – taking, gṛheṣu – in the home, kumatir = kumatiḥ = impractical ideas, gṛhī – household, dadhyau – focused on, pramadayā - with wife, dīno = dīnaḥ = miserable person, viprayoga = viprayoge = separate, upasthite – happened

were objects of *I-and-mine* for him. Whatever he thought of taking from the household was impractical. He focused on his wife but as it happened, he was separated and was a miserable person. (4.28.17)

Detail

With the hundred-year period near expiration, Purañjan and the queen had no idea of the future. They could no longer afford to ignore the fact that their contract for companionship was limited. The beautiful woman was the one to speak the limit but she did not ponder it. She issued that limit by an intuitive urge only. She had no understanding of the duration.

Purañjan was still focused through the feelings of *I-and-mine,* emotions that served him well for favorable relationship with their dependents, attendants, and even his belongings, houses, and valuables. By focusing on how he loved the queen and their retinue, he relieved himself of the stress about the city's demolition.

He realized however that he could take nothing when he made the effort to escape from the city. The situation was dire. Finally, he focused on the queen, his lovely catering wife. Then he realized that her rescue was impossible. He had no weapons to fight the enemy. Besides, he was unfamiliar with their strategy. He had no confidence that he could rescue even himself from the situation.

In the psyche, the coreSelf is possessed by a sense of identity, which is even more influential than its intellect. This causes an intuitive sense of possession of *I-and-mine.*

Its identity focus is fused to the core, which cannot separate from it. Thus, when in a crisis where the core feels that its adjuncts may become unavailable, there is uncertainty and fear because the core is left only with the unapplied identity focus. The core may try to grab the intellect, or another adjunct, but it finds that it is unable to grasp that psychic tool. This is unsettling.

Purañjan was distraught when he realized that he could not escape with the beautiful queen. If anything, he would escape by himself. He was like a man who travel out to sea with a woman he loved. A storm arose which sunk their boat. A wave appeared which separated them by a large distance. This wave pushed him far away. He lost track of his companion. There was no possibility of him saving the woman in that raging ocean. The concern was grand but the opportunity for a rescue was absent.

लोकान्तरं गतवति मय्य् अनाथा कुटुम्बिनी a
वर्तिष्यते कथं त्व् एषा बालकान् अनुशोचती (४॥२८॥१८)

lokāntaraṃ gatavati
mayy anāthā kuṭumbinī /
vartiṣyate kathaṃ tv eṣā
bālakān anuśocatī (4.28.18)

lokāntaraṃ - some other dimension, gatavati – goes, mayy = mayi = my passage, anāthā – without a reliable man, kuṭumbinī – mother of the family, vartiṣyate – will exist, kathaṃ - how, tv = tu = but, eṣā – this lady, bālakān – children, anuśocatī – sad concerning

Purañjan considered.
"When I go to some other dimension, and being without a reliable man, how will the mother of the family endure, being sad concerning the children? (4.28.18)

Detail

Purañjan was unable to focus on his wellbeing. Before he met the queen, he spent his time seeking a companion and a living situation to his liking. He was nervous, being by himself. He had a companion who was invisible even to himself. Not experiencing that person, he was lonely and could not self-reflect. He was extroverted.

When Excitement City was demolished, Purañjan pondered the situation. He suspected that he would have to go elsewhere and would be unable to assist the queen in any way. The one hundred years would soon expire. There was no telling what else he would encounter.

He regretted the situation, where the queen would be without a reliable man, without himself. Even at this time, he did not ponder his situation. He continued to divest his interest to others as if he was in a secured position.

When this is applied to the coreSelf and its psyche, the lesson is that the core occupies itself, or is induced to give itself to the concerns of the adjuncts. This begins with the concerns of the sense of identity which is attached to the intellect, which in turn is attached to the kundalini Power Central and memories. These preoccupations of the core deprived it from the impetus to research its origins.

When the physical body is demolished by time, the core is baffled. For the time being, for a period it does not control, it is deprived of some uses of the adjuncts. It realizes that its situation is one of uncertainty. Still, it does not focus on its wellbeing. Instead, it maintains the diverging interest in one or more of the adjuncts.

न मय्य् अनाशिते भुङ्क्ते नास्नाते स्नाति मत्-परा /
मयि रुष्टे सुसन्त्रस्ता भर्त्सिते यत-वाग् भयात् (४॥२८॥१९)

na mayy anāśite bhuṅkte
nāsnāte snāti mat-parā /
mayi ruṣṭe susantrastā
bhartsite yata-vāg bhayāt (4.28.19)

na – nothing, mayy = mayi = by me, anāśite – eaten, bhuṅkte – would eat, nāsnāte = na (not) + asnāte (bathe), snāti – she bathes, mat-parā = devoted to me, mayi – by me, ruṣṭe – was offended, susantrastā – very anxious, bhartsite – threatened, yata-vāg = special speech, bhayāt – from fear

"When nothing was eaten by me, she would not eat. If I did not bathe, she refrained. She was so devoted to me that when I was offended, she would be very anxious. When I threatened her, due to fear she would not reply. (4.28.19)

Detail

The secret to Purañjan's appreciation for the beautiful woman, that queen of Excitement City, is laid here for all to see. It applies to the situation in the psyche regarding the coreSelf and its reliance on the intellect, the psychic instrument which gives conclusions, imagines possibilities, and illustrates memories.

Can the core, or alternately Purañjan, directly perform those functions? Can it not derive its own conclusions, imagine some possibilities, and illustrate its memories?

Purañjan praised the queen for her dedication. To his view, her attachment was impeccable. From one angle, this was the case. From another, it put him in a dangerous situation of reliance on a woman whose discretion was correct only part of the time.

When Purañjan wandered over the earth, he lacked the rapid calculative capacity of the queen. When he avoided her association, and ventured to hunt, he did not have the proper discrimination. He put himself to fault by whimsically killing animals. By himself, he was ill-equipped to draw the proper conclusions.

From the report of Nārad, once Purañjan met the queen, he was relieved of loneliness. Prior to that he was alone, as a handsome male wanderer. He wanted a capable woman but he found none until he got to the southern Himalayas.

The beautiful woman was so loving, that he imagined that when nothing was eaten by him, she fasted. If he did not bathe, he thought that she did likewise. She was so devoted that when he was offended, she was anxious. He felt that when he threatened her, she did not reply due to fear of being alienated.

प्रबोधयति माविज्ञं व्युषिते शोक-कर्शिता /
वर्त्मैतद् गृह-मेधीयं वीर-सूर् अपि नेष्यति (४॥२८॥२०)

prabodhayati māvijñaṃ
vyuṣite śoka-karśitā /
vartmaitad gṛha-medhīyaṃ
vīra-sūr api neṣyati (4.28.20)

prabodhayati – she gave good advice, māvijñaṃ = mā (to me) + avijñaṃ (insensible), vyuṣite – absent from the place, śoka – sorrow, karśitā –unhappy, vartmaitad = vartma (course) +etad (this), gṛha – household, medhīyaṃ - responsibilities, vīra-sūr = vīra-sūḥ = mother of heroes, api – also, neṣyati – will she manage

"She gave good advice to me when I was insensible. When I was absent from the residence, she was sorrowful and unhappy. Regarding this course of household responsibilities, how will this mother of heroes manage without me? (4.28.20)

Detail

This description given by Nārad exposes the status of Purañjan in regards to what he lacked, when he wandered alone. His sense of discrimination was insufficient. He needed someone to manage the psyche. He lacked analytical skill.

Could the coreSelf develop that through observation of the operation of the sometimes faulty, and sometimes correct, intellect. The analytical tool utilizes information which is collected by the sensual energies. Could those reports from the senses reach the core directly instead of being routed through the conclusive organ of the intellect. These are issues which the core should address?

Despite the glories of the coreSelf, the *ātma* or jiva (Sanskrit), on close observation, its actions without adjuncts are brought to question. It is not an independent reality. The attempts to award it infallibility can be challenged. The fact is that in the Nature environment, it should take assistance before it makes decisions. Can it develop analytical ability where it does not require adjuncts?

When the core was confronted with the impending destruction of its physical body, it began to appreciate the services rendered by the charming intellect. Anticipating that it would be separated and not knowing if it would be unified with that adjunct again, the core mused to itself like this.

"When I was insensible, this intellect gave advice. When I was confused and indecisive, it was sorrowful and unhappy. Regarding the social responsibilities, how will this monitor of my psyche manage without me?"

The awkwardness of the self is thus revealed!

कथं नु दारका दीना दारकीर् वापरायणाः /
वर्तिष्यन्ते मयि गते भिन्न-नाव इवोदधौ (४॥२८॥२१)

kathaṃ nu dārakā dīnā
dārakīr vāparāyaṇāḥ /
vartiṣyante mayi gate
bhinna-nāva ivodadhau (4.28.21)

kathaṃ - how, nu – and it may happen, dārakā = dārakāḥ = sons, dīnā = dīnā = helpless someone, dārakīr = dārakīḥ = daughters, vāparāyaṇāḥ = vā (or) +aparāyaṇāḥ (having no capable guardian), vartiṣyante – will happen, mayi – I, gate – gone, bhinna – wrecked, nāva = nāvaḥ = boat, ivodadhau = iva (like) + udadhau (in the sea)

"How would it happen that my sons and helpless daughters will survive with no capable guardian? When I am dead and gone, they will be like a boat, wrecked at sea." (4.28.21)

Detail

Purañjan occupied his mind with the concern of others. When Excitement City, was destroyed, he lamented the predicament of his woman and their children. Once he understood that he was doomed to be separated from them, he began to imagine the awful conditions.

Even though he did not provide security for the family when there was no crisis and their lifestyle was posh, he thought about it when he was stricken with old-age and could do nothing to defend them. At that time, his life was one of abject regret.

When it finds itself to be alive as a physical body, the coreSelf should eagerly investigate its origin.

Once it realizes that it does not have a permanent existential footing, and that for the most it may function as the body for some years, it should figure a transit.

एवं कृपणया बुद्ध्या शोचन्तम् अतद्-र्हणम् /
ग्रहीतुं कृत-धीर् एनं भय-नामाभ्यपद्यत (४॥२८॥२२)

evaṃ kṛpaṇayā buddhyā
śocantam atad-arhaṇam /
grahītuṃ kṛta-dhīr enaṃ
bhaya-nāmābhyapadyata (4.28.22)

evaṃ - thus, kṛpaṇayā – by the hopeless someone, buddhyā – intelligence, śocantam – of sad disposition, atad = atat = not that, arhaṇam – sensible person, grahītuṃ - to arrest, kṛta-dhīr = kṛta-dhīḥ = acting focused, enaṃ - him, bhaya – Fear, nāmābhyapadyata = nāmā (so called) + abhyapadyata (came there)

Thus, like a helpless person, that intelligent fellow, who was of a sad disposition, not being sensible, became positioned to be arrested by Fear itself, who was focused, and who came there. (4.28.22)

Detail

In the circumstance just before death, the person may be saturated with fear. This is due to uncertainty, to having no control over events.

A physical body dies once. The transit is a one-time passage. It has no return to this side, where one can reawaken as the physical being. In dreams and astral projections, one may experience the transit from here to the psychic side but while that allows a return to this side, at death one cannot reclaim the physical body.

The person is left on the psychic side with no access to physical existence. This deprivation entertains the energy of fear.

पशुवद् यवनैर् एष नीयमानः स्वकं क्षयम् /
अन्वद्रवन्न् अनुपथाः शोचन्तो भृशम् आतुराः (४॥२८॥२३)

paśuvad yavanair eṣa
nīyamānaḥ svakaṃ kṣayam /
anvadravann anupathāḥ
śocanto bhṛśam āturāḥ (4.28.23)

paśuvad = paśuvat = like an animal, yavanair = yavanaḥ = by the uncivilized people, eṣa = eṣaḥ = City Person, nīyamānaḥ - being arrested, svakaṃ - their own, kṣayam – place, anvadravann = anvadravan = followed, anupathāḥ - attendants, śocanto = śocantaḥ = distressful, bhṛśam – much, āturāḥ - aggrieved

Being treated like an animal, arrested by the barbarians, Purañjan was taken to their place. He was followed by his attendants who were distressful and even more aggrieved. (4.28.23)

Detail

Once Purañjan met the queen and was afforded her privileges, he lost interest in touring the earth. He was so satisfied being catered by the queen's staff and being protected by her security officer, that except for one incidence, he always complied with the queen.

When the city was demolished, he saw places which were not toured by him previously. The conquerors of the city, arrested him. They took him and the attendants to their place. This was distressing. It spooked Purañjan.

It was demeaning for him, a person who was catered by a queen. In the history of the world, one thing that is baffling to one and all, is the death experience. No matter how established one is, or how wealthy or famous one may be, still, when death claims the body, it is as if one was arrested, and is deprived of honors.

At death, one must go elsewhere. One does so with one's psyche, which contains the psychological traits.

पुरीं विहायोपगत उपरुद्धो भुजङ्गमः /
यदा तम् एवानु पुरी विशीर्णा प्रकृतिं गता (४॥२८॥२४)

purīṃ vihāyopagata
uparuddho bhujaṅgamaḥ /
yadā tam evānu purī
viśīrṇā prakṛtiṃ gatā (4.28.24)

purīṃ - city, vihāya – without access, upagataḥ - departed from, uparuddho = uparuddhaḥ = besieged, arrested, bhujaṅgamaḥ - serpent, yadā – when, tam – him, evānu = eva (sure) + anu (after), purī – place, viśīrṇā – pulverized, prakṛtiṃ - basic elements, gatā – converted,

With no access to the city, being besieged, the serpent which was arrested, departed from the place. He followed Purañjana as the place was pulverized into basic elements. (4.28.24)

Detail

Before the final destruction of the city, the serpent, took cues from the queen. As she explained to Purañjan initially, the serpent, followed wherever she went. However, in the time of crisis with Purañjan, the queen, their family, and the staff, besieged, everyone was fearful and bewildered. The serpent changed priority and looked to see how Purañjan responded to the crisis.

Being that there was no longer a city to protect because of the wholesale razing of the buildings, and being cornered and herded by the enemy, the serpent decided to do whatever the enemy suggested.

The evidence is that near the end of an old body, the lifeForce becomes entrapped somewhere in the body. It loses authority. As a matter of survival, it tries to get ideas from the coreSelf directly.

विकृष्यमाणः प्रसभं यवनेन बलीयसा /
नाविन्दत् तमसाविष्टः सखायं सुहृदं पुरः (४॥२८॥२५)

vikṛṣyamāṇaḥ prasabhaṃ
yavanena balīyasā /
nāvindat tamasāviṣṭaḥ
sakhāyaṃ suhṛdaṃ puraḥ (4.28.25)

vikṛṣyamāṇaḥ - dragged, prasabhaṃ - forcibly, yavanena – by uncivilized people, balīyasā – very powerful, nāvindat = na (not) + avindat (apprehend), tamasāviṣṭaḥ = tamasā (confusion) + āviṣṭaḥ (possessed), sakhāyaṃ - friend, suhṛdaṃ -well-wisher, kind, puraḥ - long ago

Though Purañjan was forcibly dragged by the very powerful uncivilized people, he was so possessed by confusion, that he did not think of his friend and well-wisher from long ago. (4.28.25)

Detail

The situation was dire. Purañjan was the only person in the queen's retinue who could make a sensible decision about what to do in the crisis. Even though, except for the queen and Purañjan everyone was accustomed to serving the queen's behests, in this circumstance, they looked to Purañjan for directions. They wanted him to make a decision in their interest. They were prisoners of war in a trying situation.

This means that near the time of death, when one knows for sure that the body has a terminal condition, it is only the coreSelf which becomes the focus. Even the serpent which was created just to protect the intellect and its accessories, looks to the core to get hints on the best course of action.

However, being dragged like a common prisoner, Purañjan could not think sensibly. He was confused. How did this happen, that suddenly the city was pulverized? Why did the serpent not contain the assault? Who were the enemies?

Nārad declared that Purañjan did not think of his friend and well-wisher from long ago. That person was Not-Recognized (Avijñāta), a person who was with Purañjan even when the wanderer met the queen outside the Excitement City.

If only the wanderer could recall this person, he could get the insight needed to understand the circumstance. His doubts could be resolved.

The coreSelf relied on the intellect, which was symbolized by the queen. However, there was someone else whose information was better than that of the intellect. The core needed to get in touch with that superCore.

तं यज्ञ-पशवो ऽनेन संज्ञप्ता ये ऽदयालुना /
कुठारैश् चिच्छिदुः क्रुद्धाः स्मरन्तो ऽमीवम् अस्य तत् (४॥२८॥२६)

tam̩ yajña-paśavo 'nena
sam̩jñaptā ye 'dayālunā /

kuṭhāraiś cicchiduḥ kruddhāḥ
smaranto 'mīvam asya tat (4.28.26)

taṃ - him, yajna – sacrificial ceremony, paśavo = paśavaḥ = concerning animals, 'nena = anena = by him, saṃjñaptā = saṃjñaptāḥ = sacrificed, ye – them, 'dayālunā = adayālunā = with no compassion, heartlessly, kuṭhāraiś – with sharp horns, cicchiduḥ - cut repeatedly, kruddhāḥ - angry, smaranto = smarantaḥ = remembering, 'mīvam = amīvam =offences, asya – him, tat – that

The animals which were heartlessly killed in sacrificial ceremonies by him, being angry, repeatedly cut him. They remembered his offences. (4.28.26)

Detail

Purañjan was confused. He lacked clarity regarding what happened during the death transition. He was in and out of observational consciousness. While being dragged inside the ruined old body, he had nightmares with the animals which he heartlessly killed in sacrificial ceremonies.

They appeared to him through psychic perception. They were angry. As they remembered his vicious attacks which killed their physical bodies, they repeatedly gored him.

These psychic events were just as real as physical ones could be. Purañjan could not escape from this psychic reality. His physical body no longer responded to his willpower.

The indication is that just a little before the death of the physical body, and just after it dies, a coreSelf may be confronted by psychic persons who hold resentments. These people get the opportunity to avenge grievances.

This applied to the lifestyle of King Barhi, a person whom Nārad scolded about using the excuse of religious sacrifices to kill animals. Human beings have a history of killing animals for various reasons. Some animals too are maneaters.

Humans kill some animals for sport. Some animals are killed for dietary needs. Some animals are killed because they damage agricultural farming. Some are killed by humans who feel the necessity to offer the life of animals in religious ceremony.

In general, a human being classifies animals as being of less value than a human. Killing of a human is regarded as murder but it is not so for an animal. The worth of a human body is higher than an animal. If a man shoots a bird, he will not be condemned for murder. Even though a person uses the bird form, still the worth of its body is lower.

Nārad wanted King Barhi to understand that even though the value of an animal is underrated in human society, it is not so in the world hereafter. On that side of existence, the animal's resentment for being killed has an impact which is comparable to physical feelings.

When one is near death and when one just passed from a body, one will perceive the subtle existence. At that time, efforts to escape the dream side of existence are futile. One's focus shifts from the physical realm to the dreamy shifty astral situations.

अनन्त-पारे तमसि मग्नो नष्ट-स्मृतिः समाः /
शाश्वतीर् अनुभूयार्तिं प्रमदा-सङ्ग-दूषितः (४॥२८॥२७)

ananta-pāre tamasi
magno naṣṭa-smṛtiḥ samāḥ /
śāśvatīr anubhūyārtiṃ
pramadā-saṅga-dūṣitaḥ (4.28.27)

ananta-pāre = unlimited elsewhere, tamasi – confusion, magno = magnaḥ = mentally submerged, naṣṭa-smṛtiḥ = lacking memory, samāḥ - years, śāśvatīr = śāśvatīḥ = eternity, anubhūyārtiṃ = anubhūya (experienced) + ārtiṃ (misery), pramadā – of women, saṅga – by relation, dūṣitaḥ - by vulgar activity

He was mentally submerged in unlimited confusion. He lacked memory. For an eternity in years, he experienced misery which was due to his vulgar activity with women. (4.28.27)

Detail

This details what happened to Purañjan after he was arrested and dragged out of Excitement City by Fear Personified. His experience there was repeated in many lives, where he again wondered through the earth and found a beautiful woman who was the accommodating queen of a luxurious city.

Due to the lack of memory, Purañjan could not tally the experiences in each life. He could not draw the proper conclusions about the operation of destiny. And as far as intelligence was concerned, Purañjan was unable to integrate events even though in each lifetime, similar things occurred. He became involved in the queen's lifestyle. He experienced the old age of each new body, and was humiliated by hostile psychic agencies.

One event which kept him aspiring was sexual intercourse. The excitement in it destroyed his inquest into the origin of existence. Due to that he never analyzed the experiences to understand how it was that he repeatedly became a physical being.

ताम् एव मनसा गृह्णन् बभूव प्रमदोत्तमा /
अनन्तरं विदर्भस्य राज-सिंहस्य वेश्मनि (४॥२८॥२८)

tām eva manasā gṛhṇan
babhūva pramadottamā /
anantaraṃ vidarbhasya
rāja-siṃhasya veśmani (4.28.28)

tām – them, eva – it so happened, manasā – with the mind, gṛhṇan - taking, babhūva – became, pramadottamā = pramadā (woman) + uttamā (most beautiful woman), anantaraṃ - after, vidarbhasya – of Vidarbha, raja – king), siṃhasya – of the lion-like, veśmani – at the residence

Thinking of the females, it so happened that after the physical life with his mind assuming that mood, he became the most beautiful woman in the royal palace of King Rājasiṃha of Vidarbha. (4.28.28)

Detail

Because Purañjan was repeatedly catered by females, and due to the pleasure he derived from them, he remained focused on the feminine format. He lost track of the masculine profile while doing this.

Gradually over time, he assumed the psychic behavior of a beautiful woman. She was born in the royal family of King Rājasiṃha of Vidarbha. This time Purañjan had no idea about masculinity. His feelings were feminine only. His psyche assumed the format of a princess.

उपयेमे वीर्य-पणां वैदर्भीं मलयध्वजः /
युधि निर्जित्य राजन्यान् पाण्ड्यः पर-पुरञ्जयः (४॥२८॥२९)

upayeme vīrya-paṇāṃ
vaidarbhīṃ malayadhvajaḥ /
yudhi nirjitya rājanyān
pāṇḍyaḥ para-purañjayaḥ (4.28.29)

upayeme – married, vīrya – heroic acts, paṇāṃ - reward, vaidarbhīṃ - daughter of King Vidarbha, malayadhvajaḥ - named Malayadhvaja, yudhi – warfare, nirjitya – conquered, rājanyān – other kings, pāṇḍyaḥ - someone from Pandu country, para – other than, purañjayaḥ - conqueror of the city

As a reward for his heroic acts, a king named Malayadhvaja was married to Vaidarbhī, that daughter of King Vidarbha. Malayadhvaja conquered other kings in warfare. That conqueror of cities was from Pāndya country. (4.28.29)

Detail

In that life, Purañjan, in that female format, had no idea of the masculine profile. Even though he was male in many lives prior, there was no memory of the past lives as a wandering adventurer. Purañjan, as a woman named Vaidarbhī, was married to a heroic king named Malayadhvaja.

This was predictive of the potential future of King Barhi. Nārad alerted the king that his assumption that he was an eternal male being, could be disrupted as he transmigrated. Based on his focus for sexual pleasure, Nature could cause him to be the other gender in some other life.

Males feel that they are the dominant species. This is based on their chauvinistic psychology. However, the continuous exploitation of females by males, could cause those males to be switched to female beings. Verily, the reverse could occur, where females who exploit males, may be rendered as males.

The coreSelf transmigrates from body to body. To do this, it must have a subtle form. In that format it must carry adjuncts which assist it to process experiences. Because the self relies on adjuncts, it is unable to draw the proper conclusions. Instead, it is served ideas by the intellect, which makes suggestions as to what should be permitted or rejected. This causes the core to be liable for the experiences. That results in confusion because it is forced to experience pleasures and agonies, regardless of whether it desires these or not.

तस्यां स जनयां चक्र आत्मजाम् असितेक्षणाम् /
यवीयसः सप्त सुतान् सप्त द्रविड-भूभृतः (४॥२८॥३०)

tasyāṃ sa janayāṃ cakra
ātmajām asitekṣaṇām /
yavīyasaḥ sapta sutān
sapta draviḍa-bhūbhṛtaḥ (4.28.30)

tasyāṃ - through her, sa – he, the King Malayadhvaja, janayāṃ cakra = produced, ātmajām – daughter, asitekṣaṇām = asita (blue) + īkṣaṇām (eyes), yavīyasaḥ - younger brother, sapta – seven, sutān – sons, sapta – seven, draviḍa – of Draviḍa Province, bhūbhṛtaḥ - rulers of the land

Through her, that King Malayadhvaja produced a blue-eyed daughter, who had younger brothers, who were seven sons of the king. They were rulers of seven regions of Dravida Province. (4.28.30)

Detail

The birth process with changes in gender of the bodies, occurs time and time again. For as long as there are environments in the physical situation, so long as there are psychic levels which are sensitive to ideation and mental operations, there will be assumptions of forms with little or no understanding of how someone came to be.

When Purañjan was switched into a female format, she, as a woman, had no idea that the changed occurred. This is because the Nature energy which was used to craft the format, used his consciousness energy in the birthing environment, in the parents' forms.

Nature is so sensitive and proficient, that in one life, one may be male, and in another female. One may have no idea that there was a switch. Someone may be sensitive to the change but he may lack clarity. For him it is confusing. He feels himself as a certain gender emotionally but finds himself to be another gender physically, according to how the new body was formatted.

When one is in the state of subjectivity, one's objective witnessing self is disabled, such that a form which developed, happened without one's witnessing awareness of its production.

Nārad informed King Barhi, that Purañjan found himself to be a beautiful woman with aristocratic privileges and with a husband who was an emperor, named King Malayadhvaja. They had a blue-eyed daughter, who had seven younger brothers. The princes were rulers of seven regions of Dravida Province in the south of India.

The point is that the status was maintained. Since Purañjan the wandering hero was used to luxurious surroundings, Nature honored his sensual needs. Due to his focus on sexual intercourse, Nature switched the gender to facilitate the desire for enjoying the sexual access of a voluptuous woman. If one craves a fulfillment or becomes addicted to it, Nature may use that energy to format a future event in which one must participate.

Nārad hinted to King Barhi, that as a beautiful aristocratic woman, who was the senior to her siblings, Vaidarbhī keenly observed the privilege of her daughters in contrast to her seven sons who were rulers of seven regions of Dravida Province. Vaidarbhī instinctively compared the advantages of having a male format to that of having a female one.

एकैकस्याभवत् तेषां राजन्न् अर्बुदम् अर्बुदम् /
भोक्ष्यते यद्-वंश-धरैर् मही मन्वन्तरं परम् (४॥२८॥३१)

ekaikasyābhavat teṣāṃ
rājann arbudam arbudam /
bhokṣyate yad-vaṃśa-dharair
mahī manvantaraṃ param (4.28.31)

ekaikasyābhavat = ekaikasya (one after another) + ābhavat (was), teṣāṃ - them, rājann = rājan = O king, arbudam arbudam = hundred thousand and more, bhokṣyate – exploit, yad – whose, vaṃśa-dharair = by the clan, mahī – world, manvantaraṃ - one primal progenitor's reign, param –beyond

There was one after the other son of his sons, O king. A hundred thousand and more of them, who exploited the earth. Their clan ruled the earth for a period longer than the time of a reign of one primal progenitor. (4.28.31)

Detail

In terms of dominance, the male version of the body is the one which engages the most. This pertains to the external activities. In terms of emotions, the females are the factor.

From the human viewpoint, this existence has to do with reproduction. It begins and ends with that. Therein is the mystery. One is produced as a human body either as male or female or having a mixed gender. One either reproduces or does not do so. Then one dies to the physical history. Then again, one is reformatted by Nature with gender. One again repeats this behavior. It happens by the development of natural energies.

Even though a specific self is an observer, still the range of the observation is limited by the sensual reach and the intuition one has at any given moment.

अगस्त्यः प्राग् दुहितरम् उपयेमे धृत-व्रताम् /
यस्यां दृढच्युतो जात इध्मवाहात्मजो मुनिः (४॥२८॥३२)

agastyaḥ prāg duhitaram
upayeme dhṛta-vratām /
yasyāṃ dṛḍhacyuto jāta
idhmavāhātmajo muniḥ (4.28.32)

agastyaḥ - Agastya, the supernatural yogi, prāg = prāk = first, duhitaram - daughter, upayeme – married, dhṛta-vratām = holder of vows, yasyāṃ - through whom, dṛḍhacyuto = dṛḍhacyutaḥ = named Dṛḍhacyuta, a resolute person, jāta = jātaḥ = born, idhmavāhātmajo = idhmavāha (named Idhmavāha, tough and carried firelogs) + ātmajaḥ (son), muniḥ - yogi philosopher

Agastya, the supernatural yogi, married the first daughter, who was a holder of vows, and through whom was born Dṛḍhacyuta, a resolute person, who in turn produced a son named Idhmavāha,

who was tough and provided firelogs. He was a yogi philosopher. (4.28.32)

Detail

Somehow, Purañjan the wandering adventurer met a beautiful woman who had a furnished city. After that life which ended inconveniently, he was converted to being a princess, named Vaidarbhī. As that female, Purañjan had many children. One daughter married the supernatural yogi named Agastya. The sons were remarkable people who were inclined to righteous lifestyle.

विभज्य तनयेभ्यः क्ष्मां राजर्षिर् मलयध्वजः /
आरिराधयिषुः कृष्णं स जगाम कुलाचलम् (४॥२८॥३३)

vibhajya tanayebhyaḥ kṣmāṃ
rājarṣir malayadhvajaḥ /
ārirādhayiṣuḥ kṛṣṇaṃ
sa jagāma kulācalam (4.28.33)

vibhajya – divided, tanayebhyaḥ - of sons, kṣmāṃ - territory, rājarṣir = rājarṣiḥ = yogiKing, malayadhvajaḥ - named Malayadhvaja, ārirādhayiṣuḥ - wanting to worship, kṛṣṇaṃ - Deity Krishna, sa = saḥ =he, jagāma – went, kulācalam – place called Kulācala

Dividing the territory among his sons, that yogiKing Malayadhvaja, who wanted to worship the Deity Krishna, went to a place called Kulācala. (4.28.33)

Detail

Purañjan as the woman Vaidarbhī, who married the yogiKing Malayadhvaja, was cooperative in the relationship, even when the king abdicated and divided his territory among his sons. To focus totally on the Deity Krishna, Malayadhvaja and Vaidarbhī went to a shrine called Kulācala.

हित्वा गृहान् सुतान् भोगान् वैदर्भी मदिरेक्षणा /
अन्वधावत पाण्ड्येशं ज्योत्स्नेव रजनी-करम् (४॥२८॥३४)

hitvā gṛhān sutān bhogān
vaidarbhī madirekṣaṇā /
anvadhāvata pāṇḍyeśaṃ
jyotsneva rajanī-karam (4.28.34)

hitvā – abandoning, gṛhān – residence, sutān – children, bhogān – sources of enjoyment, vaidarbhī – Princess of Vidarbha, madirekṣaṇā = madira (enchanting) + īkṣaṇā (eyes), anvadhāvata – followed, pāṇḍyeśaṃ = pāṇḍya (Pāṇḍya country) + īśaṃ (ruler), jyotsneva = jyotsna (moonlight) + iva (like), rajanī – night, karam – master

Abandoning the residence, children, and sources of enjoyment, the Princess of Vidarbha, with the enchanting eyes, followed the ruler of the Pāṇḍya country, just as moonlight follows the moon, that master of the night. (4.28.34)

Detail

The hope is that eventually, after countless transmigrations in various species, someone would mature sufficiently, to be resistant to the physical experience. One should at some point switch one's interest to the psychic side of life.

There is a hint however that if it uses a female body the personSelf is unlikely to develop the extreme detachment required. But it can do so, if in such a body, it follows the lead of an ascetic who uses a male form.

As the wanderer, Purañjan failed to study the clockwork of the time factor. Instead, he focused on a woman, especially on her sexual access. He passed from that body and took a female form.

Using that female format, somehow, Purañjan got married to a realized ruler. Following the lifestyle of that man, Purañjan got the clue about defocusing from physical existence.

With the assistance of Nature and of great people, the female formatted Purañjan began extracting her interest from physical existence. She witnessed the example of the yogiKing Malayadhvaja, who pushed aside the focus on physical existence and yielded to psychic reality.

Purañjan though being in a female-body, adopted the technique of ignoring the sensations which highlighted physical reality.

Purañjan, a particular coreSelf, witnessed the detachment of another coreSelf who was known as Malayadhvaja. Even though at the time, Purañjan was circumstantially in a female format, she saw the application of the technique of applicable detachment which was displayed by Malayadhvaja. That learning was a favorable turn in the existence of Purañjan.

A core may transmigrate for millions of years, in many species, even in the human one, and still, that person may have no idea how to apply itself to the psychic side of existence. If somehow one can be in close association with a master of the technique, one has every chance of learning how to apply oneself to transit from this existence. It requires exposure to advanced yoga practice.

As Nārad described the events, Purañjan as a queen known as Vaidarbhī mimicked her husband who was known as Malayadhvaja. She mimicked his subtle activities. She learnt by observing how he reduced sensitivity to physical experience and increased perception to psychic life.

When Malayadhvaja abandoned their residence, children, and sources of enjoyment, she did so as well. With sincerity, she followed him just as moonlight follows the lunar planet.

तत्र चन्द्रवसा नाम ताम्रपर्णी वटोदका /
तत्-पुण्य-सलिलैर् नित्यम् उभयत्रात्मनो मृजन् (४॥२८॥३५)

tatra candravasā nāma
tāmraparṇī vaṭodakā /
tat-puṇya-salilair nityam
ubhayatrātmano mṛjan (4.28.35)

tatra – there, candravasā – Candravasā, nāma – so named, tāmraparṇī - Tāmraparṇī, vaṭodakā - Vaṭodakā, tat – of those, puṇya – sanctifying, salilair = salilaiḥ = with water, nityam – perpetual, ubhayatrātmano = ubhayatra (in both ways) + ātmanaḥ (of the self), mṛjan - purifying, washing

There were the Candravasā, Tāmraparṇī, and Vaṭodakā rivers. These had sanctifying water, which perpetually purified both the physical and psychic self. (4.28.35)

Detail

As the renounced Queen Vaidarbhī, Puranjana the wandered with physical focus, broke the spell of physical objects. She became aware that whatever was physical had a psychic counterpart.

In the remote place where she lived with the yogiKing, she perceived both physical and psychic existence. She perceived two realities functioning, one being related to the other, where physical acts like purification of the body, had parallel acts occurring on the psychic plane. Thus, she dismissed the physical circumstances as like a shadow with little significance.

कन्दाष्टिभिर् मूल-फलैः पुष्प-पर्णैस् तृणोदकैः /
वर्तमानः शनैर् गात्र- कर्शनं तप आस्थितः (४॥२८॥३६)

kandāṣṭibhir mūla-phalaiḥ
puṣpa-parṇais tṛṇodakaiḥ /
vartamānaḥ śanair gātra- karśanaṃ
tapa āsthitaḥ (4.28.36)

kandāṣṭibhir = kandāṣṭibhiḥ = kanda (bulb) + aṣṭibhiḥ (by seeds), mula – root, phalaiḥ - by fruits, puṣpa – flower, parṇais = parṇaiḥ = by leaves, tṛṇodakaiḥ = tṛṇa (grass) + udakaiḥ - by water, vartamānaḥ - subsisting, śanair = śanaiḥ = gradually, gātra – limb, karśanaṃ = skin and bones, tapa = tapaḥ = deprivation, āsthitaḥ - established

With bulbs, seeds, roots, fruits, flowers, leaves, grass, and water, Malayadhvaja subsisted over time, such that his limbs were skin and bones. That was due to the deprivation which he established. (4.28.36)

Detail

Malayadhvaja was a proficient yogi who was partially dedicated to the practice of yoga during the years that he managed human society as a king. Once he left that responsibility, he applied himself fully to yoga. This was observed and learnt by Queen Vaidarbhī. Whatever Malayadhvaja did, the queen who in a former life was Purañjan, did likewise.

The yogiKing used bulbs, seeds, roots, fruits, flowers, leaves, grass, and water, and so did she, with the observation of how each substance either reinforced or diminished the impact of physical existence.

By reducing the urge for physical sustenance, Malayadhvaja's physical body became mere skin and bones. That was due to the deprivation which he established for himself and which the queen imitated.

This is interesting because initially when Purañjan agreed to accept the services and accommodations of the queen of Excitement City, he imitated that beautiful woman, where whatever she did, he mimicked.

Now again he mimics someone but this time, it was the adoption of the acts of an advanced yogi. The same mimicking tendency will now give a different result. Instead of procuring for him another physical body with physical privileges, he will gain psychic advantages with access to higher dimensions.

The secret to liberation while using a female profile is divulged here. Either gender may be freed from focus on physical factors. A male or female requires the opportunity to be trained by, or to mimic, an advanced ascetic. The observation however must be of the psychic actions of the yogi. Merely following the physical behavior with little or no focus on the movements in the subtle body, will not cause the student to develop the technique.

शीतोष्ण-वात-वर्षाणि क्षुत्-पिपासे प्रियाप्रिये /
सुख-दुःखे इति द्वन्द्वान्य् अजयत् सम-दर्शनः (४॥२८॥३७)

śītoṣṇa-vāta-varṣāṇi
kṣut-pipāse priyāpriye /

sukha-duḥkhe iti dvandvāny
ajayat sama-darśanaḥ (4.28.37)

śītoṣṇa = śīta (cold) + uṣṇa (heat), vāta – wind, varṣāṇi - rain, kṣut – hunger, pipāse - thirst, priyāpriye = priya (pleasant) + apriye (disagreeable), sukha – happiness, duḥkhe – in distress, iti – hence, dvandvāny = dvandvāni = opposing conditions, ajayat – he subdued, sama – emotional quiescence, darśanaḥ - perception

Heat and cold, wind and rain, hunger, and thirst, what is pleasant or disagreeable, happiness or distress, whatever opposing conditions there is, he subdued by applying emotional quiescence when perceiving the variations. (4.28.37),

Detail

Malayadhvaja achieved complete emotional quiescence when his psyche perceived the variations of sense conditions which exude from mundane objects. Somehow Purañjan, who served as Malayadhvaja's woman, also did the same.

Previously, Purañjan, that wandering hero met a woman and mimicked the beautiful lady's behavior. Now this same Purañjan mimicked a great yogi and achieved focus on the psychic side of existence.

With the beautiful queen of Excitement City, Purañjan easily imitated the excitements which the queen felt when her senses were occupied with their objects. Now something else was achieved. In opposing conditions, either desirable or undesirable, her sensual outreach was stabilized so that she remained in emotional quiescence when perceiving the objects. The mood variations occurred but the self neither pursued nor was repelled from the incidences.

This technique is one of remaining at the center of consciousness, while observing the psychic variations. Initially, this is done in reference to physical sensation. In the proficient stage, the self no longer darts here or there in its quest to consume desirable sensations and to escape from undesirable feelings.

तपसा विद्यया पक्व- कषायो नियमैर् यमैः /
युयुजे ब्रह्मण्य् आत्मानं विजिताक्षानिलाशयः (४॥२८॥३८)

tapasā vidyayā pakva-
kaṣāyo niyamair yamaiḥ /
yuyuje brahmaṇy ātmānaṃ
vijitākṣānilāśayaḥ (4.28.38)

tapasā – by deprivation, vidyayā – by realization, pakva – disintegrated, kaṣāyo = kaṣāyaḥ. = psyche contamination, niyamair = niyamaiḥ = by approved behavior, yamaiḥ = by ceasing unacceptable activities, yuyuje – he linked, brahmaṇy = brahmaṇi = exclusive spiritual existence, ātmānaṃ - coreSelf, vijitākṣānilāśayaḥ = vijita (psychological control) + akṣa (perception ability) + anila (life energy) + āśayaḥ (self-awareness)

By deprivation and realization, Malayadhvaja's psychic contamination was disintegrated. By doing approved behavior, and ceasing unacceptable activities, he linked the coreSelf to the exclusive spiritual existence. His psychological control resulted in his having perception ability into his life energy and self-awareness. (4.28.38)

Detail

Nārad did not detail the methods because King Barhi, the audience of this conversation, was familiar with the processes. Even though the king knew of them, he did not practice any method to proficiency. The routine for kings at that time, was to abdicate by installing a son to rule the kingdom. Once this was done, the retired monarch honed the skill of yoga to proficiency. Thus, Nārad did not elaborate but simply sketched what Malayadhvaja did which was learnt and applied by Vaidarbhī, the queen who formerly was in a male configuration as Purañjan.

By sensual deprivation, and by realization of the lures which cause the self to be interested in physical existence, Malayadhvaja's psychic contamination was removed. By having the power to restrict the self to approved behavior, and by ceasing unacceptable activities, he linked the coreSelf to the exclusive spiritual existence.

Now as Queen Vaidarbhī, Puranjan did whatever psychic action her husband took. She was precise in mimicking his psychological control. She saw the reality of how physical actions shadow psychic behavior. She re-evaluated everything and reduced the quest for physical existence.

आस्ते स्थाणुर् इवैकत्र दिव्यं वर्ष-शतं स्थिरः /
वासुदेवे भगवति नान्यद् वेदोद्वहन् रतिम् (४॥२८॥३९)

āste sthāṇur ivaikatra
divyaṃ varṣa-śataṃ sthiraḥ /
vāsudeve bhagavati
nānyad vedodvahan ratim (4.28.39)

āste – remains stationary, sthāṇur = sthāṇuḥ = immoveable, ivaikatra = iva (like) + ekatra (at one place), divyaṃ - supernatural people, varṣa – year, śataṃ - one hundred, sthiraḥ - steady, vāsudeve – to Lord Vāsudeva, bhagavati – that God, nānyad = no (not) + anyat (other), vedodvahan = veda (knew) + udvahan (got), ratim – what is desired

He remained stationary and immoveable, like something positioned at one place. For one hundred years of the supernatural people, he was focused on Lord Vāsudeva, that God and no other. Thus, he knew and got what he desired (4.28.39)

Detail

King Malayadhvaja was a super-ascetic. It was Queen Vaidarbhī's fortune to observe even his subtle actions which could not be perceived with physical vision.

Malayadhvaja's body remained stationary and immoveable like a post in the ground. Within the consciousness, he was focused on supernatural people, especially on Lord Vāsudeva, that God and no other.

Yogis who use that method extract their attention fully from the physical objects. To free every bit of attention from extraneous diversion, they remain stationary and immovable like something positioned at one place.

They make contact with supernatural people and reach the cherished deity in the psychic existence. They remain focused on that Lord, forgoing other interests.

स व्यापकतयात्मानं व्यतिरिक्ततयात्मनि /
विद्वान् स्वप्न इवामर्श- साक्षिणं विरराम ह (४॥२८॥४०)

sa vyāpakatayātmānaṃ
vyatiriktatayātmani /
vidvān svapna ivāmarśa-
sākṣiṇaṃ virarāma ha (4.28.40)

sa = saḥ = he, vyāpakatayātmānaṃ = vyāpakatayā (everywhere diffused) + ātmānaṃ (coreSelf), vyatiriktatayātmani = vyatiriktatayā (localized) + ātmani (in the coreSelf), vidvān – self-realized person, svapna = svapna = in dream, ivāmarśa = iva (like) + amarśa(similarity), sākṣiṇaṃ - observer, virarāma – different, ha – certainly

He realized his coreSelf to be diffused and to be localized as itself. As a self-realized person, like in a dream, he as the observer, is different to what is observed, certainly. (4.28.40)

Detail

A yogi must parcel the aspects of the psyche. This gives the insight into what is the self, and what is not the self, but what seems to be it because the energy of the self is diffused to objects. The spread of the power-energy of the self, may be considered to be the self. When this happens, the self may falsely feel that it is the object which its rays penetrated.

The objective self is distinct when compared to what it observes. Hence the idea that the self is all-pervasive is erroneous. A self is localized and is only realizable to itself when it retracts its diffusive powers. The penetration of objects other than itself, happens because the self's radiance which is forever leaving it, is interspaced into other objects.

The self may erroneously feel that its spread through an item causes it to become that item. By withdrawal of its diffusion, the self can understand its limits and learn how to focus on its radiance.

साक्षाद् भगवतोक्तेन गुरुणा हरिणा नृप /
विशुद्ध-ज्ञान-दीपेन स्फुरता विश्वतो-मुखम् (४॥२८॥४१)

sākṣād bhagavatoktena
guruṇā hariṇā nṛpa /
viśuddha-jñāna-dīpena
sphuratā viśvato-mukham (4.28.41)

sākṣād – direct, bhagavatoktena = bhagavat (pertaining to God) + uktena (instructed), guruṇā – by the spiritual teacher, hariṇā = by Hari (God), nṛpa – O King, viśuddha – purity, jñāna-dīpena = by the light of insight perception, sphuratā – enlightening, viśvato = viśvataḥ = everywhere, -mukham – facing

By direct perception, as instructed by God who was his spiritual teacher, by the God known as Hari, O King, due to purity and the light of insight perception, he was enlightened about what faces everywhere. (4.28.41)

Detail

Nārad detailed the achievement of Malayadhvaja. This yogiKing got direct spiritual perception through insight vision. This was more than intuition and inspiration. He was directly instructed by the God who is known as Hari.

Due to purity of self and with the light of insight perception, Malayadhvaja was perceptive of the reality presence who faces everywhere. Queen Vaidarbhī followed closely after the king. She too got perceptions because she was afforded the opportunity to mimic his behavior, which caused doors of perception to open from within her psyche.

परे ब्रह्मणि चात्मानं परं ब्रह्म तथात्मनि /
वीक्षमाणो विहायेक्षाम् अस्माद् उपरराम ह (४॥२८॥४२)

pare brahmaṇi cātmānaṃ
paraṃ brahma tathātmani /

vīkṣamāṇo vihāyekṣām
asmād uparārāma ha (4.28.42)

pare - beyond this existence, brahmaṇi – in the exclusive spiritual energy, cātmānaṃ = ca (and) + ātmānaṃ (coreSelf), paraṃ - supreme, brahma – spiritual self, tathātmani = tathā (as well) + ātmani (in the coreSelf), vīkṣamāṇo = vīkṣamāṇaḥ = stopped perceiving, vihāyekṣām = vihāya (separating) + īkṣām (consider, viewing), asmād = asmāt = I, sense of identity, uparārāma – ceasing, ha – sure

His self was beyond this existence, being in the exclusive spiritual energy. His consciousness was aware of the supreme spiritual self as well. His normal self ceased separating, as its normal sense of identity, ceased for sure. (4.28.42)

Detail

For Malayadhvaja, the normal sense of identity which imposes on a coreSelf, ceased to function. There was no application of his focus to the intellect, kundalini Power Central and memory. The mundane psychology which he was known as, ceased to exist in the physical and subtle worlds.

पतिं परम-धर्म-ज्ञं वैदर्भी मलयध्वजम् /
प्रेम्णा पर्यचरद् धित्वा भोगान् सा पति-देवता (४॥२८॥४३)

patiṃ parama-dharma-jñaṃ
vaidarbhī malayadhvajam /
premṇā paryacarad dhitvā
bhogān sā pati-devatā (4.28.43)

patiṃ - husband, param – supreme, dharma – righteous lifestyle, jñaṃ - awareness of, vaidarbhī – Princess of Vidarbha, malayadhvajam – relating to the king named Malayadhvaja, premṇā – with endearing love, paryacarad = paryacarat = serve in close proximity, dhitvā = hitvā =

abandoned, bhogān – enjoyment, sā – she, pati – husband, devata – god

Regarding her husband who was aware of righteous lifestyle, as being superior, the Princess of Vidarbha, the wife of King Malayadhvaja, with endearing love, served him in close proximity. She abandoned the enjoyments and focused on regarding her husband as a god. (4.28.43)

Detail

Queen Vaidarbhī lagged in progress, but she observed enough of the yogic mystic behavior of the king, to continue the practice, if perhaps he would pass from his physical body. Still from attachment and a sense of duty, she served him in close proximity. She abandoned the enjoyments and focused to regard him as a deity. He was her informal guru to be sure.

At this time, the tendency to imitate someone served the purpose. Just as in the life as the male adventurer, Purañjan mimicked the queen, so now the same Purañjan in a female format as Queen Vaidarbhī, repeated whatever mystic method was used by the yogiKing Malayadhvaja.

As Purañjan had high regard for the queen, so with Vaidarbhī there was extreme regard because her partner was a self-realized person whose spiritual master was God.

चीर-वासा व्रत-क्षामा वेणी-भूत-शिरोरुहा /
बभाव् उप पतिं शान्ता शिखा शान्तम् इवानलम् (४॥२८॥४४)

cīra-vāsā vrata-kṣāmā
veṇī-bhūta-śiroruhā /
babhāv upa patiṃ śāntā
śikhā śāntam ivānalam (4.28.44)

cīra-vāsā = using old clothing, vrata-kṣāmā = skinny due to observing harsh vows, veṇī-bhūta = unbraided, knotted, śiroruhā - hair, babhāv = babhau = she radiated, upa patiṃ = near the husband, śāntā = śāntā = serenity, śikhā – flame, śāntam – steady, ivānalam = iva (like) + analam (fire)

Using old clothing, being skinny due to observing harsh vows, having unbraided hair, she radiated serenity. Being near her husband, she was like a flame of a steady fire. (4.28.44)

Detail

When Excitement City was ravished by Fear personified, one of the destructive forces was old-age in person. That was a supernatural woman who was rejected by nearly everyone. Her name was Durbhagā the Unlucky Woman.

Because she systematically degrades everyone's body, everyone was scared of this witch. Purañjan disliked her because she assaulted his libido, making it impossible for him to enjoy sexual pleasure. Despite his rejection, she entered his body and made him impotent.

In a new life however, as a female individual named Queen Vaidarbhī, Puranjan had no ill feelings toward old-age.

Vaidarbhī left the luxurious surrounds of Pāndya country to live a destitute life in the forest. Being that she followed her husband with confidence, it did not concern her to lament their poverty.

Using old clothing and having no concern with physical appearance, being skinny due to observing harsh dietary vows, having unbraided hair, she radiated serenity. Because she was psychically linked to her husband, she was like the flame of a steady fire.

अजानती प्रियतमं यदोपरतम् अङ्गना /
सुस्थिरासनम् आसाद्य यथा-पूर्वम् उपाचरत् (४॥२८॥४५)

ajānatī priyatamaṃ
yadoparatam aṅganā /
susthirāsanam āsādya
yathā-pūrvam upācarat (4.28.45)

ajānatī – does not know, priyatamaṃ - dearest, yadoparatam = yadā (when) + uparatam (died), aṅganā – woman, susthirāsanam = susthira (steady) + āsanam (seat), āsādya – reaching, yathā – so it was, pūrvam – prior, upācarat – attending

Not knowing when her dearest husband died, the woman, noticing his steady posture, continued attending as before. (4.28.45)

Detail

Queen Vaidarbhī failed to notice that King Malayadhvaja died. The king himself was unconcerned about his physical condition. He was focused on the transcendental reality. To him, the death of the body had no significance.

If before the physical body dies, a yogi transfers to the spiritual side of existence, he is not affected by the unserviceable condition of the physical system.

यदा नोपलभेताङ्घ्राव् ऊष्माणं पत्युर् अर्चती /
आसीत् संविग्न-हृदया यूथ-भ्रष्टा मृगी यथा (४॥२८॥४६)

yadā nopalabhetāṅghrāv
ūṣmāṇaṃ patyur arcatī /
āsīt saṃvigna-hṛdayā
yūtha-bhraṣṭā mṛgī yathā (4.28.46)

yadā – when, nopalabhetāṅghrāv = na (not) + upalabheta (perceive) +aṅghrau (in the feet), ūṣmāṇaṃ - heat, patyur =

patyuh = husband, arcatī – serving, āsīt - was, saṃvigna – nervous, hṛdayā – heart felt, yūtha-bhraṣṭā = is separated from the herd, mṛgī - doe, yathā – as it was

When not feeling heat in the feet of her husband while serving him, she was nervous at heart, like a doe which is separated from its herd. (4.28.46)

Detail

Queen Vaidarbhī's meditation practice was advanced but she had more proficiency to develop. There was still a part of her consciousness which was reliant on physical references.

His death made her nervous. She felt abandoned. His presence, even in an old starved body, was the point of reference. She was not fully confident of his psychic entity. She would have to practice the techniques he used for some time, before her awareness would be referenced fully to the spiritual side.

आत्मानं शोचती दीनम् अबन्धुं विक्लवाश्रुभिः /
स्तनाव् आसिच्य विपिने सुस्वरं प्ररुरोद सा (४॥२८॥४७)

ātmānaṃ śocatī dīnam
abandhuṃ viklavāśrubhiḥ /
stanāv āsicya vipine
susvaraṃ praruroda sā (4.28.47)

ātmānaṃ - of this self, śocatī – she lamented, dīnam – wretched person, abandhuṃ - with no friend, viklavāśrubhiḥ = viklava (bewildered) + aśrubhiḥ (by tears), stanāv = stanau = breasts, āsicya – wetting, vipine – in the forest, susvaraṃ - loud, praruroda – cried, sā – she

For herself, she lamented, feeling wretch. She had no friend, and was bewildered. Her tears wet her breasts. In that forest she cried aloud. (4.28.47)

Detail

It happens that a yogi/yogini may suddenly lack physical access to a great teacher. This could cause lamentation and regret. However, the key to a relationship with a guru is to practice his teaching. Though she lost tract of that great yogi, Vaidarbhī already integrated the practice to a degree. His physical presence was not required for her to be successful in the methods.

Her sorrowful condition occurred because once she realized that his body died, her interest became focused on having physical access to his person. She was in shock, stunned beyond belief.

उत्तिष्ठोत्तिष्ठ राजर्षे इमाम् उदधि-मेखलाम् /
दस्युभ्यः क्षत्र-बन्धुभ्यो बिभ्यतीं पातुम् अर्हसि (४॥२८॥४८)

uttiṣṭhottiṣṭha rājarṣe
imām udadhi-mekhalām /
dasyubhyaḥ kṣatra-bandhubhyo
bibhyatīṃ pātum arhasi (4.28.48)

uttiṣṭhottiṣṭha – stand stand, rājarṣe – O yogi of the kings, imām – this place, udadhi – by the sea, mekhalām – surrounded, dasyubhyaḥ - from the criminals, kṣatra-bandhubhyo = kṣatra-bandhubhyaḥ = rogues who are warriors, bibhyatīṃ - fearful, pātum – to secure, arhasi – you can

(Vaidarbhī exclaimed.)
"Stand! Please stand! O yogi of the kings! Protect this country which is surrounded by the sea. Shield it from criminals and warrior rogues. It is fearful. Only you can secure it." (4.28.48)

Detail

The protection of a country is the business of a king. Once Malayadhvaja retired, it was not his concern. The queen however was of the view that it was to be considered because otherwise. If there were criminals and warrior rogues inflicting criminal and military violence on the citizens, such conditions should be corrected by the king.

For his part, however, Malayadhvaja relinquished the authority to govern Pāndya country. He withdrew his interest long ago. He transferred it to his sons.

We can conclude that Queen Vaidarbhī did not complete her detachment from the role of being the wife of a king. Her observation of the king's precise detachment was difficult to imitate. She did not complete it. She would have to practice to release herself from the tendency to rule either as a monarch or as the spouse of a ruler.

Queen Vaidarbhī pronounced that Malayadhvaja was the only person in the country who could silence unruly elements. Was this a fact?

This indicates more about the queen than about Malayadhvaja. This arrogance should be removed by the queen in meditation, where she locates her vanity and removes it from the psyche.

King Malayadhvaja had no illusions or grand designs about his ruling power. It was not his. It was part of Nature's energy operation. He relinquished it to the entities who appeared in history as the bodies of his sons. If those persons were fit or incompetent, that was part of history, a scene which a king could not control. With disinterest in the future of Pāndya country, he gave the ruling authority to other persons who were to function as the succeeding rulers.

In her meditations, Queen Vaidarbhī would have to examine her tendencies. She would have to sort the facets of her psyche to determine which were in her interest as a spiritual being, and which dulled her spirituality. Then using the methods demonstrated by Malayadhvaja, she would reinforce the beneficial aspects and eliminate the negative factors.

एवं विलपन्ती बाला विपिने ऽनुगता पतिम् /
पतिता पादयोर् भर्तू रुदत्य् अश्रूण्य् अवर्तयत् (४॥२८॥४९)

evaṃ vilapantī bālā
vipine 'nugatā patim /
patitā pādayor bhartū
rudaty aśrūṇy avartayat (4.28.49)

evaṃ - thus, vilapantī – distressed, bālā – woman, vipine – in the forest, 'nugatā = anugatā = followed, patim – husband, patitā – fell, pādayor = pādayoḥ = at the feet, bhartū = bhartūḥ = of the husband, rudaty = rudati = she cried, aśrūṇy = aśrūṇi = tears, avartayat – she lamented

Thus, that distressed woman who went with her husband to the forest, fell at his feet. She cried with tears, lamenting. (4.28.49)

Detail

On the spiritual path, when a yogi/yogini is near completion, there is a final accounting, where one must parcel out. One should eliminate specific corrosive tendencies. At some point one must come to terms with faults. Irrespective of what is imposed by the environment, one should sort the adjuncts and energies which are in the individual psyche. Then one can understand what has value and what is worthless.

With the retired King Malayadhvaja dead and gone, his widow, Queen Vaidarbhī, had no one as the reference. With the king's body dead, she was left with no physical partner. Thus, that distressed woman who went with her husband to the forest, fell at his feet. She cried with tears, lamenting.

With only partial reach into the psychic existence, which was the only place to find the man who was the husband, she pinned herself to physical reality which was certain in contrast to the subtlety of the psychic world. She would have to release herself from the physical scene and established a presence on the astral plane.

चितिं दारुमयीं चित्वा तस्यां पत्युः कलेवरम् /
आदीप्य चानुमरणे विलपन्ती मनो दधे (४॥२८॥५०)

citiṃ dārumayīṃ citvā
tasyāṃ patyuḥ kalevaram /
ādīpya cānumaraṇe
vilapantī mano dadhe (4.28.50)

citiṃ - funeral pyre, dārumayīṃ - of logs, citvā – piled, tasyāṃ - of that, patyuḥ - of the husband, kalevaram – body, ādīpya – after igniting, cānumaraṇe = ca (and) +anumaraṇe (dying immediately after), vilapantī – regreting, mano = manah = mind, dadhe – determined

For the funeral, she piled logs with the body of her husband. And before igniting it, she was determined to die immediately after him. Though regretting what happened, she was mentally determined. (4.28.50)

Detail

Queen Vaidarbhī may have continued the austerities to complete the yoga process but it seems that she was motivated to practice in a way which did not permit her to complete the practice after his death. She had no confidence that she could remain as a lone forest ascetic.

Her motive for following the mystic process used by the now deceased king was to be with the king as his consort in whatever lifestyle he adopted. Now that he was dead, she felt that her only alternative was to follow him to the psychic existence, the world hereafter.

From this situation, one can deduce that the wanderer, Purañjan, up to this point, did not develop the motivation required for someone to be liberated through self-effort. Even though in the female body format, Purañjan gained training through imitating the psychological actions of King Malayadhvaja, he/she did not develop the impetus to practice yoga to become liberated.

As Purañjan, he skillfully mimicked the actions of the queen of Excitement City. When in that life, he independently acted to kill animals, he regretted it, and had to apologize to the queen. After death, when he got a female format as Queen Vaidarbhī, the tendency of following remained the same.

This suggest that one is limited by his/her natural method of learning and observation. Since she did not see the end procedure of yoga, which was used by King Malayadhvaja, she could not implement it. Her psyche was so designed that the opportunity she saw, was that of killing her body to reach the king wherever he transited hereafter.

For the funeral, she piled logs with his body. Before igniting it, she planned to die on the pyre. Though regretting that she did not die at the same moment he did, using whatever mystic transit he used, she was determined to kill her body.

तत्र पूर्वतरः कश्चित् सखा ब्राह्मण आत्मवान् /
सान्त्वयन् वल्गुना साम्ना ताम् आह रुदतीं प्रभो (४॥२८॥५१)

tatra pūrvataraḥ kaścit
sakhā brāhmaṇa ātmavān /
sāntvayan valgunā sāmnā
tām āha rudatīṃ prabho (4.28.51)

tatra – at the place, pūrvataraḥ - previously, kaścit – someone, sakhā – friend, brāhmaṇa – brahmin spiritually focused person, ātmavān – someone familiar with spiritual existence, sāntvayan – person who knows reality, valgunā – speaking nicely, sāmnā – kind, tām – to her, āha – he said, rudatīṃ - crying state, prabho – O King Barhi

At that place, someone whom she knew before, a friend who was spiritually focused, and who was familiar with spiritual existence, who knows reality, spoke nicely with kindness, to her who was in that crying state. That happened, O King Barhi. (4.28.51)

Detail

The idea of Queen Vaidarbhī was to reach the yogiKing Malayadhvaja in the psychic existence. She felt that she could continue the yoga practice and perfect it in his association in the world hereafter. She assumed that the yogi would wait for her in a dimension where they could be together and transit to supernatural places.

This idea was based on assumptions. A question arises. If the queen's reasoning was correct, why did King Malayadhvaja not show a technique for the transit he instituted?

The queen assumed that if she acted to cremate her body in the fire which roasted his, she would arrive in his presence somewhere in the astral existence.

Even though King Malayadhvaja did not object to the queen's viewing and imitating some of his mystic movements, still he did not tell her to imitate the actions. She did that of her own accord. He never told her to cremate his body and to commit suicide by entering the conflagration. He never assured that she would reach him hereafter by that physical action of jumping into the pyre.

Who can guarantee that anyone would reach someone hereafter merely by dying at the same moment in a similar circumstance?

Lucky for Queen Vaidarbhī, a friendly person appeared. This was someone she knew before, a friend who was spiritually focused, and who was familiar with spiritual existence. One who knew reality. To her who was in that depressed state, he spoke with kindness.

Her plan to reach the king by self-immolation was filled with uncertainty. It is possible for someone, a spouse, to reach another through killing the body soon after the target person dies, but what is the guarantee?

Can a spouse be sure that he/she will reach the psychic destination of the deceased loved one, merely by entering the fire in which the target person's body is burnt?

ब्राह्मण उवाच
का त्वं कस्यासि को वायं शयानो यस्य शोचसि /
जानासि किं सखायं मां येनाग्रे विचचर्थ ह (४॥२८॥५२)

brāhmaṇa uvāca
kā tvaṃ kasyāsi ko vāyaṃ
śayāno yasya śocasi /
jānāsi kiṃ sakhāyaṃ māṃ
yenāgre vicacartha ha (4.28.52)

brāhmaṇa – the spiritual focused person, uvāca – said, kā – who, tvaṃ - you, kasyāsi = kasya(whose) + asi (are you), ko = kaḥ = who, vāyaṃ = vā (or) + ayaṃ (this), śayāno = śayānaḥ = reclined body, yasya – for whom, śocasi – you weep, jānāsi – you recognize, kiṃ - why, sakhāyaṃ - friend, māṃ - me, yenāgre = yena (with whom) + agre (previously), vicacartha – you wandered about, ha- for sure

The spiritually focused person said.
"Who are you? Whose relative, are you? Who was the reclined body for whom you weep? Do you recognize me, your friend, with whom previously you wandered? (4.28.52)

Detail

Initially when the adventurer, the one named Purañjan, met the queen of Excitement City, he questioned about her parents and pedigree. He did not declare to her, his relations. He was so eager to enjoy her facilities, that without knowing her lineage, and with being informed by her that she had no idea about her parents or producer, he agreed to be her sexual companion for one hundred years.

Now Purañjan in a crisis of sorrow, in a female body, is approached by someone who inquired about her lineage and situation. Some of these are the same questions which Purañjan asked when he met the queen of Excitement City. Nearly every living being who finds itself to be a self, ignores these inquiries. Instead of investigating to get the information, the self ignores the inquiries and pursues experiences with a voracious appetite.

That causes excessive focus into the physical reality with little or no perception of what happens on the psychic side. Then the self finds itself to be subjected to an elderly body with no idea of what will happen when that form dies. That was the predicament of Purañjan when he surfaced again in history as the wife of King Malayadhvaja.

The daunting problem of death surfaces in every lifetime. Up to this point in his reincarnation history, Purañjan successfully avoided dealing with it. In the last years, when his body as a male or female was afflicted with debilitating illnesses, he/she focused on relatives. This was enough to ward off the uncertainty of what would happen at death.

Lurking in the background of the psyche, was Fear personified, who was assisted by Pyrexia Fever and by Old Age itself. These always attacked Purañjan's body and brought it nearer and nearer to its end.

The questions asked of the widowed Queen Vaidarbhī, should be sorted. These are the queries.

- Who are you?
- Whose relative, are you?
- Who is the reclined body for whom you weep?
- Do you recognize me, your friend, with whom previously you wandered?

Who are you?

In every lifetime, this first query should be answered at the onset. Even though the fetus is connected to its mother for nutrition, still when it is delivered, it becomes obvious that it is different to its mother. Before accosting anyone, a self should identify itself to itself. It should research its origin.

Whose relative, are you?

If it is that one cannot explain one's presence as a reality unto itself, as a superSource even, then one may identify oneself as a relation to someone whose identity is established. We experience that at the onset of the life of an infant. People tag that someone to its parent, relative or ward. The identity crisis is abated for some time by claiming oneself as a relative of someone who is known.

Who is the reclined body for whom you weep?

If one cannot identify the self and cannot show that the self is related to a known person, one may identify the self with someone who is known, but who is deceased. Pointing to a dead body, one may say, "I am related to him but he died recently."

Do you recognize me, your friend, with whom previously you wandered?

This is perplexing. The lady had no recall of the person who presented himself as her friend. She had neither a recent memory nor any recall about wandering through any lives with him.

अपि स्मरसि चात्मानम् अविज्ञात-सखं सखे /
हित्वा मां पदम् अन्विच्छन् भौम-भोग-रतो गतः (४॥२८॥५३)

api smarasi cātmānam
avijñāta-sakhaṃ sakhe /

hitvā māṃ padam anvicchan
bhauma-bhoga-rato gataḥ (4.28.53)

api – what? smarasi – you remember, cātmānam = ca (and) + ātmānam (coreSelf), avijñāta – Not-Recognized, sakhaṃ - friend, sakhe – o friend, hitvā – abandoning, māṃ - me, padam – place, anvicchan – desiring, bhauma – physical, bhoga – enjoyment, rato = rataḥ = sex pleasure, gataḥ - went

"Do you not remember the self who is known as Not-Recognized (Avijñāta), your friend. Having abandoned me at this place, and desiring physical enjoyment especially sex pleasure, you went away. (4.28.53)

Detail

This reminds one of the first mention of this unrecognized self. When Nārad began the narration about the fabled wanderer, Purañjan, Nārad introduced this special friend.

> ***O King Barhi, there was a king named Purañjan City Person, who is great to hear of. His friend, whose movements was imperceptible, was named Not-Recognized (Avijñāta). (4.25.10)***

Needless to say, Purañjan as Queen Vaidarbhī had no idea about such a friend. The only person the queen thought of recently, was the dead King Malayadhvaja.

It is interesting that Not-Recognized (Avijñāta) gave the location where the two friends were separated from each other. It was the place at which Queen Vaidarbhī was confronted with impending death and the place at which the same queen, as Purañjan was about to begin a lifetime as the lover of the queen of Bhogavatī. It is the place of existential crisis regarding losing or acquiring a physical body.

The background support for this amnesia is declared as physical enjoyment, especially sexual pleasure. The pull to the experiences of history, is itself the method of breaking whatever insight a self may have, about the psychic side of existence.

Since the self who is known as Not-Recognized (Avijñāta) did not register on the physical side, Purañjan in any life as a male or female, could not perceive this transcendental person, his perpetual friend.

The friend reported that Purañjan turned his back and did not look to the special friend for solutions to the challenges. Not-Recognized (Avijñāta) is invisible to people who are focused into the physical world.

हंसाव् अहं च त्वं चार्य सखायौ मानसायनौ /
अभूताम् अन्तरा वौकः सहस्र-परिवत्सरान् (४॥२८॥५४)

hamṣāv ahaṃ ca tvaṃ cārya
sakhāyau mānasāyanau /
abhūtām antarā vaukaḥ
sahasra-parivatsarān (4.28.54)

haṃsāv = haṃsau = two swans, ahaṃ - I, ca – and, tvaṃ - you, cārya = ca (and) + ārya (noble person), sakhāyau – friends, mānasāyanau = mānasa (Manasa Lake) + ayanau (staying), abhūtām – became, antarā – separated, vaukaḥ = vā (from) + okaḥ (residence), sahasra – thousand, parivatsarān – successive years

"Two swans, you and I, noble persons, friends, stay on the Manasa Lake. Somehow, we became separated from our residence for a thousand years. (4.28.54)

Detail

The friends were compared to swans, which are select avians, with the power of flight. A swan can distance itself from any location on the earth. That is a power of detachment.

The special friend declared that instead of chasing sensational experiences in the physical world, they should adhere to their residence on the Manasa Lake. The friend observes Purañjan and never loses sight of him, but the wanderer is hardly aware of his confidant.

For a thousand years, they were separated but only in the sense of Purañjan being unaware of the psychic presence of his fellow. Not-Recognized (Avijñāta) never lost track of Purañjan, even though the physically focused one lost psychic contact.

स त्वं विहाय मां बन्धो गतो ग्राम्य-मतिर् महीम् /
विचरन् पदम् अद्राक्षीः कयाचिन् निर्मितं स्त्रिया (४।।२८।।५५)

sa tvaṃ vihāya māṃ bandho gato
grāmya-matir mahīm /
vicaran padam adrākṣīḥ
kayācin nirmitaṃ striyā (4.28.55)

sa – that male person, someone, tvaṃ - you, vihāya – left, māṃ - me, bandho – O friend, gato = gataḥ = went, grāmya – basic, matir = matiḥ = mental occupation, mahīm – to the earth, vicaran – wandering, padam – place, adrākṣīḥ - you saw, kayācin = kayācit = someone, nirmitaṃ - designed, striyā – by a woman

"You, a male being, left me, O friend. You wandered to places on the earth. This was due to mental occupation with basic things. You saw a place which was designed by a woman. (4.28.55)

Detail

Not-Recognized (Avijñāta) identified Purañjan as a male being, a dear friend, from long ago. Purañjan wandered through the physical worlds making history. That was due to the mental occupation with basic things and the lack of interest in what is perpetual.

Purañjan was attracted to a place which was designed as if by a woman. It was the existential niche called Nature. Due to being endowed with physical perception, Purañjan only perceived physical existence. He was familiar with nothing else.

पञ्चारामं नव-द्वारम् एक-पालं त्रि-कोष्ठकम् /
षट्-कुलं पञ्च-विपणं पञ्च-प्रकृति स्त्री-धवम् (४॥२८॥५६)

pañcārāmaṃ nava-dvāram
eka-pālaṃ tri-koṣṭhakam /
ṣaṭ-kulaṃ pañca-vipaṇaṃ
pañca-prakṛti strī-dhavam (4.28.56)

pañcārāmaṃ - five parks, nava-dvāram = five entries, eka-pālaṃ = one security officer, tri-koṣṭhakam = three enclosing walls, ṣaṭ - six, kulaṃ - families, pañca – five, vipaṇaṃ - businesses, pañca – five, prakṛti – materials, strī – woman, dhavam – governor

"It had five parks, nine entries, one security officer, three enclosing walls, six families and, five businesses. It was made of five materials and was governed by a woman. (4.28.56)

Detail

Not-Recognized (Avijñāta), the invisible friend explained what happened over time. Initially when Purañjan met the queen of Excitement City, he, by good luck, successfully propositioned the wealthy woman, for whom servants and a security officer maintained the luxurious surroundings of her place.

It had five parks which were places where one could indulge each of the five senses. There were nine restricted entrances into the city. Each of these functioned for access to the parks. Some provided a means for expelling pollutants from the place.

There was a park for aural communication, where pleasing or displeasing sounds were heard. To access this place, the queen and Purañjan travelled through the two gates which were the ears.

There were two other gates through which they exited the city to perceive colors. Those were the eyes. There were two gates which opened to a park which had aromas. Those gates were double functioned. They ventilated the city by expelling its polluted air and acquiring fresh breezes.

One other gate opened to a park which had flavors. The queen and Purañjan went there through the mouth which accessed through the sense of taste. This same gate allowed speech.

One other gate which was lower than the ones already mentioned was the genital. That opened facilities for sexual pleasure through the touch sensation. This opened for sexual contact. This same gate was used for excreting urine, for menstruation, for acceptance of sperm and for parturition of a fetus.

With these there was another special gate which was the lowest entry out of the city. That gate, the anus, was used for excretion of waste.

The one security officer was the kundalini lifeForce Power Central. Its residence was near the anus gate. It had a contingency which was the sensual detection device. In coordination with the needs of the queen, this security system protected the city.

पञ्चेन्द्रियार्था आरामा द्वारः प्राणा नव प्रभो /
तेजो-ऽब्-न्नानि कोष्ठानि कुलम् इन्द्रिय-सङ्ग्रहः (४॥२८॥५७)

pañcendriyārthā ārāmā
dvāraḥ prāṇā nava prabho /
tejo-'b-annāni koṣṭhāni
kulam indriya-saṅgrahaḥ (4.28.57)

pañcendriyārthā = pañca (five) + indriya (sensual targets) + arthāḥ (valued), ārāmā = ārāmāḥ = gardens, dvāraḥ - entrances, prāṇā - lifeForce, nava – nine, prabho – O respected sir, tejo = tejaḥ = heat, 'b = ab = water, annāni – earth, koṣṭhāni – ramparts, kulam – family, indriya – senses, saṅgrahaḥ - collective mental function

"The five valued sensual targets are the gardens. Of the entrances for the lifeForce, there are nine. O respected sir, the heat, water, and earth are the ramparts. The family is represented as the senses and the collective mental function. (4.28.57)

Detail

Nārad detailed the symbolism of the legend of Purañjan. The five gardens were symbolic of the five valued targets of sound, surface, color, flavor, and odor. To access these pleasures or annoyances, the attention of the coreSelf must be routed through specific gates.

Through the orifices of the ears, Purañjan's attention was focused as a receptacle for agreeable or unwanted sound.

From the skin he accessed sensation through touch. Using sight energy, he exits the body to go through gate which is the eye. Using that, he hunts for colors.

Through the gate which is the mouth, he expressed the tasting function. With this he tastes a variety of flavors. Through the nostrils which are open continuously for collecting and expelling air, he also expresses the smell sense to appreciate odors.

The city has ramparts. These massive walls were made from heat, water, and rock. The physical body is constructed by nature in a similar way. When one eats food which comprise of water, and different types of vegetation or flesh, that is recomposed in the body to produce blood, flesh, and bones.

When the queen met Purañjan, she had a staff. At the time, he had no servants. This meant that initially the coreSelf travelled with no adjuncts which could supply information about the environment. From the onset however, the intellect received services from the five senses but those facilities were not divested.

Once the queen adopted Purañjan as her spouse, they reproduced children, who produced other progeny. This represents the fact, that once the queen and her servants had the company of Purañjan, the children they produced increased their sensual range. The coreSelf with an intellect and rudimentary senses, divests into a wide range of sensuality, which expands outwards for acquiring objects to experience in the world. The collective of Purañjan, the queen, her security officer, her servants, the children, and grandchildren, was a massive mental and emotional operation. It kept Purañjan occupied.

विपणस् तु क्रिया-शक्तिर् भूत-प्रकृतिर् अव्यया /
शक्त्य्-धीशः पुमांस् त्व् अत्र प्रविष्टो नावबुध्यते (४॥२८॥५८)

vipaṇas tu kriyā-śaktir
bhūta-prakṛtir avyayā /
śakty-adhīśaḥ pumāṃs tv atra
praviṣṭo nāvabudhyate (4.28.58)

vipaṇas – businesses, tu – then, kriyā – activity energy, śaktir = śaktiḥ = sensual power, bhūta – types of energy, prakṛtir = prakṛtiḥ = Nature, avyayā – perpetual, śakty = śakti = sensual intelligence, adhīśaḥ - governor, pumāṃs = pumān = coreSelf, tv = tu = but, atra – here, praviṣṭo = praviṣṭaḥ = influenced, subdued, nāvabudhyate = na (not) + avabudhyate (is unaware of)

"The businesses are the activity energy with the sensual power, which are the types of natural energy in Nature and which are perpetual. Then there is the governor, which is sensual intelligence. The coreSelf comes under its influence. The core is not aware that it is subdued. (4.28.58)

Detail

As vendors and customers are busy conversing and exchanging in a market, so the activity energy interacts with the sensual power. This is observed by the coreSelf, which indulges or curtails the sensual experiences. Whatever that self consents to or dispels, is sprayed over the self, such that it makes decisions based on those influences.

The sensual energies do not look to the core, for approval. They check with the intelligence which renders conclusions.

Just as Purañjan mimicked the mistress of Excitement City, such that when she relaxed, he did likewise, and when she got busy, he did the same, so the core mimics the functions of the intellect.

When the core is induced to submit itself to the decisions of the intellect, the influence is so smooth and pervasive, that the core does not suspect its bewilderment. Instead, it confidently renders permission for the intellect's ideas. This is similar to Purañjan's posturing behind the beautiful lady whom he met outside Excitement City.

He mused, "This is ideal. How fortunate! After searching this earth for an opportunity, I became fated to have this woman, her servants, her security official and her affluent city. What could be better than this?"

तस्मिंस् त्वं रामया स्पृष्टो रममाणोऽश्रुत-स्मृतिः /
तत्-सङ्गाद् ईदृशीं प्राप्तो दशां पापीयसीं प्रभो (४॥२८॥५९)

tasmiṃs tvaṃ rāmayā spṛṣṭo
ramamāṇo 'śruta-smṛtiḥ /
tat-saṅgād īdṛśīṃ prāpto
daśāṃ pāpīyasīṃ prabho (4.28.59)

tasmiṃs = tasmin = in that, tvaṃ - you, rāmayā – with the lady, spṛṣṭo = spṛṣṭaḥ = touching, ramamāṇo = ramamāṇaḥ = enjoying, 'śruta = aśruta not aware of spirituality, smṛtiḥ - what should be remembered, tat – that, saṅgād = saṅgāt = from association, īdṛśīṃ - similar to this, prāpto = prāptaḥ =

got, daśāṃ - condition, pāpīyasīṃ - full of faults, prabho – respected sir

"In that phase, with the lady, touching and enjoying, you were not aware of spirituality which should be remembered. From that association O respected sir, you got a condition which was full of faults. (4.28.59)

Detail

The stranger, the perpetual friend, alerted Purañjan that the conveniences enjoyed which were funded by the lady, the queen of Excitement City, were faulty. This was due to the fact that Purañjan was unaware of his status as a spiritual being.

Purañjan submitted to the queen. For one hundred years, he was to approve and mimic her physical and psychological actions. He experienced whatever she did. His discrimination was inoperative.

Near the end of the period however, Excitement City was charred. Purañjan, the queen, her attendants, the security officer, and their children, were captured. They were forced from the city by natural and supernatural enemies.

This exit meant death for the physical form. Losing the queen's luxurious surroundings, Purañjan had to reorganize himself. After being like this, in that type of birth for a time, he assumed the feminine format as Queen Vaidarbhī, the beautiful modest wife of King Malayadhvaja. But that situation also developed to the extent of ruin. As the woman, Vaidarbhī, her body aged. Her husband had the nerve to abandon his rulership role as the King of Pāndya country. She followed him sincerely, thinking that it was the best plan for the long term, for providing a better life hereafter. That king died. Then on the basis of superstition, she planned to kill her body in his pyre.

It was all a matter of playing various roles in physical existence, in one lifetime after another. Who was the essential person? Was it the man Purañjan? Was it the woman, Vaidarbhī?

न त्वं विदर्भ-दुहिता नायं वीरः सुहृत् तव /
न पतिस् त्वं पुरञ्जन्या रुद्धो नव-मुखे यया (४॥२८॥६०)

na tvaṃ vidarbha-duhitā
nāyaṃ vīraḥ suhṛt tava /
na patis tvaṃ purañjanyā
ruddho nava-mukhe yayā (4.28.60)

na – not, tvaṃ - you, vidarbha-duhitā = daughter of King Vidarbha, nāyaṃ = not this, vīraḥ - heroic one, suhṛt – good friend, tava – your, na – not, patis = patiḥ = husband, tvaṃ - you, purañjanyā – husband of Purañjani, ruddho = ruddha = compelled, nava-mukhe = nine entrances in the place, yayā – by that (influence)

"You are not the daughter of King Vidarbha. Nor was this hero your good friend. You were not Purañjana, the husband of Purañjani. You were compelled by her influence to be in the city with nine entrances. (4.28.60)

Detail

Who was the coreSelf which assumed the various roles and costumes, playing this character of this gender and then some other feature in one life and then in another?

Once he met the queen of Excitement City, Purañjan became a willing slave. Due to the enjoyment, he got by becoming preoccupied with the woman's routine, he could not rate the inconvenience.

Prior to meeting her, he was a researcher who travelled the earth with an adventurous attitude. It was about experience and learning. The high point in these lives however, was reached when he stumbled on the southern Himalayan area where Excitement City was located.

Having a male human body proved to be only part of the human attainment. In that experience, something was lacking. When he saw the queen, he realized what it was. To further captivate him, providence provided not just a beautiful woman, but luxurious furnishings, a staff, and a security officer. The highlight was sexual pleasure derived by sexual linkage.

Purañjan was of the view that he was in control. He was not. Once when he ventured to sportingly kill animals, he found that the exercise of independence was offensive to the queen. He could not endure her ire. He had no independence because he could not afford her anger and cold attitude.

माया ह्य् एषा मया सृष्टा यत् पुमांसं स्त्रियं सतीम् /
मन्यसे नोभयं यद् वै हंसौ पश्यावयोर् गतिम् (४॥२८॥६१)

māyā hy eṣā mayā sṛṣṭā yat
pumāṃsaṃ striyaṃ satīm /
manyase nobhayaṃ yad vai
haṃsau paśyāvayor gatim (4.28.61)

māyā – Nature's influence, hy = hi = sure, eṣā – this, mayā – by Me, sṛṣṭā – created, yat – from which, pumāṃsaṃ - male, striyaṃ - female, satīm – modest, manyase – you think, nobhayaṃ = na (not) + ubhyam (both), yad = yat = with, vai – certainly, haṃsau – swan-like beings, paśyāvayor = paśya (see) + āvayoḥ (our), gatim – reality, objective

"Surely, by Nature's influence which was created by me, you thought you were the male and then you considered yourself as a modest female. You are neither. Both of us are swan-like beings. Please see the reality. (4.28.61)

Detail

Not-Recognized (Avijñāta) provided a fresh outlook based on information which Purañjan was unaware of. Initially when Purañjan met the beautiful queen, he inquired about her situation, and background. She was unable to explain because she just happened to exist. She had no idea of parents.

Purañjan never declared his tradition and lineage. He, like the queen was ignorant of the origin. Now, he was informed by the invisible person.

It was declared by Not-Recognized (Avijñāta) that Purañjan was neither the man, the adventurer, nor the chaste lady who was the wife of the yogiKing Malayadhvaja.

Who was he? Who was she?

He/She was declared as being similar to the invisible person. Both were compared to legendary swans, graceful creatures who should remain free to fly here or there, observing.

अहं भवान् न चान्यस् त्वं त्वम् एवाहं विचक्ष्व भोः /
न नौ पश्यन्ति कवयश् छिद्रं जातु मनाग् अपि (४॥२८॥६२)

ahaṃ bhavān na cānyas tvaṃ
tvam evāhaṃ vicakṣva bhoḥ /

na nau paśyanti kavayaś
chidraṃ jātu manāg api (4.28.62)

ahaṃ - I, bhavān – you, na – not, cānyas = ca (and) + anyaḥ (other than), tvaṃ tvam = you and you, evāhaṃ = eva (sure) + aham (I), vicakṣva – see this, bhoḥ - friend, na – not, nau – of us, paśyanti – they see, kavayaś = kavayaḥ = informed person, chidraṃ - alienate, jātu – sometime, manāg = manāk – in the least, api – even

"I am familiar with you. You are not opposed to me. You and I are in constant association. See this, O friend! Regarding our relationship, informed persons do not see us as being alienated, not in the least. (4.28.62)

Detail

When Purañjan met the queen of Excitement City, he had in effect become blind and deaf to the level of existence, where his perpetual friend existed. Purañjan had no cognizance of the previous relationship. Due to being attracted to physical existence, he lost perception of Avijñāta, his informed friend

Somehow just when Purañjan, as that woman Queen Vaidarbhī, was to commit suicide, she (Purañjan) began to experience the subtle perception. Thus, she saw her friend. He never abandoned her. He stood by her through many lives. She however had no memory of their relationship because as soon as she was aware of physical existence, she lost awareness of the higher plane where the friend focused.

There is a tendency in the limited self, to move away from this dear friend, the supreme person. Thus, Not-Recognized (Avijñāta) alerted Purañjan not to reject the association and to realize that there was no alienation between them.

यथा पुरुष आत्मानम् एकम् आदर्श-चक्षुषोः /
द्विधाभूतम् अवेक्षेत तथैवान्तरम् आवयोः (४॥२८॥६३)

yathā puruṣa ātmānam
ekam ādarśa-cakṣuṣoḥ /
dvidhābhūtam avekṣeta
tathaivāntaram āvayoḥ (4.28.63)

yathā – as, puruṣa = puruṣaḥ = person, ātmānam – self, ekam – one reality, ādarśa – mirror, cakṣuṣoḥ - by the eyes, dvidhābhūtam = two beings, avekṣeta – sees, tathaivāntaram = tathā (as) + eva (so it is) + antaram (contrast), āvayoḥ - between two

"As with a mirrored reflection, or even looking into the eyes, a person sees two formats of one reality, even so there is no contrast between us." (4.28.63)

Detail

To a degree, the limited self is similar to the supreme one. There is no reason for the limited person to be alienated from the supreme being.

The limited self should befriend his eternal friend, who is the supreme one. If the limited person turns away from the supreme, it will deprive itself of higher association. Then the limited one will be left with the intellect. That would be like when Purañjan submitted to live under the auspices of the queen. Purañjan was guided by a flawed influence and was subjected to traumas which were beyond his control.

एवं स मानसो हंसो हंसेन प्रतिबोधितः /
स्व-स्थस् तद्-व्यभिचारेण नष्टाम् आप पुनः स्मृतिम् (४॥२८॥६४)

evaṃ sa mānaso haṃso
haṃsena pratibodhitaḥ /
sva-sthas tad-vyabhicāreṇa
naṣṭām āpa punaḥ smṛtim (4.28.64)

evaṃ - thus, sa = saḥ = he, mānaso = mānasaḥ = Mānasa Lake, haṃso = hamsaḥ = swan, haṃsena - by the swan, pratibodhitaḥ - inspired, sva – real identity, sthas = sthaḥ = positioned, tad = tat = that, vyabhicāreṇa – separated from, naṣṭām – lost, āpa – resumed, punaḥ - again, smṛtim – remembered

Thus, as inspired by the swan from the Mānasa Lake, the other swan, which was separated and lost, was positioned in real identity. (4.28.64)

Detail

As Purañjan eventually understood that it was in his interest, to remain in association and to be influenced by the supreme self, so a coreSelf should sort its choices. If such a self wants to act with no input from the supreme, it will function under the influence of an intellect, which is a psychological adjunct which adheres itself to the self as soon as the self turns away from the supreme one.

There is no position for the self to make perfect decisions on its own. This was proven when Purañjan neglected to consult with the queen, and went on a hunting expedition. When he completed that, he realized that he lacked perfect discrimination.

If a coreSelf gets the idea that it can function on its own, without its eternal friend or an intellect, that self will make faulty actions because it will lack both an intellect and the advice of the supreme person.

The limited self is similar to its eternal friend, the supreme self, except that the limited one does not have the information to make perfect decisions. It needs to realize this predicament.

बर्हिष्मन्न् एतद् अध्यात्मं पारोक्ष्येण प्रदर्शितम् /
यत् परोक्ष-प्रियो देवो भगवान् विश्व-भावनः (४॥२८॥६५)

barhiṣmann etad adhyātmaṃ
pārokṣyeṇa pradarśitam /
yat parokṣa-priyo devo
bhagavān viśva-bhāvanaḥ (4.28.65)

barhiṣmann - O King Barhi, etad = etat = this, adhyātmaṃ - subject of the supreme self, pārokṣyeṇa – by what is difficult to perceive, pradarśitam - explained, yat – which, parokṣa-priyo = parokṣa-priyaḥ = abstract to physical perception but endearing to the self, devo = devaḥ = God, bhagavān – Person of God, viśva-bhāvanaḥ = the existential basis of everyone

O King Barhi, this subject of the supreme self which is difficult to perceive, was explained. That supreme person is abstract to physical perception but is endearing to the self. God, the Person of God, is the existential basis of everyone. (4.28.65)

Detail

The experiences of Purañjan in many lives, some as a male being, some as a female one, culminated in the realization that all of this is misleading. It does not render events which continually point to the supreme self, the friend of the limited entity. Due to focus on physical existence, a limited self does not know the supreme one.

Chapter 5
Purañjan Explained

प्राचीनबर्हिर् उवाच
भगवंस् ते वचो ऽस्माभिर् न सम्यग् अवगम्यते /
कवयस् तद् विजानन्ति न वयं कर्म-मोहिताः (४॥२९॥१)

prācīnabarhir uvāca
bhagavaṃs te vaco 'smābhir
na samyag avagamyate /
kavayas tad vijānanti na
vayaṃ karma-mohitāḥ (4.29.1)

prācīnabarhir = prācīnabarhiḥ = King Barhi, uvāca – responded, bhagavaṃs = bhagavan = respectful someone, te – your, vaco = vacaḥ = conversation, 'smābhir =asmābhiḥ = by us, na – not, samyag = samyak = correctly, avagamyate - intellectually grasps, kavayas = kavayaḥ = educated person, tad = tat = that, vijānanti – they understand, na – not, vayaṃ - we, karma – socio-cultural activities, mohitāḥ - enchanted

King Barhi responded.
"O respectful self, your conversation to us was not correctly grasped. The intellectual persons! They understand this, but not us. We are enchanted by social activities." (4.29.1)

Detail

King Barhi could not understand the allegory. He knew there was an explanation in terms of human lifestyle but he could not fathom it.

नारद उवाच
पुरुषं पुरञ्जनं विद्याद् यद् व्यनक्त्य् आत्मनः पुरम् /
एक-द्वि-त्रि-चतुष्-पादं बहु-पादम् अपादकम् (४॥२९॥२)

nārada uvāca
puruṣaṃ purañjanaṃ vidyād yad
vyanakty ātmanaḥ puram /
eka-dvi-tri-catuṣ-pādaṃ
bahu-pādam apādakam (4.29.2)

nārada – Nārada, uvāca – said, puruṣaṃ - that person, purañjanaṃ - City-Tenant, vidyād = vidyāt = know, yad = yat = that which, vyanakty = vyankti = manifested, ātmanaḥ - of the self, puram – residence, eka-dvi-tri-catuṣ = one, two, three, four (catuḥ), pādaṃ - legs, bahu-pādam = multiple legs, apādakam- without limbs

Nārada said.
That person, Purañjan, should be known as the self which manifested its residence which has one, two, three, four, or multiple legs, or which is without limbs. (4.29.2)

Detail

In the allegory, Purañjan represents the limited coreSelf, the *ātma.* He has an eternal friend but his awareness about this other person is indefinite. While the supremeSelf is inclined to the spiritual plane of existence, the limited self has a tendency to experience on lower levels. This difference between the two is telling for the limited one.

The limited self has a tendency to desire perception of physical things. This naturally allows for that self, a psyche which adapts to physical forms, one which yields physical perception. According to the species, that is the perception which a limited self is afforded.

Using the attention of the limited self, Nature creates for that someone a particular body with one, two, three, four or more legs. It may also provide a form which is limbless and has very little sensual variation.

Nature uses the focusing energy of a limited self to create a form which that self identifies with. In such a format the self is wired to adjuncts which function for the experiences that form can have.

Nārad informed the King that a limited self is allied to a certain lifeform in the physical existence. That form serves as the self's address or residence.

योऽविज्ञाताहृतस् तस्य पुरुषस्य सखेश्वरः /
यन् न विज्ञायते पुम्भिर् नामभिर् वा क्रिया-गुणैः (४॥२९॥३)

yo 'vijñātāhṛtas tasya
puruṣasya sakheśvaraḥ /
yan na vijñāyate pumbhir
nāmabhir vā kriyā-guṇaiḥ (4.29.3)

yo = yaḥ = who, 'vijñātāhṛtas = avijñāta (Not-Recognized) + āhṛtaḥ (described), tasya – of his, puruṣasya – of the person, sakheśvaraḥ - Lord who is the friend, yan = yat = so, na – not, vijñāyate – understood, pumbhir = pumbhiḥ = by person, nāmabhir = nāmabhiḥ = by names, vā – or, kriyā-guṇaiḥ = by function and tendency

The one described as Not-Recognized, who is a person, is the Lord, the friend of the self. He is not identified as a person with names, function, or tendency. (4.29.3)

Detail

The difference between the limited self and the supreme being is presented in this verse in part. The similarity of the two is that they are persons (*puruṣa*), specific selves. Each can be targeted, except that the supreme self registers on the spiritual plane distinctly, while the limited self is drawn to the physical level.

Because it is focused into the physical world and has an inborn interest to participate in this history, the limited self is identified with names, functions and tendencies which pertain to physical situations.

Conversely, the supreme self, due to its slight focus into physical existence, is not tagged as a person with physical names, functions, or tendencies. That supreme self is the Lord but he is also the friend of the limited person. He is described as Not-Recognized. He rarely exhibits a pronounced register on the physical side.

यदा जिघृक्षन् पुरुषः कार्त्स्न्येन प्रकृतेर् गुणान् /
नव-द्वारं द्वि-हस्ताङ्घ्रि तत्रामनुत साध्व् इति (४॥२९॥४)

yadā jighṛkṣan puruṣaḥ
kārtsnyena prakṛter guṇān /
nava-dvāraṃ dvi-hastāṅghri
tatrāmanuta sādhv iti (4.29.4)

yadā - when, jighṛkṣan – eager to experience, puruṣaḥ - person, kārtsnyena – entirely, prakṛter = prakṛteḥ = of Nature, guṇān – temperaments of Nature, nava-dvāraṃ = nine entrances, dvi – two, hastāṅghri = hasta (hands) + aṅghri (legs), tatrāmanuta = tatra (there) + amanuta (he considered), sādhv = sadhu (suitable, preferred), iti – thus

When being eager to experience, someone is totally involved with the temperaments of Nature, it uses the nine entranced, two handed, two-legged format, which it considers as the preferred residence. (4.29.4)

Detail

The eagerness to experience is the driving force behind the coreSelf's submission to its intellect. The core becomes entranced and consents to the conclusions of the intellect. The core turns away from its dear friend, the supreme self. This happens because of the core's hastiness for accommodations and sexual companionship, the same experiences which Purañjan got from the queen.

A limited self, once it fuses with Nature, becomes subjected to Nature's moods. This was presented by Nārad when he described that Purañjan mimicked the queen, such that when she enjoyed, Purañjan did that. When she was in distress, he felt miserable too.

In its original format, the coreSelf has the potential for inquiry. It is curious about experience. Since at first it effortlessly develops an interest in Nature, and it lacks a compelling interest to relate to its friend, the supreme spirit, its conjunction with and submission to Nature, happens instantly.

The self may use any of the simple or complex lifeforms which are produced by Nature. However, the nine entranced, two handed, two-legged format of the human body is what Purañjan preferred.

बुद्धिं तु प्रमदां विद्यान् ममाहम् इति यत्-कृतम् /
याम् अधिष्ठाय देहे ऽस्मिन् पुमान्
भुङ्क्ते ऽक्षभिर् गुणान् (४॥२९॥५)

buddhiṃ tu pramadāṃ vidyān
mamāham iti yat-kṛtam /
yām adhiṣṭhāya dehe 'smin
pumān bhuṅkte 'kṣabhir guṇān (4.29.5)

buddhiṃ - intellect, tu – but, pramadāṃ - lady, vidyān = vidyāt = know, mamāham = mama (my) + aham (I), iti – thus, yat by that, kṛtam – done, yām – which, adhiṣṭhāya – situated, dehe – in the body, 'smin = asmin = this, pumān –

individual, bhuṅkte – experiences, 'kṣabhir = akṣabhiḥ = by the senses, guṇān – Nature's influences

The intellect is represented as the young woman. Know that the *my-and-I* feelings are produced by that. It is situated in the body and gives the individual experiences through the senses and by Nature's influences. (4.29.5)

Detail

Nārad breaks apart the analogy of the wandering adventurer who was captivated when he met a beautiful maiden who had all trappings as a wealthy seductive woman.

That lady represented the intellect, which the coreSelf became fused to. Due to the affiliation between the core and its intellect, a sense of identity of *my-and-I* spontaneously arose. It is not that the wanderer lacked identity prior to that. In fact, the identity was there but it was not applied. It was not even applied to the perpetual friend who was focused on the transcendental side of existence.

The supreme self identified himself as the friend of the core, but the core did not have a feeling of kinship with the supreme person. Instead, the core felt strongly attached to the queen whom he met and also to the children they produced.

As we heard, whatever the queen did, the wanderer imitated. He identified the queen's actions as his own. This misidentification caused him to live a trivial existence pursuing the objects which the queen craved.

Stated differently, the coreSelf spends its days and nights pursuing whatever the intellect proposes. In that way time whittles away needlessly for the core, which did not, even for a moment, consider its origin or existential support.

The intellect supervises the activities of the senses, which are used to gather information about the external, and internal environments. The internal environment, the psyche, includes the mind. In that there are adjuncts. These impulsively render experiences to the self.

Because the core relies on the intellect, it fails when it tries to divorce itself from any of the adjuncts. In fact, as we heard in the story of Purañjan, when once, he acted independently, that distressed the queen which caused her to be unhappy with him. He could not bear her indifference. Subsequently he apologized and gained her favor as before.

This shows that if the coreSelf ignores the intellect, that core suffers because of getting a neglect energy in response. The core can hardly command the other adjuncts, like the kundalini lifeForce Power Central, the senses, and memory, even the sense of identity. It is as if the queen, the intellect, is the mistress in command.

सखाय इन्द्रिय-गणा ज्ञानं कर्म च यत्-कृतम् /
सख्यस् तद्-वृत्तयः प्राणः पञ्च-वृत्तिर् यथोरगः (४॥२९॥६)

sakhāya indriya-gaṇā jñānaṃ
karma ca yat-kṛtam /
sakhyas tad-vṛttayaḥ prāṇaḥ
pañca-vṛttir yathoragaḥ (4.29.6)

sakhāya = sakhāyaḥ = male escorts, indriya-gaṇā = collection of the senses, jñānaṃ - information, karma – actions, ca – and, yat-kṛtam = done by that, sakhyas – female associates, tad = tat = of that, vṛttayaḥ - frantic activity, prāṇaḥ - lifeForce, pañca – five, vṛttir = vṛttiḥ = psychological movement, yathoragaḥ = yathā (so as) + uragaḥ (serpent)

The male escorts are the collection of senses which cause information and action. The female associates represent frantic activity. The lifeForce which exhibits five psychological movements is represented by the serpent. (4.29.6)

Detail

In the legend of Purañjan, the City Person, that wanderer travelled everywhere on earth. He was a loner with no companion. He experienced much in his travels but he felt that there was someone somewhere who suited his needs.

When he met the queen of Excitement City, he felt that she was the perfect match. Not only was she beautiful beyond compare, she had a staff, an affluent city, and tight five-sectioned security. She put this at his disposal for one hundred years.

Her male escorts correspond to the collection of senses which cause one to be informed about events. These also are involved with physical and psychological actions.

The female staff corresponded to frantic sensual activity which is impulsive and reactionary. These are necessary operations which are due to sensitivity triggers in the psyche. These give alerts and show spontaneous behavior according to the time and place.

The serpent which followed the queen wherever she went, which protected her from every side, is the lifeForce which exhibits five psychological movements for the kundalini Power Central energy to diverge and energize every part of the physical body and psychic systems.

बृहद्-बलं मनो विद्याद् उभयेन्द्रिय-नायकम् /
पञ्चालाः पञ्च विषया यन्-मध्ये नव-खं पुरम् (४॥२९॥७)

bṛhad-balaṃ mano vidyād
ubhayendriya-nāyakam /
pañcālāḥ pañca viṣayā
yan-madhye nava-khaṃ puram (4.29.7)

bṛhad – super, balaṃ - strong, mano = manaḥ = mind, vidyād = vidyāt = know, ubhayendriya = ubhaya (both) + indriya (collection of senses), nāyakam – monitor, pañcālāḥ - Pañcālā country, pañca – five, viṣayā = viṣayāḥ = sense objects, yan = yat = of which, madhye – in the middle, nava – nine, khaṃ - entrances, puram – city

The Super-Strong one is the mind. Know it as the monitor of both collection of the senses. There is the Pañcālā country which has five sense objects, which surround the city with nine entrances, (4.29.7)

Detail

The powerful willpower force which usually directs physical and psychic activities, is the mind. This is when it seems that a collective decision is executed in a definite way. The mind as a whole, which includes the intellect, is the monitor of the senses.

What was rendered as the Pañcāla country are the five sense objects which the mind constantly procures. These surround the city which has nine entrances. The idea is that the coreSelf is fused with the intellect, which monitors the information seized by the senses. Once the intellect forms a conclusion, the mind acts as a super-strong person would. To grasp the sense object, the mind moves to take that target.

अक्षिणी नासिके कर्णौ मुखं शिश्न-गुदाव् इति /
द्वे द्वे द्वारौ बहिर् याति यस् तद्-िन्द्रिय-संयुतः (४॥२९॥८)

akṣiṇī nāsike karṇau
mukhaṃ śiśna-gudāv iti /
dve dve dvārau bahir yāti
yas tad-indriya-saṃyutaḥ (4.29.8)

akṣiṇī – two eyes, nāsike – two nostrils, karṇau – two ears, mukhaṃ - mouth, śiśna – genitals, gudāv = gudau = anus, iti – thus, dve dve = two, two, dvārau – entrances, bahir = bahiḥ = outdoor, yāti – goes, yas = yaḥ = who, tad = tat = that, indriya – senses, saṃyutaḥ - utilized

which are the eyes, nostrils, two ears, mouth, the genitals, and anus. The first two are followed by another two entrances, which access the outdoor where the senses are utilized. (4.29.8)

Detail

Purañjan made an agreement with the queen, whereby she would provide services and accommodations for one hundred years. She did not explain that everything, including her city, would age and deteriorate. At first Purañjan considered that it was his fortune to meet such a beautiful lady who was catered by male and female servants and by a bodyguard who never slept, and was on duty every second of a day and night.

This meant that when the coreSelf is matched to an intellect, it happens spontaneously and not by a special selection of the core.

With the intellect, came certain features. This was according to the specific species that intellect operated. In this case, it was the human situation which had two eyes, two nostrils, two ears, one mouth, the genital, and anus. These were entrances on the psyche for acquiring information about events to which the psyche is subjected.

When a sense gets information, it relays that to the intellect, which processes the data and draws conclusions for indulging in an event or escaping from it.

अक्षिणी नासिके आस्यम् इति पञ्च पुरः कृताः /
दक्षिणा दक्षिणः कर्ण उत्तरा चोत्तरः स्मृतः (४॥२९॥९)
पश्चिमे इत्य् अधो द्वारौ गुदं शिश्नम् इहोच्यते /

akṣiṇī nāsike āsyam iti
pañca puraḥ kṛtāḥ /
dakṣiṇā dakṣiṇaḥ karṇa
uttarā cottaraḥ smṛtaḥ /
paścime ity adho dvārau
gudaṃ śiśnam ihocyate (4.29.9)

akṣiṇī – two eyes, nāsike – two nostrils, āsyam – mouth, iti – thus, pañca – five, puraḥ - front, kṛtāḥ - located, dakṣiṇā – right, dakṣiṇaḥ - right, karṇa – ear, uttarā – left, cottaraḥ = ca (and) + uttaraḥ (left), smṛtaḥ - as declared, paścime - to the bottom, ity = iti = thus, adho = adhaḥ = lower, dvārau – two entrances, gudaṃ - rectum, śiśnam – genitals, ihocyate = iha (here) + ucyate (explained)

Two eyes, two nostrils, and the mouth are the five entrances located in the front. To the right is the right ear. To the left is the left ear. So, it is declared. To the bottom are the lower two entrances, the anus, and genital. That is explained. (4.29.9)

Detail

According to the species so is the design of the body. Some species have only one sensual entrance. Some have two or more. Each entrance into the psyche has specific sensing abilities either in relationship to the events outside the body or to those within it.

In some elementary lifeforms, the mouth acts as an anus. Some forms have no visual perception. These have other types of sensing apparatus which get information about the environment through some other sensual reception.

Each species is a type of condition, a life event. The form itself is experienced as an environment, which is within another environment which we know as the physical world. Each lifeform is an address from which a coreSelf, accepts the services of an intellect, for experiences which are sensual occasions.

From a psychological perspective, the humanBody container is similar to and also different from another body type. The human walks upright. Some other species may never do that. The human has a particular visual range which some other species lack in all respects. But there is a similarity in that each body enclosure has a predominant core which is situated in the form as the primary experiencer.

खद्योताविर्मुखी चात्र नेत्रे एकत्र निर्मिते /
रूपं विभ्राजितं ताभ्यां विचष्टे चक्षुषेश्वरः (४॥२९॥१०)

khadyotāvirmukhī cātra
netre ekatra nirmite /

rūpaṃ vibhrājitaṃ tābhyāṃ
vicaṣṭe cakṣuṣeśvaraḥ (4.29.10)

khadyotāvirmukhī = khadyotā (Glow-Worm) + āvirmukhī (Peep-Hole), cātra = ca (and) + atra (here), netre – two eyes, ekatra – at one place, nirmite – formed, rūpaṃ - form, vibhrājitaṃ - Vibhrājita subdued diversions, tābhyāṃ - by two, vicaṣṭe – perceive, cakṣuṣeśvaraḥ = cakṣuṣā (with perception) + īśvaraḥ (master of the city)

Khadyotā Glow-Worm, and Āvirmukhī Peep-Hole, are the two eyes which are at one place. There is the form which is Vibrājita or subdued diversions. By the two organs, the master of the city perceives various perceptions. (4.29.10)

Detail

Of the two eyes, one operates like a glow worm. It tries to attract the attention of others. It attracts influences. The other eye focuses to discover colors which are desirable to the self. The eyes digest the colors they absorbed but they do so in a subdued way, as contrasted to the mouth which devours physical things. The hands and mouth assist the eyes to bring things into the body or even to expel things from the form.

नलिनी नालिनी नासे गन्धः सौरभ उच्यते /
घ्राणो ऽवधूतो मुख्यास्यं विपणो वाग् रसविद् रसः (४॥२९॥११)

nalinī nālinī nāse gandhaḥ
saurabha ucyate /
ghrāṇo 'vadhūto mukhyāsyaṃ
vipaṇo vāg rasavid rasaḥ (4.29.11)

nalinī – called Nalinī, nālinī – called Nālinī, nāse – two nostrils, gandhaḥ - odor, saurabha = saurabhaḥ = fragrance or Saurabha, ucyate - is named, ghrāṇo = ghrāṇaḥ = sense of smell, 'vadhūto = avadhūtaḥ = Avadhūta, wandering wiseman, mukhyāsyaṃ = mukhyā (Mukhyā primary) + āsyaṃ (mouth), vipaṇo = vipaṇaḥ = Vipaṇa vocal organ, vāg = vāk = means for speech, rasavid = rasavit = tasting organ, rasaḥ - sense of tasting flavor

Nalinī and Nālinī are the two nostrils. Odor is fragrance or Saurabha. The sense of smell was called Avadhūta, the wandering wiseman, The Mukhyā primary is the mouth. The Vipana vocal organ is the means for speech. The tasting organ is Rasavit. It renders flavor. (4.29.11)

Detail

The nostrils which house the sense of smell pursue, acquire, or reject odors. This sense has an important task which is to detect and inhale healthy air.

There is the mouth which is used for speech. That concerns the vocal organ. In the mouth, there is the tongue which renders taste, a necessary sense for evaluating edibles.

Due to not having a way to evaluate this environment, the coreSelf, Purañjan, is reliant on the assistants of the intellect. The core is responsible for the permissions it voluntarily or involuntarily gives for the operations of the intellect and its accessories.

आपणो व्यवहारो ऽत्र चित्रम् अन्धो बहूदनम् /
पितृहूर् दक्षिणः कर्ण उत्तरो देवहूः स्मृतः (४॥२९॥१२)

āpaṇo vyavahāro 'tra
citram andho bahūdanam /
pitṛhūr dakṣiṇaḥ karṇa
uttaro devahūḥ smṛtaḥ (4.29.12)

āpaṇo = āpaṇaḥ = Āpaṇa consuming place, vyavahāro = vyavahāraḥ = frantic activity, 'tra = atra = here, citram – varieties, andho = andhaḥ = foodstuff, bahūdanam - Bahūdana food variety, pitṛhūr – Pitṛhū Ancestral Ritual, dakṣiṇaḥ - right, karṇa = karṇaḥ - ear, uttaro = uttarah = left, devahūḥ - Devahū Deity Ritual, smṛtaḥ - is known as

Āpaṇa consuming place signifies frantic activity. Bahūdana food variety indicates various foodstuff. Pitṛhū Ancestral Ritual is the right ear. The left one is known as the Devahū Deity Ritual. (4.29.12)

Detail

This world provides experience which is consumed by the coreSelf. The consumption of air and food sponsors frantic activity. There is a variety of foodstuff for indulgence. The tongue and teeth are involved in eating and speaking. The core needs the assistance of the intellect and its accessories for rendering ideas into language.

Since they have an investment in the body, the ancestors access the mind through the inner right ear. They speak into this organ and influence the core to act in their interest. The other ear is used by the Devahū Deities.

प्रवृत्तं च निवृत्तं च शास्त्रं पञ्चाल-संज्ञितम् /
पितृ-यानं देव-यानं श्रोत्राच् छ्रुत-धराद् व्रजेत् (४॥२९॥१३)

pravṛttaṃ ca nivṛttaṃ ca
śāstraṃ pañcāla-saṃjñitam /
pitṛ-yānaṃ deva-yānaṃ śrotrāc
chruta-dharād vrajet (4.29.13)

pravṛttaṃ - exciting activity, ca – and, nivṛttaṃ - curtailment of excitement, ca – and, śāstraṃ - religious texts, pañcāla – Pañcāla, saṃjñitam = is known as, pitṛ-

yānaṃ = transit to the ancestors, deva-yānaṃ = transit to the celestial beings, śrotrāc = śrotrāt = hearing of, chruta = śruta = sound, what is heard, dharād = dharāt = collector of, vrajet – should tour

The exciting activity, and the curtailment of that, which are described in the religious texts, are listed as the Pañcāla country. The transit to the ancestors and that to the celestial beings, are heard of by the collector of sound, known as Śrutadharā. That allows one to tour (the worlds hereafter). (4.29.13)

Detail

The five territories known as the Pañcāla country, are the haunts of the coreSelf. Those were the sense object locations which it searched for experiences. The intellect was sure to arrange these facilities for the maximum enjoyment. This kept the core occupied so that it had no time for noticing the flow of time.

Even though Purañjan was told that he had a limit of one hundred years, he never paused to consider the allotted time. Due to that, he was in a fix when the timer was near the end of its ticking.

Because of its reliance on the intellect for sensing and concluding, a coreSelf remains unaware of the time factor. Time keeps clocking. It will enforce duration and termination. It is unforgiving. It never offers a pardon. It is exacting.

There is exciting activity and curtailment of that. For one's benefit, one may follow the scripture and superstitions which put one in the graces of the ancestors. They have social power.

Alternately, one may follow the texts which promote the interest of the celestial beings. What happens hereafter is related to one's compliance with the influence of the departed relatives and the supernatural controllers.

आसुरी मेढ्रम् अर्वाग्-द्वार् व्यवायो ग्रामिणां रतिः /
उपस्थो दुर्मदः प्रोक्तो निर्ऋतिर् गुद उच्यते (४॥२९॥१४)

āsurī meḍhram arvāg-dvār
vyavāyo grāmiṇāṃ ratiḥ /
upastho durmadaḥ prokto
nirṛtir guda ucyate (4.29.14)

āsurī – Āsurī, meḍhram – genitals, arvāg = arvāt = downward, dvār = dvāḥ = entrance, vyavāyo = vyavāyaḥ = copulation, grāmiṇāṃ - vulgar people, ratiḥ - sexual love, upastho = upasthaḥ = sexual organs, durmadaḥ - infatuation, prokto = proktaḥ = spoken, informed, nirṛtir = nirṛtiḥ = Nirṛti death, guda = gudaḥ = rectum, ucyate – is assigned

Āsurī is the genitals which is an entrance which faces downward. Copulation is for vulgar people who are infatuated by Rati, sexual love. It is said that Nirṛti or death is assigned as the anus. (4.29.14)

Detail

The Āsurī is the genitals. For humans, these face downward. They are adored by vulgar people who are infatuated by Rati, sexual love. In every case even for the modest persons, sexual involvement is necessary for the birth of a body. The operation of the genitals produced feelings which are interpreted by the mind as ecstatic pleasure.

Nirṛti or death is the end for the time being. That confiscates one's opportunity to participate in history. This is a temporary suspension since sooner or later one may again surface in this world as an infant. As the anus is at the end of the trunk of the body, so death of a form is the termination of an opportunity in history.

वैशसं नरकं पायुर् लुब्धको ऽन्धौ तु मे शृणु /
हस्त-पादौ पुमांस् ताभ्यां युक्तो याति करोति च (४॥२९॥१५)

vaiśasaṃ narakaṃ pāyur
lubdhako 'ndhau tu me śṛṇu /
hasta-pādau pumāṃs tābhyāṃ
yukto yāti karoti ca (4.29.15)

vaiśasaṃ - Vaiśasa Death Locale, narakaṃ - hell dimension, pāyur = pāyuḥ = evacuation power, lubdhako = lubdhakaḥ = Lubdhaka, Greed, 'ndhau = andhau = two blind persons, tu – but, me – to me, śṛṇu – listen, hasta-pādau = hands and legs, pumāṃs = pumān = person, tābhyāṃ - with them, yukto = yuktaḥ = effort, yāti – goes, karoti – does, ca – and

The Death Locale (Vaiśasa) is the hell dimension. It is related to the evacuation power which is based on Greed (Lubdhaka). About the two blind persons, listen to me. Those are the hands and legs, which assist the person with the effort of moving and acting. (4.29.15)

Detail

To get the best from Excitement City, Purañjan should properly maintain its facilities. Instead, he followed the queen at every step and was unconcerned except to enjoy the pleasure and accommodations which her staff provided. He relied on the five-hooded snake which was responsible for maintenance. Purañjan did not lift a finger to help in the up-keep of the city.

This parodies the coreSelf, which relies on the intellect and its accessories which include the kundalini Power Central. The core expects to enjoy many exciting events at the expense of the intellect. What actually happens, however, is that the core is tagged for the costs of these enjoyments.

The physical body deteriorates. This causes inefficient use of energy. That affects the focus of the core. It is experienced as discomforting scenes. When the core decides to leave the body, it may have neither the means nor will to do so. Then it must wait for the turn of time to bring the diseased form to an end.

Vaiśasa Death Locale is the hell dimension. Its highway is paved with decay. Purañjan had no plan to deter it. In fact, whatever he did to imitate the queen, funded it.

The greed tendency supports death. Its immediate benefit is satisfaction. Its long-term situation is diseased vital organs.

There were two blind persons on the queen's staff. These were the hands and legs. They assisted readily in the first years but as they aged, they became unserviceable and were an inconvenience.

अन्तः-पुरं च हृदयं विषूचिर् मन उच्यते /
तत्र मोहं प्रसादं वा हर्षं प्राप्नोति तद्-गुणैः (४॥२९॥१६)

antaḥ-puraṃ ca hṛdayaṃ
viṣūcir mana ucyate /
tatra mohaṃ prasādaṃ vā
harṣaṃ prāpnoti tad-guṇaiḥ (4.29.16)

antaḥ-puraṃ = inner room, bedroom, ca – and, hṛdayaṃ - heart, viṣūcir = viṣūciḥ = checking everywhere, mana = manaḥ = mind, ucyate – is said, tatra – there, mohaṃ - infatuation, prasādaṃ - what is fulfillment, vā – or, harṣaṃ - happy excitement, prāpnoti – got, tad = tat = of that, guṇaiḥ - by Nature's influences

The bedroom is the heart. There is checking everywhere which is conducted by the mind. There is infatuation which renders fulfillment. It gives happy excitement. These are produced by Nature's influences. (4.29.16)

Detail

The bedroom is where the coreSelf resides during meditative focus and where it is positioned when it is focused on the intelligence. Purañjan and the queen had their private quarters at that place.

The mind as a whole, as a functioning apparatus, conducts actions through the use of willpower. This is the combination of the coreSelf and the intellect, which acts spontaneously to fulfill movements for accessing sense gratification.

Purañjan accessed the physical world but he did so through the medium of the queen and her staff. His contact with the sense objects was indirect. The coreSelf should detached itself from the intellect and its accessories. That is how it could rate its value.

यथा यथा विक्रियते गुणाक्तो विकरोति वा /
तथा तथोपद्रष्टात्मा तद्-वृत्तीर् अनुकार्यते (४॥२९॥१७)

yathā yathā vikriyate
guṇākto vikaroti vā /
tathā tathopadraṣṭātmā
tad-vṛttīr anukāryate (4.29.17)

yathā yathā = just as, vikriyate – stirred to action, guṇākto = guṇāktaḥ = affected by Nature's influences, vikaroti - vigorously does, vā = or, tathā tathopadraṣṭātmā = tathā tathā (so as) + upadraṣṭā (witness) +ātmā (coreSelf), tad = tat = that, vṛttīr = vṛttīḥ = frantic psychological activity, anukāryate – mimics

As it happens, one is stirred to action as one is affected by Nature's influence. One acts vigorously such that as the witness, the coreSelf mimics the frantic psychological activity. (4.29.17)

Detail

The rapid movements of the intellect fascinate the core. The intellect appears to flicker in the blank dark space that is the mind. This bewilders the core.

देहो रथस् त्व् इन्द्रियाश्वः संवत्सर-रयो ऽगतिः /
द्वि-कर्म-चक्रस् त्रि-गुण- ध्वजः पञ्चासु-बन्धुरः (४॥२९॥१८)

deho rathas tv indriyāśvaḥ
saṃvatsara-rayo 'gatiḥ /
dvi-karma-cakras tri-guṇa-
dhvajaḥ pañcāsu-bandhuraḥ (4.29.18)

deho = dehah = body, rathas = rathaḥ = chariot, tv = tu = but, indriyāśvaḥ = indriya (senses) + aśvaḥ (horses), saṃvatsara – years, rayo = rayaḥ = course, 'gatiḥ = agatiḥ = not moving, dvi – two, karma – cultural activities, cakras = chakraḥ = wheels, tri-guṇa = Nature's three influences, dhvajaḥ - flag, pañcāsu – five vital airs, bandhuraḥ - reins

The body is similar to a chariot but with the senses functioning like the horses. In the course of a year, it feels as if it did not move. The two types of cultural activities are its wheels. Nature's three influences are its flag. The five vital airs are its five reins. (4.29.18)

Detail

One way to consider this situation is to rate it as a chariot. Such a conveyance is pulled by horses. In this case, five steeds. According to how the horses move to the left, center or right, that is how the chariot will convey. If the horses stand still, the chariot will remain in place. If one horse refuses a command, the chariot will be affected according to the strength of that animal.

Sense control is one way of directing what the horses may or may not do. That involves controlling the reins. A driver may cause the chariot to move in one, or the other direction, by the way the reins are tensioned or released. If there was one horse, one tug to the right would cause the animal to move in that direction but with five animals, in this case five senses, the control of the animals is complicated.

Bhogavatī, Excitement City, represents the psyche which is an inner environment. It is similar to a physical city but it has a subtle complement which runs parallel and which is to an extent coordinate. The coreSelf experiences the physical and subtle enclosure through feelings which are in every part of the physical and subtle bodies.

The two forms are interspaced one into the other. The subtle one is experienced simultaneously with the physical system, except that in dream, the subtle one becomes aware of itself with little or no reference to the physical system. It is as if the physical system is the address of the subtle body.

In the course of a year many events take place in the physical body and in the subtle one, but the coreSelf may not be aware of the changes. This means that time passes with little accounting by the core. Hence the core is bewildered when suddenly it realizes that such changes occurred when it did not observe the alterations.

This happened to Purañjan who was caught off-guard when Excitement City was ravaged by destructive forces of Fear and Old Age. By the time Purañjan realized the chaos, it was too late for counter-actions.

It seemed that time suddenly disfavored him. Actually, it was a gradual conquest which was not observed until it was near completion. By the time Purañjan understood, it was too late to act. In any case, there was nothing he could do to stop the assault. If he knew of it early on, he could prepare a transit plan to escape when the one hundred years expired.

A chariot moves on wheels. In the psyche, the operations are sponsored by the acceptable and unacceptable activities. One is motivated to act by an urge. That is like a fuel which when ignited causes energy release.

A chariot may have insignia. In the psyche, there are the three influences of nature. This is such that clarifying activities vent one type of energy that makes the driver see clearly. But there are two other influences. One is passionate energy. The other is a dulling psychological force. According to which influence prevails, that is how the charioteer determines the course. At any given time, he is influenced by either of the three influences, either by one or by a combination.

To control the horses, a charioteer must manipulate the reins. These straps are essential. If these are not properly connected, the charioteer will be unable to direct the horses. Then it will be such that the horses will jostle and pull the chariot in an undesirable direction.

Control of the reins corresponds to control of the senses by the coreSelf. Since the core is influenced by one of the three influences, his mental condition when trying to manipulate the senses, may be successful or unsuccessful according to if an influence undermines or supports a suggestion.

मनो-रश्मिर् बुद्धि-सूतो हृन्-नीडो द्वन्द्व-कूबरः /
पञ्चेन्द्रियार्थ-प्रक्षेपः सप्त-धातु-वरूथकः (४ ॥२९ ॥१९)

mano-raśmir buddhi-sūto
hṛn-nīḍo dvandva-kūbaraḥ /
pañcendriyārtha-prakṣepaḥ
sapta-dhātu-varūthakaḥ (4.29.19)

mano = manaḥ = mind, raśmir = raśmiḥ = reins, buddhi – intellect, sūto = sūtaḥ = charioteer, hṛn = hṛt = central position, nīḍo = nīḍaḥ = seat, dvandva – dual, kūbaraḥ - yoke bar, pañcendriyārtha = pañca (five) + indriyārtha (sensations), prakṣepaḥ - weapons, sapta – seven, dhatu – substances, varūthakaḥ - armor

The mind is like the reins. The intellect is the charioteer. The central position is the seat of the chariot. The dual conditions are the yoke bar. The five sensations are weapons. The seven substances are its armor. (4.29.19)

Detail

The controlling lever is the reins. The controller is supposed to be the coreSelf but on a close inspection, one discovers that it is the intellect which directly checks the reins which in turn triggers changes in the attitude and motion of the horses. The hidden but spooked passenger is in a precarious situation, where it wants to direct the intellect but it finds that it cannot.

Instead of controlling the intellect, the passenger, that coreSelf, is intimidated so that it absorbs the intellect's decisions and is subjected to various crises. The mind is not one single item. It is a combination of the core, the intellect, and sensual energies. Collectively these cause a decision to be made but with the intellect being the controller and with the rest as subdued assistants.

The coreSelf is alert to the actions of the intellect but mostly as an observer, not as a director. The intellect collects permitting energy from the core. This gives the intellect its autonomy so that it acts with authority over the psyche. At times however, the sensual conglomerate overrides the intellect, and forces the psyche to act impulsively.

There is a central position. That is where the core is located. Even though it is at the existential center of the psyche, still the core is subjected to compelling suggestions by the intellect. Being in the central position, the coreSelf could control the psyche but its subordination to the intellect and even to the sensual energies, causes the core to assume a submissive posture, where it can only give permission for the plans of the intellect and the sensual functions.

There is a yoke bar which transfers the power of the animals to the chariot. According to how this modifies the power of the animals, it causes tension for impeding or granting the desire of the charioteer.

The five sensations are the quest of the psyche. In the hunt for objects of desire, Purañjan went to five resorts just outside the city. He enjoyed these five pleasures when he was within the city but he had a need to acquire them outdoors as well.

These were variations of sounds, surfaces, colors, flavors, and odors. These occur in unlimited varieties and combinations. These baffled Purañjan. The coreSelf is attacked by these targets which afflict it for permissions for contact. The core helplessly exposes itself to the impressions which penetrate the psyche and cause mood changes which can be comforting or disturbing.

आकूतिर् विक्रमो बाह्यो मृग-तृष्णां प्रधावति /
एकादशेन्द्रिय-चमूः पञ्च-सूना-विनोद-कृत् (४॥२९॥२०)

ākūtir vikramo bāhyo
mṛga-tṛṣṇāṃ pradhāvati /
ekādaśendriya-camūḥ
pañca-sūnā-vinoda-kṛt (4.29.20)

ākūtir = ākūtiḥ = means of action, vikramo = vikramaḥ = motion, bāhyo = bāhyaḥ = external, mṛga-tṛṣṇāṃ = craving like an animal, pradhāvati - chases, ekādaśendriya – eleven senses, camūḥ - army, pañca – five, sūnā – slaughter, - vinoda – amusement, kṛt - done

The Ākūti, means of action, are its external motion. Craving like an animal, he chases with his army of eleven senses. The five types of slaughter are done for his amusement. (4.29.20)

Detail

The actions of the body are conducted by the hands, forearms, arms, feet, legs, thighs, and even by the jaws and neck. These operate for offence and defense. Acting on impulse, craving like lower lifeforms, the self chases sense objects. It operates like a warlord and his ravishing warriors.

Using eleven senses, namely five types of urges and five mental commands and the mind, the entity rushes to interact with what is outside its body-psyche. This is how it acts like an animal without considering the consequences which will be imposed on it in the future.

These activities are of five types, and are compared to the slaughter of animals by a cruel hunter, who kills for the sport of it.

- The hunter may use sound to lure or stun an animal. Once the animal is hypnotized, an arrow is dispatched to kill it.
- The hunter may use a certain surface which the animal licks. Once it comes to the place, the hunter will kill it.
- He may use a color which attracts the animal.
- He may use some food which the animal may taste.
- He may use an odor which the animal cannot resist. The hunter will kill it when it gets within range.

Just as a hunter will enjoy outsmarting the animals which he kills, so in the mind, the intellect may draft plans to entice the coreSelf to indulge any or a combination of the five senses.

When Purañjan acted independently, when once and once only, he did not mimic the queen who rested in her quarters, he went hunting for the sport of it. He did not consult any other intellect. He got no assessment about the unfavorable reactions to his behavior.

In that way, the coreSelf on its own, or as advised by the intellect, should estimate how Nature would serve returns, to urges and actions.

संवत्सरश् चण्डवेगः कालो येनोपलक्षितः /
तस्याहानीह गन्धर्वा गन्धर्व्यो रात्रयः स्मृताः /
हरन्त्य् आयुः परिक्रान्त्या षष्ट्य्-उत्तर-शत-त्रयम् (४॥२९॥२१)

saṃvatsaraś caṇḍavegaḥ
kālo yenopalakṣitaḥ /
tasyāhānīha gandharvā
gandharvyo rātrayaḥ smṛtāḥ /
haranty āyuḥ parikrāntyā ṣa
ṣṭy-uttara-śata-trayam (4.29.21)

saṃvatsaraś = saṃvatsaraḥ = year, caṇḍavegaḥ = Caṇḍavega massive reaction, kālo = kālaḥ = time, yenopalakṣitaḥ = yena (by which) + upalakṣitaḥ (noticed), tasyāhānīha = tasya (of what) + āhāni (days) + iha (now), gandharvā = gandharvāḥ = male psychic people, gandharvyo = gandharvyaḥ = Gandharvis, female psychic people, rātrayaḥ - nights, smṛtāḥ - are experienced, haranty = haranti = they deduct, āyuḥ - lifespan, parikrāntyā – by the motion, ṣaṣṭy = ṣaṣṭi = sixty, uttara – over, śata – hundred, trayam – three

The year is Caṇḍavega Massive Reaction by which time is noticed. Regarding the days there are male psychic beings. The female psychic people are experienced as nights. They deduct the lifespan by the motion of time. (4.29.21)

Detail

The hidden cruel and precise factor is time. It neither rests nor sleeps. Its dominion is absolute. It pardons no one. It gives no exception. When it favors someone, it uses the favor as a distraction to enforce its movement. Whatever time constructs is dismantled just the same.

When Caṇḍavega Massive Reaction appears, an entity realizes that he/she is cornered. For Purañjan the break-down of his body in the elderly years, was such, that he was forced to note it. That was due to diseases of the vital organs.

On the psychic level, Purañjan suffered as well. His mental and emotional faculties were afflicted with the ailments of old age. With the passing of days and nights, which were like male and female enemies present in his body, he was distressed. He was helpless and could not reverse the damage.

Day after day, there was the countdown as the one hundred years steadily diminished. He had to face the fact, that each day and night reduced his time for living with the conveniences provided by the queen.

काल-कन्या जरा साक्षाल् लोकस् तां नाभिनन्दति /
स्वसारं जगृहे मृत्युः क्षयाय यवनेश्वरः (४॥२९॥२२)

kāla-kanyā jarā sākṣāl
lokas tāṃ nābhinandati /
svasāraṃ jagṛhe mṛtyuḥ
kṣayāya yavaneśvaraḥ (4.29.22)

kāla-kanyā – time's daughter, jarā – aging process, sākṣāl = sākṣāt = as that, lokas = lokaḥ = humanity, tāṃ - her, nābhinandati = na (not) + abhinandati (approve), svasāraṃ - his sister, jagṛhe – adopted, mṛtyuḥ - death, kṣayāya – for destruction, yavaneśvaraḥ - Leader of the barbarians

Time's daughter is the aging process itself. It is that exactly. Humanity does not approve her. For the purpose of destroying the world, she was adopted by Death as a sister. (4.29.22)

Detail

The aging process, known also as Jarā, has Time as her guardian. No limited being can resist her. Generally, humanity does not like the elderly years, but this disliking feature could serve to encourage Jarā to increase her hold on someone.

It depends on how one objects to her advances. One should understand that she is authorized by her father to destroy the body one uses. One does not own the body. It was leased for some years. For Purañjan it was one hundred years and the same amount of nights.

Hence, the destruction of the body, from within and without, must occur. One should use the time allotted to figure how to transmigrate from this body to some other realm.

Jarā was adopted as a sister by Death personified. He is the ultimate fear. From the moment the body becomes aware of itself, just before it is delivered from the mother's passage, it is fearful of injury. This is the introduction to the fear of death.

Since it is a one-time instance, death itself is not recurrent. Still, the fear of it is present at all times. The fear is the one of injury but since the ultimate injury causes death, people mistake the fear of injury for the fear of death.

Survivors who see that someone's body dies without injury, feel that such a death was a blessing indeed. Hence it is injury which is the cause of the ongoing fear of death. However, since Nature bridged the fear of injury to the instance of death, one is traumatized by it continually.

आधयो व्याधयस् तस्य सैनिका यवनाश् चराः /
भूतोपसर्गाशु-रयः प्रज्वारो द्वि-विधो ज्वरः (४॥२९॥२३)

ādhayo vyādhayas tasya
sainikā yavanāś carāḥ /

bhūtopasargāśu-rayaḥ
prajvāro dvi-vidho jvaraḥ (4.29.23)

ādhayo = ādhayaḥ = physical distress, vyādhayas = vyādhayaḥ = psychological problems, tasya – of him, sainikā = sainikāḥ = soldiers, yavanāś = yavanaḥ = barbarians, carāḥ - followers, bhūtopasargāśu = bhūta (people) + upasarga (misfortune) + āśu (shortly), rayaḥ - forceful, prajvāro = prajvāraḥ = pyrexia fever, dvi – two. vidho = vidhaḥ = type, jvaraḥ - fever

Physical distress and psychological problems are his soldiers, the uncivilized troops. The people are quickly afflicted with misfortune which is enforced as pyrexia fever, having two types. (4.29.23)

Detail

Even though death is a final event only, the fear of it lingers through the years. From the onset of discovering oneself as a physical body, one is haunted by death. Part of the reason for this confusion is the fact that death is allied to physical and psychological problems. Those are ongoing features which challenged one from moment to moment. They act like uncivilized troops which ravish a city. They pillage and rape at random. They see no point in maintaining a civilization.

When Purañjan first met the queen, she had all accommodations. Everything was new and handy for his satisfaction. When the place was attacked by its enemies, the city was disordered.

This means that Nature does its best to design and produce the body, but in the course of time, those complex facilities are no longer kept in order. In fact, they are systematically ruined. There is nothing Purañjan nor any limited being could do about it.

One could take a hint and prepare to transmigrate. Otherwise, there is nothing one could do, to prevent the wholesale destruction of the very same body, which Nature invented for one's usage, in enjoying her intellectual and sensual faculties.

If one has the attitude of Purañjan which was to mimic the queen's behavior when she enjoyed the services, one will give no thought to the movement of the time factor. That means that one will not be ready to transmigrate, when the life of the body is terminated.

Irregular temperature, pyrexia fever, has two sways. Either as chills or fevers, it upsets the health of the body. As a double-sided axe cuts either way, pyrexia fevers or chills, systematically damage the organs of the body. At last, the form is killed.

One great affliction is the realization that one is ignorant about the maintenance of the body. One discovers oneself as this body but with no information of how best to keep it in the healthiest condition. The operation of the psyche is such that one may act regularly to increase the ailments. This causes psychosis which reduces whatever little happiness one may extract from operating the body.

एवं बहु-विधैर् दुःखैर् दैव-भूतात्म-सम्भवैः /
क्लिश्यमानः शतं वर्षं देहे देही तमो-वृतः (४॥२९॥२४)

evaṃ bahu-vidhair duḥkhair
daiva-bhūtātma-sambhavaiḥ /

kliśyamānaḥ śataṃ varṣaṃ
dehe dehī tamo-vṛtaḥ (4.29.24)

evaṃ - thus, bahu – many, vidhair = vidhaiḥ = kinds, duḥkhair = duḥkhaiḥ = by distress, daiva – supernatural power, bhūtātma = bhūta (ordinary people) + ātma (self), sambhavaiḥ - by production, kliśyamānaḥ - being inconvenienced, śataṃ - hundred, varṣaṃ - years, dehe – in the body, dehī – embodied self, tamo = tamaḥ = retardative influence, vṛtaḥ - harassed

Thus, many kinds of distress due to supernatural power, and due to ordinary people as well, afflict the self. For one hundred years the self is inconvenienced in the body. This embodied self is harassed by the retardative influence. (4.29.24)

Detail

From the very onset when it is created in the father's testes, and is transferred to the mother's conduit, and is then developed and evicted into the world, the body was under attack to end its bid for survival.

The embryo which survives and is born, is assaulted just the same by different kinds of distress. Some afflictions are applied by supernatural power, some by natural tensions, some are self-inflicted. Purañjan was given a guarantee of one-hundred years. That was exceptional. Unusually an entity is allowed to be a physical body for less duration. Usually, one is harassed by the retardative influence, which blocks insight.

प्राणेन्द्रिय-मनो-धर्मान् आत्मन्य् अध्यस्य निर्गुणः /
शेते काम-लवान् ध्यायन् ममाहम् इति कर्म-कृत् (४॥२९॥२५)

prāṇendriya-mano-dharmān
ātmany adhyasya nirguṇaḥ /
śete kāma-lavān dhyāyan
mamāhaṃ iti karma-kṛt (4.29.25)

prāṇendriya = prāṇa (lifeForce) + indriya (senses), mano = manaḥ = mind, dharmān – tendencies, ātmany = ātmani = to the self, adhyasya – wrongly assigning, nirguṇaḥ - without Nature's influences, śete – reclines, kāma – enjoyment, lavān – fragmenting, dhyāyan – meditative absorption, mamāham = my, I, iti – thus, karma-kṛt = conductor of social activities

Though the self is without Nature's influences, the lifeForce and the senses, as well as the mind, and the tendencies, adhere to it. The self reclines enjoying and being fragmented, with its meditative focus expressed through *my-and-I*. Thus, it conducts social activities. (4.29.25

Detail

Theoretically, the self is attributed as being transcendental to Nature but in practice, it is discovered to be absorbent to Nature's influences. The lifeForce, the senses, as well as the mind and the tendencies adhere to the core and utilize its radiance.

In this existence, the self discovers itself expressing attention which seeks for physical or psychic objects. It renders interest through a sense of identity where it aspires to claim anything by applying its sense of possession. It constantly seeks to make claims using its clutching tool of *my-and-I*.

यदात्मानम् अविज्ञाय भगवन्तं परं गुरुम् /
पुरुषस् तु विषज्जेत गुणेषु प्रकृतेः स्व-दृक् (४॥२९॥२६)

yadātmānam avijñāya
bhagavantaṃ paraṃ gurum /
puruṣas tu viṣajjeta
guṇeṣu prakṛteḥ sva-dṛk (4.29.26)

yadātmānam = yadā (when) + ātmānam (coreSelf), avijñāya – not realizing, bhagavantaṃ - supreme person, paraṃ - foremost, gurum – spiritual master, puruṣas = puruṣaḥ = personSelf, tu – but, viṣajjeta – attached, guṇeṣu – influences, prakṛteḥ - Nature, sva – self, dṛk – focus

When the coreSelf does not realize the Supreme Person, the foremost spiritual master, then that personSelf in the psyche, is attached to the influences of Nature which absorbs the self's focus. (4.29.26)

Detail

The limited self is not a reality unto itself. It has the inborn tendency to be influenced. When it challenges Nature, the self absorbs Nature's mood. Conversely, if the self is exposed to the Supreme Person, the foremost spiritual master, that self absorbs the Lord's superRadiance.

गुणाभिमानी स तदा कर्माणि कुरुते ऽवशः /
शुक्लं कृष्णं लोहितं वा यथा-कर्माभिजायते (४॥२९॥२७)

guṇābhimānī sa tadā
karmāṇi kurute 'vaśaḥ /
śuklaṃ kṛṣṇaṃ lohitaṃ vā
yathā-karmābhijāyate (4.29.27)

guṇābhimānī = guna (Nature's influences) + abhimānī (assertion about), sa = saḥ = he, tadā – then, karmāṇi - social activities, kurute – does, 'vaśaḥ = avaśaḥ = impulsive, śuklaṃ - white, kṛṣṇaṃ - black, lohitaṃ - red, vā – and, yathā – accordingly, karmābhijāyate = karma (cultural situations) + abhijāyate - become, born

The assertions are due to Nature's influences. Thus, he does social activities impulsively. Some are white, some black, and some red. This is according to the situations in which the self discovers itself. (4.29.27)

Detail

As Purañjan wandered aimlessly and without a purpose when he was alone, as he settled down when he agreed to accept the accommodations and sexual companionship of the queen, as he lost perception of his friend, Not-Recognized (Avijñāta), so the limited self aligns itself to an intellect and functions under that influence.

On one occasion, Purañjan acted on his own. When he did so, he was abandoned by the queen. He was unhappy without her. He begged her pardon. Thus, it appears that the limited self requires advisory support. That can be acquired from its intellect or from its invisible friend. However, the intellect is easily accessible. The self would require special vision to see the invisible person, the Supreme Lord.

Depending on the environment, the self is influenced by a higher or lower agency. The activities performed under this or that power, results in positive, median, or negative reactions, which the self absorbs.

शुक्लात् प्रकाश-भूयिष्ठा लोकान् आप्नोति कर्हिचित् /
दुःखोदर्कान् क्रियायासांस् तमः-शोकोत्कटान् क्वचित् (४॥२९॥२८)

śuklāt prakāśa-bhūyiṣṭhā
lokān āpnoti karhicit /
duḥkhodarkān kriyāyāsāṃs
tamaḥ-śokotkaṭān kvacit (4.29.28)

śuklāt – faultless, prakāśa – sheer existential light, bhūyiṣṭhā = bhūyiṣṭhān = saturation, lokān – dimensions, āpnoti – attains, karhicit – alternately, duḥkhodarkān = duḥkha (distressful situation) + udarkān (consequence), kriyāyāsāṃs = kriyā (efforts) + āyāsān (troublesome), tamaḥ - mentally depressive, śokotkaṭān = śoka (grief) + utkaṭān (excessive), kvacit – sometimes

From faultless acts, he attains illuminative dimensions which are saturated with sheer existential light. Alternately distressful situation will be the consequence of the troublesome efforts which cause mentally depressive states with excessive grief. (4.29.28)

Detail

The faultless acts and the troublesome efforts happen deliberately or impulsively. In some incidences, the self is inspired by others, or he/she may have a revelation which motivates a spiritually elevating status. At any other time, there may be an incidence which is willfully done and which causes grief.

The best acts are those which result in the transfer to illuminative dimensions which are saturated with sheer existential light. That is contrasted to actions which have mentally depressive states as the outcome.

क्वचित् पुमान् क्वचिच् च स्त्री क्वचिन् नोभयम् अन्ध-धीः /
देवो मनुष्यस् तिर्यग् वा यथा-कर्म-गुणं भवः (४॥२९॥२९)

kvacit pumān kvacic ca strī
kvacin nobhayam andha-dhīḥ /
devo manuṣyas tiryag vā
yathā-karma-guṇaṃ bhavaḥ (4.29.29)

kvacit - sometimes, pumān - male, kvacic = kvacit = sometimes, ca – and, strī – female, kvacin = kvacit = again, nobhayam = na (not) + ubhyam (both), andha – blind, dhīḥ = intelligent person, devo = devaḥ = supernatural governor, manuṣyas = manuṣyaḥ = human being, tiryag = tiryak = animal, vā – or, yathā – as so, karma – cultural activities, guṇaṃ - Nature's influences, bhavaḥ - birth experience

Sometimes one functions as a male, then as a female, then again being neither, but being blind or intelligent, or being a supernatural governor, or human being, or animal, according to the cultural activities enacted under Nature's influences. Thus is a birth experience. (4.29.29)

Detail

In any lifeform, the *ātma* or coreSelf aligns itself with the intellect. When the *ātma* uses a female format, even then it is faced to the intellect as if the intellect is a feminine principle. Those who sit to be chauffeured, sit in the passenger seat, irrespective of if that person is of either gender.

Each entity, regardless of using a male, female, bisexual, or neuter format, absorbs the influence of the intellect and should endeavor to subjugate that adjunct. The core should not accept every mental proposal.

Each birth is an opportunity to be educated about how Nature operates the particular body one inhabits. From the onset one should prepare to transmigrate to some other time and place. Each body will end. That is mandatory.

क्षुत्-परीतो यथा दीनः सारमेयो गृहं गृहम् /
चरन् विन्दति यद्-दिष्टं दण्डम् ओदनम् एव वा (४॥२९॥३०)

kṣut-parīto yathā dīnaḥ
sārameyo gṛhaṃ gṛham /
caran vindati yad-diṣṭaṃ
daṇḍam odanam eva vā (4.29.30)

kṣut – hunger, parīto = parītaḥ = afflicted, yathā – as, dīnaḥ - pitied someone, sārameyo = sārameyaḥ = dog, gṛhaṃ gṛham = house to house, caran – wander, vindati – receives, yad = yat = whose, diṣṭaṃ - as destined, daṇḍam – flogging, odanam – food, eva – sure, vā – or

Afflicted by hunger, a pitied dog wanders from house to house. As destined it receives either a flogging or some food. (4.29.30)

Detail

As Purañjan wandered on earth, so the living entity is shifted from one dying body to a new infant form. It does this with little or no recall of the previous situation.

A pitied dog wanders from house to house. Its preoccupation is food. It thinks "If only this human would let me in. If only I could get a bone." This quest for accommodations, especially for food, is pressing. Without food there would be no survival of any lifeform.

As it is however, there is fate. A dog may receive either a flogging or some food. The coreSelf wanders from one body to another, either one that is similar to the one it currently has, or to one that is higher or lower. It shifts as dictated by fate. Sometimes what happens is beyond expectation. Sometimes it is disappointing.

By studying the psychic existence, one gets insight about the laws of rebirth. The system is similar to that of a dog who goes from door to door in the hope of meeting a compassionate human. As the coreSelf moves from one physical body to another, it is like a beggar who pleads with others for accommodation. It seeks kind parents who would sponsor an infant form, and carry the responsibility for its upbringing.

तथा कामाशयो जीव उच्चावच-पथा भ्रमन् /
उपर्य् अधो वा मध्ये वा याति दिष्टं प्रियाप्रियम् (४॥२९॥३१)

tathā kāmāśayo jīva
uccāvaca-pathā bhraman /
upary adho vā madhye vā
yāti diṣṭaṃ priyāpriyam (4.29.31)

tathā – just so, kāmāśayo = kāma (desires) + āśayaḥ (psyche), jīva – individual self, uccāvaca – higher or lower, pathā – course of existence, bhraman – wandering, upary = upari = high, adho = adhaḥ = low, vā – or, madhye – in the midst, vā – or, yāti – goes, diṣṭaṃ - as fated, priyāpriyam = pleasing and displeasing situations

Just so, by desires which are embedded in the psyche, the individual self is higher or lower, wandering on the course of existence, being high, low, or median, as fated, going to pleasing or displeasing situations. (4.29.31)

Detail

One is subjected to the bewildering course of transmigration because one does not have the power to resist. When one stands against it successfully, that happens because one part of Nature supports one in the resistance against another part of the same Nature.

Standing alone, pitting oneself in full contrast to Nature, is not a feat a limited being can successfully perform. Such a self needs support to be in an advantageous position in reference to Nature.

A log which is propelled up and out of an ocean but which was projected by forces of the ocean itself, cannot claim to be independent. The propulsion happened because of the buoyancy and wave action. It was sponsored.

By desires which are embedded in the psyche, the individual finds itself to be in a higher or lower species. It wanders as it is flung through the course of existence, being high, low, or median, as fated, going to pleasing or displeasing situations.

दुःखेष्व् एकतरेणापि दैव-भूतात्म-हेतुषु /
जीवस्य न व्यवच्छेदः स्याच् चेत् तत्-तत्-प्रतिक्रिया (४॥२९॥३२)

duḥkheṣv ekatareṇāpi
daiva-bhūtātma-hetuṣu /
jīvasya na vyavacchedaḥ
syāc cet tat-tat-pratikriyā (4.29.32)

duḥkheṣv = duḥkheṣu = in distress, ekatareṇāpi = ekatarena (in one kind) + api (as well), daiva – supernatural force, bhūtātma = bhūta (common people) + ātma (coreSelf), hetuṣu – cause, jīvasya – of the individual self, na – not, vyavacchedaḥ - diminished, separation, syāc = syāt = may happen, cet – although, tat-tat = that then that, pratikriyā – reaction

Regarding distress of one kind or the other, as well as that which comes by supernatural force, or due to common people, or the self, the cause cannot be diminished by the individual when the reaction comes from this, and then from that event. (4.29.32)

Detail

Distress and happiness are fabricated in a natural flow of the compound energy of Nature as it is mixed with the attention of the limited entities. Above the plane of ordinary events, there is the Supreme Lord and the Primal Nature. The mix of those two super realities is a compelling force which a limited being cannot resist. It may be attracted to some part of the cosmic mix, where it finds itself in an advantageous or distressful circumstance, but it cannot control the energy layout.

If it can, it may act to shift itself from one part to some other position but even that must be done with support. Hence events which come by supernatural force, or due to common people, or the self, cannot be diminished by the individual when the reaction comes from this, and then from that event.

Consider what happened to the mythical Purañjan, where he realized himself as a wanderer on this earth. He travelled with no set purpose, except with a certain curiosity to see the environment. Eventually he met an attractive woman. She had no idea how she came to be. She could not explain how she was the queen of a furnished city, nor why she was provided with constant security.

Purañjan then committed himself to live with the beautiful lady on her terms for one-hundred years. Once when he broke the commitment, he apologized for the misbehavior and for not consulting her for permission to hunt animals in a forest near her city. Killing animals was an activity which the lady detested.

Eventually however their city became so ruined that they could not enjoy as before. Purañjan could do nothing about it. His manliness, which on one occasion exhibited violence, could not be put to use to defend the city. The place was ruined. Through the years, Purañjan became a weak old man. There was nothing he could do to stop the demolition.

Such is the usual life of an entity after it assumes a self as a certain infant body in some species. Again and again, we experience this. We witness this in the lives of others.

यथा हि पुरुषो भारं शिरसा गुरुम् उद्वहन् /
तं स्कन्धेन स आधत्ते तथा सर्वाः प्रतिक्रियाः (४॥२९॥३३)

yathā hi puruṣo bhāraṃ
śirasā gurum udvahan /
taṃ skandhena sa ādhatte
tathā sarvāḥ pratikriyāḥ (4.29.33)

yathā – for instance, hi – take the example, puruṣo = puruṣaḥ = person, bhāraṃ - burden, śirasā – on the head, gurum – heavy, udvahan – carry, taṃ - that, skandhena – with the shoulder, sa = saḥ = he, ādhatte – feels, tathā – so. sarvāḥ - all, pratikriyāḥ - change

For instance, take the example of a person who carries a burden on his head, something heavy. He shifts it to his shoulder. Despite the change he feels it all the same. (4.29.33)

Detail

The effort to dissociate a condition or event which is being applied by Nature, may result in a switch from a discomfort in one place in the psyche to some other place in the same body.

Sometimes one desires to clear a condition and event, but one finds that one can move neither. One may consider separating one from the other but one may realize that one cannot partition one from the other. The discomfort remains.

नैकान्ततः प्रतीकारः कर्मणां कर्म केवलम् /
द्वयं ह्य् अविद्योपसृतं स्वप्ने स्वप्न इवानघ (४॥२९॥३४)

naikāntataḥ pratīkāraḥ
karmaṇāṃ karma kevalam /
dvayaṃ hy avidyopasṛtaṃ
svapne svapna ivānagha (4.29.34)

naikāntataḥ = na (not) + ekāntataḥ (only), pratīkāraḥ - counteraction, karmaṇāṃ - of culturality activities, karma – fresh action, kevalam – only, alone, dvayaṃ - both, hy = hi = due to the fact, avidyopasṛtaṃ = avidyā (ignorance) + upasṛtaṃ (basis), svapne – in dream, svapna – dream, ivānagha = iva (like) + anagha (faultless one)

Neither a counteraction nor a fresh action would dissolve a previous action. This is due to the fact that both attempts are based on ignorance. That is like a dream within a dream, O faultless one. (4.29.34)

Detail

A dream within a dream, even if the second dream seems to be a duplicate of the first, is still a separate incidence, which yield a slightly or vastly difference value reference. The registry of events causes the roll of history to advance in an orderly way.

There is this idea that one can suppress, counteract, or eliminate a particular incidence. Actually, whatever one does in that regard merely establishes a new incidence, which rolls out as new history.

अर्थे ह्य् अविद्यमाने ऽपि संसृतिर् न निवर्तते /
मनसा लिङ्ग-रूपेण स्वप्ने विचरतो यथा (४॥२९॥३५)

arthe hy avidyamāne 'pi
saṃsṛtir na nivartate /
manasā liṅga-rūpeṇa
svapne vicarato yathā (4.29.35)

arthe – in placing a value, hy = hi = for the reason, avidyamāne – not present, 'pi = api = also, saṃsṛtir = saṃsṛtiḥ = being subjected to existential events, na – not, nivartate – cessation, manasā – by the mind, liṅga – characteristic, rūpeṇa – with form, svapne – in a dream, vicarato = vicarataḥ = participation, yathā – so as

In placing a value in something that is not present, we are further subjected to its existential events with no cessation. This is due to the mind and to characteristic forms, just as in a dream one is forced into participation. (4.29.35)

Detail

In a dream, one's attention is shifted to another plane of activity. That causes values to be inserted even to trivial occurrences. One does not have to be willfully involved for this to happen. Even trivial or momentary contact with something in a flimsy dream, is registered and is referred to a stronger reality. The individual involved is tagged appropriately.

If something is absent, a value can be inserted into it. This depends on the impact force, and reach of the energy emitted. It produces other existential events which serve as new basis for fresh wavelengths.

अथात्मनो ऽर्थ-भूतस्य यतो ऽनर्थ-परम्परा /
संसृतिस् तद्-व्यवच्छेदो भक्त्या परमया गुरौ (४॥२९॥३६)

athātmano 'rtha-bhūtasya
yato 'nartha-paramparā /
saṃsṛtis tad-vyavacchedo
bhaktyā paramayā gurau (4.29.36)

athātmano = athātmanaḥ = atha (thus) + ātmanaḥ (of coreSelf), 'rtha = artha = value, bhūtasya – of things, yato = yataḥ = from which, 'nartha = anatha = unwanted, paramparā – serial factors, saṃsṛtis = saṃsṛtiḥ = confusing existential events, tad= tat= of that, vyavacchedo = vyavacchedaḥ = eradicated, bhaktyā – by devotion, paramayā – by the highest, gurau – to the spiritual master

Thus, regarding the coreSelf, and the value of things, there are unwanted serial factors. The confusing existential events are eradicated by the highest devotion to the spiritual master. (4.29.36)

Detail

The toss of objects which a self encounters, has to do with the value of the items. 'According to the awarded value, that is the impact which an item makes on the self.

In running an estimate about worth, there will be unwanted serial factors. The result will be negative for the self. Hence it is recommended that one should be advised by a spiritual master who is familiar with the pitfalls and who advises in one's interest.

वासुदेवे भगवति भक्ति-योगः समाहितः /
सध्रीचीनेन वैराग्यं ज्ञानं च जनयिष्यति (४॥२९॥३७)

vāsudeve bhagavati
bhakti-yogaḥ samāhitaḥ /

sadhrīcīnena vairāgyaṃ
jñānaṃ ca janayiṣyati (4.29.37)

vāsudeve – to Vāsudeva, bhagavati – cherished lord, bhakti-yogaḥ = application of yoga to devotion, samāhitaḥ - psychologically applied, sadhrīcīnena - by one focus, vairāgyaṃ - detachment, jñānaṃ - realization, ca – and, janayiṣyati – will result in

To Vāsudeva, the cherished Lord, the application of yoga to devotion, which is psychologically applied with one focus, will result in detachment and realization. (4.29.37)

Detail

Bhaktiyoga is bhakti *and* yoga. That is the application of yogic mystic process to the devotional interest in the cherished Lord, in Vāsudeva.

Nārad informed King Barhi of this necessary process for anyone to breach serial transmigrations, where life after life, one remains in bewilderment regarding the self.

Queen Vaidarbhī, a life of Purañjan, was in distress when her husband died. Vaidarbhī wanted to commit suicide but she was approached by someone who was this very Lord Vāsudeva.

The devotion (bhakti) which Vaidarbhī applied to her deceased husband, King Malayadhvaja, should be applied to the Lord instead. She needed to shift to the spiritual plane. To be effective however, that devotion would have to be applied with yogic focus.

सो ऽचिराद् एव राजर्षे स्याद् अच्युत-कथाश्रयः /
शृण्वतः श्रद्दधानस्य नित्यदा स्याद् अधीयतः (४॥२९॥३८)

so 'cirād eva rājarṣe
syād acyuta-kathāśrayaḥ /
śṛṇvataḥ śraddadhānasya
nityadā syād adhīyataḥ (4.29.38)

so = saḥ = that, 'cirād = acirāt = soon, eva – certainly, rājarṣe - O yogi among the kings, syād = syāt = perhaps, acyuta – infallible one, kathāśrayaḥ = relying on lectures, śṛṇvataḥ - someone who listens, śraddadhānasya – of one who is confident, nityadā – perpetual, syād = syāt = perhaps, adhīyataḥ - communicating

O yogi among the kings, that (application of Yoga to devotion) will certainly, and soon, cause focus on the infallible one. It relies on lectures about him, and on listening, by one who is confident, and is perpetually communicating with the God. (4.29.38)

Detail

King Barhi is addressed respectfully as *rājarṣe*, a wise yogi among the kings. The recommendation for him concerned switching his process of focus. Barhi was dedicated to Vedic rituals which involved killing animals in sacrifices. These were supposed to be offerings to psychic entities, demigods. Nārad recommended that the king cease this and take a new process.

Barhi was to master bhaktiYoga, which would cause focus on the infallible person, the one who was the friend of Purañjan at the onset, but whom Purañjan could not perceived due to focusing on physical existence.

Initially, this process hinged on listening to lectures about Lord Vāsudeva, given by one who is confident of, and who perpetually communicates with the God.

यत्र भागवता राजन् साधवो विशदाशयाः /
भगवद्-गुणानुकथन- श्रवण-व्यग्र-चेतसः (४॥२९॥३९)

yatra bhāgavatā rājan
sādhavo viśadāśayāḥ /
bhagavad-guṇānukathana-
śravaṇa-vyagra-cetasaḥ (4.29.39)

yatra – wherever, bhāgavatā = bhāgavatāḥ = those who adore God, rājan – O king, sādhavo = sādhavaḥ = saintly person, viśadāśayāḥ = viśada (brilliant) + āśayāḥ (intention, focus), bhagavad = bhagavat = of God, guṇānukathana = guṇa (features) + anukathana (narration), śravaṇa – hear, vyagra – anxious for, cetasaḥ - absorbed

Wherever there are those who adore God, O King, the saintly persons, who are brilliant and focused on him, having qualities relating to the narrations which are heard, there is the likelihood that one will be anxiously absorbed. (4.29.39)

Detail

The support for this yogically applied devotion is acquired by association with those saintly persons who are brilliant and who focus on God.

तस्मिन् महन्-मुखरिता
मधुभिच्- चरित्र-पीयूष-शेष-सरितः परितः स्रवन्ति /
ता ये पिबन्त्य् अवितृषो नृप गाढ-कर्णैस्
तान् न स्पृशन्त्य् अशन-तृड्-भय-शोक-मोहाः (४॥२९॥४०)

tasmin mahan-mukharitā
madhubhic- caritra-pīyūṣa-śeṣa-
saritaḥ paritaḥ sravanti /
tā ye pibanty avitṛṣo
nṛpa gāḍha-karṇais
tān na spṛśanty aśana-
tṛḍ-bhaya-śoka-mohāḥ (4.29.40)

tasmin – at the time, mahan = mahat = great, mukharitā = mukharitāḥ = sounding, speaking, madhubhic = madhubhit = killer of Madhu, caritra – story, pīyūṣa – nectar, śeṣa – remainder, saritaḥ - rivers, paritaḥ - encircling, sravanti - they flow, tā = tāḥ = them, ye – they who, pibanty = pibanti = they drink, avitṛṣo = avitṛṣaḥ = not satiated, nṛpa – O King, gāḍha – deep, karṇais = karṇaiḥ - with the ear, tān – them, na – not, spṛśanty = spṛśanti = they are affected, asana – hunger, tṛḍ = tṛt = thirst, bhaya – fear, śoka – sadness, mohāḥ - disillusionment

At the time, great narrations about the history of the killer of Madhu, which like nectar flowed like encircling rivers, which they drank but were not satiated. O king, with deep hearing with the ear, they were affected neither by hunger, thirst, fear, sadness, or disillusionment. (4.29.40)

Detail

When the narrations about Lord *Vāsudeva* are properly heard, it has the specific effect of causing the focus of the devotee to shift to the spiritual plane where hunger, thirst, fear, sadness, or disillusionment, are absent.

Purañjan, as Queen Vaidarbhī, had a sharp focus, on King Malayadhvaja, her ascetic husband, but that attention to him did not result in the absence of physical or psychological discomforts.

एतैर् उपद्रुतो नित्यं जीव-लोकः स्वभावजैः /
न करोति हरेर् नूनं कथामृत-निधौ रतिम् (४॥२९॥४१)

etair upadruto nityaṃ
jīva-lokaḥ svabhāvajaiḥ /
na karoti harer nūnaṃ
kathāmṛta-nidhau ratim (4.29.41)

etair = etaiḥ = by these, upadruto = upadrutaḥ = oppressed, nityaṃ - perpetual, jīva-lokaḥ = world for limited entities, svabhāvajaiḥ - natural, na – not, karoti – does, harer – of Lord Hari (God), nūnaṃ - sure, kathāmṛta – nectarine narration, nidhau – ocean, ratim - attachment

By those afflictions, they are perpetually oppressed in this world for the limited entities. They do not have the natural attraction for the ocean of Lord Hari's (God's) nectarine narrations. (4.29.41)

Detail

This world, the realm which is experienced by the limited entities, provide little challenge for the souls to seek the association with God, Lord Hari. In fact, the blaring attraction here is the objects which are easily detected by the senses the lifeforms are outfitted with.

Even though this place is the location for feeling afflictions, still, the entities are attracted and are perpetually oppressed because their attention energy is arrested by physical incidences.

The God surfaces here from time to time, and yet, the attraction to his nectarine activities, do not command the attention of every limited entity, who would benefit from hearing his glories.

प्रजापति-पतिः साक्षाद् भगवान् गिरिशो मनुः /
दक्षादयः प्रजाध्यक्षा नैष्ठिकाः सनकादयः (४॥२९॥४२)

prajāpati-patiḥ sākṣād
bhagavān giriśo manuḥ /
dakṣādayaḥ prajādhyakṣā
naiṣṭhikāḥ sanakādayaḥ (4.29.42)

prajāpati-patiḥ = Brahmā, father of original fathers, sākṣād – directly, bhagavān – Lord God, giriśo = giriśaḥ = Shiva, manuḥ - Manu Progenitor, dakṣādayaḥ = dakṣa (Dakṣa progenitor) + ādayaḥ (others), prajādhyakṣā = prajā (people) + adhyakṣāḥ (leaders of), naiṣṭhikāḥ - perpetual celibate person, sanakādayaḥ = Sanaka and others

Brahmā, the father of original fathers, the Lord God Shiva, the Manu Progenitor, the Dakṣa Progenitor, and others like him who are leaders of people, the perpetual celibate persons like Sanaka and others, (4.29.42)

Detail

This begins the list of persons with existential grip who have difficulty focusing continuously on the Supreme Lord. Purañjan was directly approached by this Supreme Person, who offered a method of switching focus from physical existence to remaining in touch with this deity as the advisor, such that the deity replaced the intellect which was relied on.

Instead of signing for the accommodation, services, and companionship of the intellect, the coreSelf should be linked to the supreme being to get whatever supplementary services it requires.

Brahmā, the father of original fathers is the creatorGod who produced the sub-creators. The Lord God Shiva restricts some parts of Brahmā's creation. He does this to assist the limited entities in resisting the influence of the Nature displays which are easily seen by selves. The Manu Progenitor, and the Dakṣa Progenitor establish moral behavior and demonstrate responsible lifestyle. The perpetual celibate persons like Sanaka and others are demonstrations of extreme resistance to social participation.

When these persons are preoccupied with the concerns of Nature, their focus on the supreme being tilts. That causes loss of contact with the Lord.

मरीचिर् अत्र्य्-ङ्गिरसौ पुलस्त्यः पुलहः क्रतुः /
भृगुर् वसिष्ठ इत्य् एते मद्-न्ता ब्रह्म-वादिनः (४॥२९॥४३)

marīcir atry-aṅgirasau
pulastyaḥ pulahaḥ kratuḥ /
bhṛgur vasiṣṭha ity ete
mad-antā brahma-vādinaḥ (4.29.43)

marīcir = marīciḥ = Marīci, atry = Atri, aṅgirasau – and Aṅgirasa, pulastyaḥ - Pulastya, pulahaḥ - Pulaha, kratuḥ - Kratu, bhṛgur = Bhṛgu, vasiṣṭha - Vasiṣṭha, ity = iti = thus, ete – these, mad = mat = me, antā = antāḥ = end, brahma – Vedic information, vādinaḥ - verbal authorities

Marīci, Atri, Aṅgirasa, Pulastya, Pulaha, Kratu, Bhṛgu, Vasiṣṭha, these and others ending with me, the verbal authorities of the Vedic information, (4.29.43)

Detail

Nārad and his existential brothers, namely Marīci, Atri, Aṅgirasa, Pulastya, Pulaha, Kratu, Bhṛgu, Vasiṣṭha, who are the verbal authorities of the Vedic information, became occupied with events in this creation. Subsequently, they lost contact with the Lord.

अद्यापि वाचस्-पतयस् तपो-विद्या-समाधिभिः /
पश्यन्तो ऽपि न पश्यन्ति पश्यन्तं परमेश्वरम् (४॥२९॥४४)

adyāpi vācas-patayas
tapo-vidyā-samādhibhiḥ /

paśyanto 'pi na paśyanti
paśyantaṃ parameśvaram (4.29.44)

adyāpi = adya (now) + api (until), vācas = vācaḥ = speech, patayas = patayaḥ = orators, tapo= tapaḥ = disciplinary deprivations, vidyā = ritual masters, samādhibhiḥ - spiritual absorption, paśyanto = paśyantaḥ = perceiving, 'pi = api = also, na – not, paśyanti – they see, paśyantaṃ - special observer, parameśvaram – supreme Lord

until now, and even the orators of speech, those who master disciplinary deprivations, those who are ritual masters, those who are spiritually absorbed, do not perceive the spiritual observer, the Supreme Lord. (4.29.44)

Detail

The task of perceiving the special spiritual observer, the Lord, eludes even the great personalities, even those who are devoted to him. This is due to the strong attraction between the attention of the entity and Nature's energy. It pulls the focus and simultaneously causes loss of contact with the supreme being.

The orators of speech have voice charisma. Just by speech, they cause others to be attentive to the information they emit. But while doing so they lose contact with the spiritual observer, the Lord. Those who master disciplinary deprivations gain the respect of others.

While others must indulge, these penance performers easily resist urges to indulge. Even these persons lose contact with the Lord because of focus on what is other than the God.

There are those who are ritual masters. They know the mantric formulae and can perfectly utter the pronunciations. They invoke supernatural beings and make request for themselves or for their clients. Persons of this caliber were employed for the rituals of King Barhi. Due to their emphasis on ceremony, they lose contact with the Lord.

There are those who are spiritually absorbed. They are the most proficient of the yogis. Even they have difficulty locating God. They may focus on the invisible aspects of Nature. When they make the effort to contact God, they do so with difficulty.

शब्द-ब्रह्मणि दुष्पारे चरन्त उरु-विस्तरे /
मन्त्र-लिङ्गैर् व्यवच्छिन्नं भजन्तो न विदुः परम् (४॥२९॥४५)

śabda-brahmaṇi duṣpāre
caranta uru-vistare /
mantra-liṅgair vyavacchinnaṃ
bhajanto na viduḥ param (4.29.45)

śabda-brahmaṇi = the information about spiritual reality, duṣpāre – insurmountable, caranta = carantaḥ = properly study, uru – expansive, vistare – extensively, mantra – matching sounds, liṅgair = liṅgaiḥ = by precise features, vyavacchinnaṃ - limited, bhajanto = bhajantaḥ = worshipful reverence, na – not, viduḥ - they realize, param – supreme

Those who study the information about spiritual reality, which is insurmountable when properly studied, and is expansive and extensive, with matching sounds and precise features, even with worshipful reverence, are limited. They do not realize the Supreme. (4.29.45)

Detail

The Supreme is subtler than what is subtle. It is not arrested by the focus of any and everyone. Even those who know the *śabda-brahmaṇi*, the information of spiritual reality, even those who realized this in a flash in meditation or who were graced with its perception, even they lose the contact, and must speak about it from memory.

As a man who climbs a jagged mountain, does so step by step, with great risk to his life, and as he must descend to low land, so the expounder of the true information about the spiritual reality, may have attained direct vision of it, but lost that perception and relied on the recall of the experience, when he resumed a lower level of awareness.

I recently spoke to two deceased masters of samadhi. Either one admitted being ejected from the brahm, the spiritual existence. When I queried about the divine eye, each yogi was at a loss for words as how they lost the use of it. This verifies these statements of Nārad.

यदा यस्यानुगृह्णाति भगवान् आत्म-भावितः /
स जहाति मतिं लोके वेदे च परिनिष्ठिताम् (४॥२९॥४६)

yadā yasyānugṛhṇāti
bhagavān ātma-bhāvitaḥ /
sa jahāti matiṃ loke
vede ca pariniṣṭhitām (4.29.46)

yadā - when, yasyānugṛhṇāti = yasya (whom) + anugṛhṇāti (is compassionate to), bhagavān – Lord, ātma – coreSelf, bhāvitaḥ - spiritually absorbed, sa = saḥ =that someone, jahāti – extracts, matiṃ - consciousness, loke – in the world, vede – in the Vedic information, ca – and, pariniṣṭhitām – established

When someone acquires compassion from the Lord, and is spiritually absorbed on the coreSelf, that person's consciousness is extracted from the

world, and from the Vedic information, because of being spiritually established. (4.29.46)

Detail

The necessary ingredients for having the association of the Lord, are explained. It requires the following.

- compassion from the Lord
- spiritual absorption on the coreSelf
- full extraction of focus from the physical world and it related levels of operation
- extraction from the Vedic information

When these achievements are in place, that person is fully established on the spiritual plane and has the infallible reference.

Two requirements rely solely on the endeavor of the person concerned. He/She is responsible to do what is necessary to be spiritual self-absorbed. When one considers how this applies to Purañjan, he would have to separate his interest from that of the queen. He would be deprived of her association and services. This would mean focusing on his coreSelf with no reliance on the intellect and its accessory adjuncts (the queen and her staff including the kundalini Power Central five-hooded snake).

The other aspect which depends on the individual's endeavor is the extraction from the Vedic information. The person must remove himself from this dogma. This is done after he examined that knowledge and tested it to find which parts accurately report the realities on various planes of existence. He/She extracts the self from the valid and invalid information which is rendered in the text.

The two remaining aspects which must be achieved are listed.

- compassion from the Lord
- full extraction of focus from the physical world and it related levels of operation

Compassion from the Lord is necessary. This means specific interest from the Lord to the devotee. This is different to an eager interest of the devotee.

When the compassion from the Lord occurs, the devotee finds that he/she has full extraction of focus from the physical world and its related levels of operation. That is the miracle that must happen before the devotee can fully be in the association of the supreme being.

तस्मात् कर्मसु बर्हिष्मन्न् अज्ञानाद् अर्थ-काशिषु /
मार्थ-दृष्टिं कृथाः श्रोत्र- स्पर्शिष्व् अस्पृष्ट-वस्तुषु (४॥२९॥४७)

tasmāt karmasu barhiṣmann
ajñānād artha-kāśiṣu /
mārtha-dṛṣṭiṃ kṛthāḥ śrotra-
sparśiṣv aspṛṣṭa-vastuṣu (4.29.47)

tasmāt – therefore, karmasu – in cultural activity, barhiṣmann = barhiṣman = O King Barhi, ajñānād = ajñānāt = not aware of, artha – what is valued, kāśiṣu - showing, mārtha = mā (not) + artha (what is valued), dṛṣṭiṃ - opinion, kṛthāḥ - do, śrotra-sparśiṣv = śrotra-sparśiṣu = pleasing to hear, aspṛṣṭa – not relating to, vastuṣu – real

Therefore, in considering cultural activity, O King Barhi, do not evaluate what shows as having value, which in reality has no worth. Those opinions though pleasing to hear, do not relate to what is real. (4.29.47)

Detail

The assessment about the value of cultural acts is fraught with miscalculation. As one shifts from this basis to that basis, one forms convenient estimations. One remains divorced from the truth.

One should not be confident about social involvement. One should not trust that it will yield favorable results. One does not know how Nature will produce new circumstances and for what purpose.

स्वं लोकं न विदुस् ते वै यत्र देवो जनार्दनः /
आहुर् धूम्र-धियो वेदं सकर्मकम् अतद्-विदः (४॥२९॥४८)

svaṃ lokaṃ na vidus te vai
yatra devo janārdanaḥ /
āhur dhūmra-dhiyo vedaṃ
sakarmakam atad-vidaḥ (4.29.48)

svaṃ - their own, lokaṃ - world, na – not, vidus = viduḥ = know, te – they, vai – indeed, yatra – where, devo = devaḥ = God, janārdanaḥ - Janārdana God Vishnu, āhur = āhuḥ = said, dhūmra – smoke-ridden rituals, dhiyo = dhiyaḥ = intelligence, vedaṃ - Vedas, sakarmakam – with Vedic ritual acts, atad-vidaḥ = someone who lack the correct information

Not knowing the actual world, where Janārdana, the God Vishnu resides, they regard the smoke-ridden rituals as intelligent actions based on the Vedas, but they lack the correct information. (4.29.48)

Detail

There is some value in Vedic rituals. These procedures, like any other actions, will result in specific outcomes, either to benefit or to inconvenience the performer. The lack of clarification is that some performers feel that the rituals, once done expertly with the correct pronunciations, and with the proper ingredients, will give purely spiritual results.

Nārad denounced those who felt that the ceremonies gave perception of Janārdana's world. Some rituals may cause the performer to reach the heaven of Indra but that is as far as that person may go. It will not result in access to God's world.

The psychic realm which corresponds to this physical situation, is not the world of the supreme being. If one attains that psychic place, one will soon return to this physical environment.

आस्तीर्य दर्भैः प्राग्-ग्रैः कात्स्न्र्येन क्षिति-मण्डलम् /
स्तब्धो बृहद्-वधान् मानी कर्म नावैषि यत् परम् /
तत् कर्म हरि-तोषं यत् सा विद्या तन्-मतिर् यया (४॥२९॥४९)

āstīrya darbhaiḥ prāg-agraiḥ
kārtsnyena kṣiti-maṇḍalam /
stabdho bṛhad-vadhān mānī
karma nāvaiṣi yat param /
tat karma hari-toṣaṃ yat
sā vidyā tan-matir yayā (4.29.49)

āstīrya – covered, darbhaiḥ - by ritual grass, prāg-agraiḥ = tips facing east, kārtsnyena – every direction, kṣiti-maṇḍalam = land of earth, stabdho = stabdhah = animals, bṛhad = bṛhat = great, vadhān = vadhāt = by killing, mānī - proud, karma – cultural activity, nāvaiṣi = na avaiṣi = do not know, yat – which, param – better, tat – which, karma – cultural activities, hari – God Hari, toṣaṃ - satisfaction of, yat – that, sā = sāḥ = that, vidyā – realization, tan= tat = to that which, matir = matiḥ = mind, yayā – by which

Covering the entire earth with ritual grass which pointed to the east, you slaughtered a great number of animals. You were proud and did not know what is a cultural activity and what is better than that. Cultural acts which give satisfaction to the God Hari is the real act. Realization with the mind referenced on him, is the real knowledge. (4.29.49)

Detail

King Barhi carved out a reputation as a person who performed Vedic rituals everywhere on earth. He was the cause of the *darbha* grass becoming a weed on earth. He was sure that he achieved the heaven described in the Vedas. He felt that at death, he would be transported to that psychic location. He was convinced that he would stay there forever because of the many sacrifices he performed.

Barhi did not figure what would happen to the resentment energy of the animals he heartlessly slaughtered. If one commits criminal acts to support a religious rite, there will be accounting for those faulty behaviors. Beneficial social acts are logged for future flybacks. Vicious assaults will produce results too. Who will compensate whom?

Cultural acts which serve the purpose of the God Hari, which were done deliberately or whimsically, will result in some association with the Lord. Those are the highest acts. They result in some association with the supreme being.

हरिर् देह-भृताम् आत्मा स्वयं प्रकृतिर् ईश्वरः /
तत्-पाद-मूलं शरणं यतः क्षेमो नृणाम् इह (४॥२९॥५०)

harir deha-bhṛtām ātmā
svayaṃ prakṛtir īśvaraḥ /
tat-pāda-mūlaṃ śaraṇaṃ
yataḥ kṣemo nṛṇām iha (4.29.50)

harir = hariḥ = God Hari, deha-bhṛtām = embodied soul, ātmā – core, svayaṃ - himself, prakṛtir = prakṛtiḥ = Nature, īśvaraḥ - Lord, tat – his, pāda – foot, mūlaṃ - sole, śaraṇaṃ - shelter, yataḥ - from which, kṣemo = kṣemaḥ = well-being, security, nṛṇām – of men, iha – here

The God Hari is himself, the core of the embodied soul. He is Nature and Lord. The soles of his feet are the shelter from which the well-being of the people in this world is derived. (4.29.50)

Detail

The Supreme Person is the subtle one who is subtler than the limited selves. That Supreme Being is the underlying basis. A psyche has a central unit consciousness which is termed as a coreSelf. There is some difficulty in realizing this core by itself. That is due to its being adhesively connected to adjuncts. Even though the adjuncts are of a lower frequency than the core, still the core has difficulty discerning itself in contrast.

If, however the core does meditation, it may come to realize itself and may objectify itself in reference to its adjuncts. A greater task is for it to perceive the Supreme Person.

In the fable of Purañjan, this wanderer paired with a queen, but when he tried to get information about the woman's lineage, he was told that she knew nothing of her parentage. This suggests that the core cannot normally check its intellect, nor any of its other adjuncts. Even though the core is reliant on the intellect for services, accommodation, and protection, still the core does not understand the existence of that intellect.

If Purañjan could neither identify nor tag his intellect, it is reasonable to assume that he could not sense his perpetual friend, Not-Recognized (Avijñāta). This is a report about the subtlety of superSoul. As for the idea that the superSoul advises the soul, that can happen only if the soul becomes aware of that superEntity.

Just after the death of her husband, the yogiKing Malayadhvaja, Purañjan as the woman, Queen Vaidarbhī, heard from a brahmin who was that Supreme Person. That was a rare experience for her. Usually, due to subtlety, this superSoul cannot be perceived by a limited entity. The nearness of the superSoul is one thing, his availability is a separate daunting issue. In terms of dimension, some aspect could be one frequency higher than another and be totally unavailable.

स वै प्रियतमश् चात्मा यतो न भयम् अण्व् अपि /
इति वेद स वै विद्वान् यो विद्वान् स गुरुर् हरिः (४॥२९॥५१)

sa vai priyatamaś cātmā
yato na bhayam aṇv api /
iti veda sa vai vidvān yo
vidvān sa gurur hariḥ (4.29.51)

sa = saḥ = he, vai – indeed, priyatamaś = priyatamaḥ = dearest, cātmā = ca (and) + ātmā (coreSelf), yato = yataḥ = from whom, na – not, bhayam – fear, aṇv = anu = under, not the least, api – also, iti – thus, veda – knows, sa = saḥ = he, vai – indeed, vidvān – educated person, sa = saḥ = he, vidvān – educated person, sa = saḥ = he, gurur = guruḥ = spiritual teacher, hariḥ - God Hari

He is the dearmost one, the self itself, from whom no fear, not the least, is sourced. One who knows this is educated indeed. A learned one is as relevant as the spiritual teacher or even the God Hari himself. (4.29.51)

Detail

The position of the limited entity, its existential insecurity, is dealt with by Nārad. He does not say that the limited self and the supremePerson are one and the same.

For Purañjan, the reach for and the perception of queen of Excitement City was easy. Purañjan needed only the opportunity to meet the woman. That was enough. The perception of her was natural for him.

However, to see Not-Recognized (Avijñāta), was near impossible. This tells us that the coreSelf easily uses the intellect. That adjunct has with it other facilities. It is accompanied by a dedicated security service, which maintains the physical body, and much of the functions in the subtle one.

Once Purañjan, as Queen Vaidarbhī, made sensual contact with the Supreme Lord, it was just a matter of maintaining that perception. Failure to do so would mean she would resume ordinary consciousness.

Nārad listed that Supreme One as the dearmost person, the self itself, the one from whom there is no fear, not the least of it. Persons who have the continuous contact with him are as relevant as the spiritual teacher or even the God Hari himself.

नारद उवाच
प्रश्न एवं हि सञ्छिन्नो भवतः पुरुषर्षभ /
अत्र मे वदतो गुह्यं निशामय सुनिश्चितम् (४॥२९॥५२)

nārada uvāca
praśna evaṃ hi sañchinno
bhavataḥ puruṣarṣabha /
atra me vadato guhyaṃ
niśāmaya suniścitam (4.29.52)

nārada - Nārada uvāca – said, praśna = praśnaḥ = question, evaṃ - thus, hi – sure, sañchinno = sañchinnaḥ = resolved, bhavataḥ - your, puruṣarṣabha – best of persons, atra – here, me – by me, vadato = vadataḥ = speech, guhyaṃ - secret, niśāmaya – contacting, suniścitam – thoroughly explained

Nārada said.
Your question is resolved, O Best of Persons. Now hear my speech about a secret which I will thoroughly explain. (4.29.52)

Detail

King Barhi requested a simplification of the story of Purañjan. Nārad related the equivalents between the life of the legendary adventurer and Barhi himself. But Nārad explained even more about something secret.

क्षुद्रं चरं सुमनसां शरणे मिथित्वा
रक्तं षडङ्घ्रि-गण-सामसु लुब्ध-कर्णम्
म्प्;ग्रे वृकान् असु-तृपो ऽविगणय्य यान्तं
पृष्ठे मृगं मृगय लुब्धक-बाण-भिन्नम् (४॥२९॥५३)

kṣudraṃ caraṃ sumanasāṃ
śaraṇe mithitvā
raktaṃ ṣaḍaṅghri-gaṇa-
sāmasu lubdha-karṇam
agre vṛkān asu-tṛpo

'vigaṇayya yāntaṃ
pṛṣṭhe mṛgaṃ mṛgaya
lubdhaka-bāṇa-bhinnam (4.29.53)

kṣudraṃ - grass, caraṃ – grazing, sumanasāṃ - flower garden, śaraṇe – under protection, mithitvā – sexually connected, raktaṃ - attached, ṣaḍaṅghri = ṣat aṅghri = six legged insect, bee, gaṇa – of group, sāmasu lubdha – anxious for,greedy, karṇam – ear, agre – before, vṛkān – wolves, asu – life, tṛpo = tṛpaḥ = satisfaction, 'vigaṇayya = avigaṇayya = be aware of, yāntaṃ - travelling, pṛṣṭhe – behind, mṛgaṃ - deer, mṛgaya – stalking, lubdhaka – hunter, bāṇa – by arrows, bhinnam – pierced

It grazes grass in a flower garden. It is sexually involved, and is attached. It sees six legged insects, bees, which it anxiously hears with its ears. Before it, are wolves who get satisfied taking the lives of others. Travelling behind the deer, stalking, is a hunter who will pierce it with arrows. (4.29.53)

Detail

This is about a creature which grazes in a flower garden, while it is oblivious of the threats to its life. The creature feels that this creation is for its satisfaction. It does not understand that it is part of a grand design which will be ruined.

This is similar to King Barhi as well as to the fabled adventurer, Purañjan, who got the idea that the queen and her accommodations were for his pleasure.

A deer is sexually involved, and is attached to various types of gratification. That makes it dependent on items in its environment. It sees six legged insects, bees, which it anxiously hears with its ears, but it does not contemplate the similarity between itself and the busy insects. With the deer, there are wolves which are satisfied by taking the lives of others. Despite that threat, the deer does not understand the danger.

More dangerous is a hunter who travels behind the deer. He stalks the animal with intentions to kill it.

सुमनः-सम-धर्मणां
स्त्रीणां शरण आश्रमे पुष्प-मधु-गन्धवत्

sumanaḥ-sama-dharmaṇāṃ
strīṇāṃ śaraṇa āśrame
puṣpa-madhu-gandhavat (4.29.54a)

sumanaḥ - flowers, sama – same, dharmaṇāṃ - course, strīṇāṃ - of women, śaraṇa – what gives relief, āśrame – in domestic affairs, puṣpa – flowers, madhu – honey, gandhavat – like fragrance,

Flowers are similar and take the same course as women in domestic affairs, where flowers, honey and fragrance give relief. (4.29.54a)

Detail

Girls and young women are appreciated for their grace and beauty. Once youth passes, Nature no longer supports a female's beauty. With each passing day, the looks fade and are replaced with the appearance of one who is aged. This is similar to the appearance, growth and wilting of flowers.

Of course, males age just the same but they are not as famous for beauty and grace. There are tugs and pulls in domestic affairs. Some are appreciated. Some are detested. In the midst of it, there are beautiful flowers, tasty honey, and lovely fragrances. These give relief.

क्षुद्रतमं काम्य-कर्म-विपाकजं
काम-सुख-लवं जैह्व्यौपस्थ्यादि
विचिन्वन्तं मिथुनी-भूय

kṣudratamaṃ kāmya-karma-vipākajaṃ
kāma-sukha-lavaṃ jaihvyaupasthyādi
vicinvantaṃ mithunī-bhūya

kṣudratamaṃ - insignificant, kāmya – what is desirable, karma – cultural activities, vipākajaṃ = consequence produced, kāma-sukha = pleasing enjoyment, lavam – small portion, jaihvyaupasthyādi = jaihvya (sense of taste, tongue) + aupasthya (sex intercourse) + ādi (the rest), vicinvantaṃ - mentally occupied, mithunī-bhūya = sexually involved, (4.29.54b)

But that is insignificant. What is desirable? Is it cultural activities which produce consequences and has small portions of pleasing enjoyment like the sense of taste? Is it sexual intercourse and the rest of the fleeting pleasures in which one becomes mentally occupied for pleasure? (4.29.54b)

Detail

Whatever is desirable in physical existence is temporary. As soon as one begins to appreciate something, one's contact with it is altered. Everything is unreliable. If there is unhappiness, one wishes to end that immediately but it may persist for a time as it is empowered by fate.

Sex pleasure is a highlight of physical existence but it does not last forever. There is the promise of enjoying it again and again. Otherwise, it is a tease for assumption of responsibility.

तद्-भिनिवेशित-मनसं
षडङ्घ्रि-गण-साम-गीतवद्
अतिमनोहर-वनितादि-जनालापेष्व् अतितराम्
अतिप्रलोभित-कर्णम् अग्रे वृक-यूथवद्
आत्मन आयुर् हरतो ऽहो-रात्रान् तान्
काल-लव-विशेषान् अविगणय्य गृहेषु विहरन्तं
पृष्ठत एव परोक्षम् अनुप्रवृत्तो लुब्धकः

tad-abhiniveśita-manasaṃ
ṣaḍaṅghri-gaṇa-sāma-gītavad
atimanohara-vanitādi-janālāpeṣv atitarām
atipralobhita-karṇam agre vṛka-yūthavad
ātmana āyur harato 'ho-rātrān tān
kāla-lava-viśeṣān avigaṇayya gṛheṣu viharantaṃ
pṛṣṭhata eva parokṣam anupravṛtto lubdhakaḥ
(4.29.54c)

tad = tat = her, abhiniveśita – absorbed about, manasaṃ - mind, ṣaḍaṅghri – six-legged insect, bee, gaṇa – of group, sāma – tranquil, gītavad = gītavat = like singing, atimanohara – very attractive, vanitādi – wife and others, janālāpeṣv = jana (people) + ālāpeṣu (to speech), atitarām – excessive, atipralobhita – very alluring, karṇam – ear, agre – before, vṛka – wolf, yūthavad – like a pack, ātmana - of oneself, āyur = āyuḥ = lifespan, harato = harataḥ = confiscating, 'ho= ahaḥ = days, rātrān – nights, tān – them, kāla-lava-viśeṣān = flowing moments of time, avigaṇayya – not figuring, gṛheṣu – in family life, viharantaṃ - enjoying here and there, pṛṣṭhata = pṛṣṭhataḥ = back, eva – even so, parokṣam – unseen, anupravṛtto = anupravṛttaḥ = from the back, lubdhakaḥ - hunter,

Being mentally absorbed with your wife, you were like bees buzzing in a swarm. You felt strongly attracted to your wife and others. You spoke excessively to others. That was alluring to the ear. You were like someone pursued by a wolf pack. Your lifespan was confiscated by the flowing

moments of time. In family life, due to enjoying here and there, one does not figure this. Time is like a hunter which is unseen. It approaches from behind. (4.29.54c)

कृतान्तो ऽन्तः शरेण यम् इह पराविध्यति
तम् इमम् आत्मानम् अहो राजन्
भिन्न-हृदयं द्रष्टुम् अर्हसीति (४॥२९॥५४)

kṛtānto 'ntaḥ śareṇa yam iha parāvidhyati
tam imam ātmānam aho rājan
bhinna-hṛdayaṃ draṣṭum arhasīti (4.29.54d)

kṛtānto = kṛtāntaḥ = angel of death, 'ntaḥ = antaḥ = psychic, śareṇa – by arrow, yam – whom, iha – here, parāvidhyati – strikes, penetrates, tam – that, imam – this, ātmānam – self, aho rājan = O King, bhinna – split, hṛdayaṃ - psyche, draṣṭum – to see, arhasīti = arhasi (you should) + iti (thus)

The angel of death is psychic. With his arrow, he pierces, O King, splitting the psyche. (4.29.54d)

Detail

Death as an incidence or death as a deity, results in the same end of the body, with the coreSelf being evicted from its residence, where it returned after every sleeping period, to repossess its reputation and social value.

The Death person or energy, causes a disturbance so that the psyche is disrupted when it occurs. This is due to the fact that when a disembodied self becomes unified with the energy of new parents, there is a feeling of singularity, as if the new body, the mental and psychic energies, are of one formation.

When death comes, that compound breaks apart. This is experienced as a dismal event, where it seems that the psyche burst. In truth the psychic aspects become incompatible with the physical ones. But the loss of the physical aspects, is interpreted as a destructive event.

स त्वं विचक्ष्य मृग-चेष्टितम् आत्मनो ऽन्तश्
चित्तं नियच्छ हृदि कर्ण-धुनीं च चित्ते
जह्य् अङ्गनाश्रमम् असत्तम-यूथ-गाथं
प्रीणीहि हंस-शरणं विरम क्रमेण (४॥२९॥५५)

sa tvaṃ vicakṣya mṛga-ceṣṭitam ātmano 'ntaś
cittaṃ niyaccha hṛdi karṇa-dhunīṃ ca citte
jahy aṅganāśramam asattama-yūtha-gāthaṃ
prīṇīhi haṃsa-śaraṇaṃ virama krameṇa (4.29.55)

sa = sa = that person, tvaṃ - you, vicakṣya – knowing, mṛga – deer, ceṣṭitam – lifestyle, ātmano = ātmanaḥ = of self, 'ntaś = antaḥ = within, cittaṃ - awareness, niyaccha – cease, fix, hṛdi – in the psyche, karṇa – ear, dhunīṃ - sounding, ca – and, citte – in consciousness, jahy = jahi = rejected, abandoned, aṅganāśramam = aṅganā (woman) + āśramam (situation), asattama – of the lowest value, yūtha – concerning everyone, gāthaṃ - gossip, prīṇīhi – be content, haṃsa – superior person, śaraṇaṃ - reliance on, virama – abstain, terminate, avoid, krameṇa – step by step

Knowing that your lifestyle is like that of a deer, keep your awareness within the psyche, and the sounding tendency of the ear within the consciousness. Abandon the female situations which are of the lowest value, and which consists of gossip about everyone. Be content in reliance on the superior person, while abstaining from everything else step by step. (4.29.55)

Detail

Up to this point, even though he was exposed to spiritual considerations, King Barhi spent the majority of his time, satisfying the senses of his kingly body. He was like Purañjan. Though the King was human, Nārad compared him to a deer. The human has a wider range of sensual quest but only in some areas, not all. The aggressive hunt for sensual satisfaction is ongoing in either species.

King Barhi was advised to keep his awareness within the psyche and to listen for inner sounds and not be lured to the sources of outer sounds which are pleasing to the ear.

Nārad suggested that Barhi should abandon the female situations. In considering how female bodies age, the pursuit for their beauty results in finding that their aged forms are of less value. In their association, instead of focusing on the concerns of the core, there would be interest in gossip.

राजोवाच
श्रुतम् अन्वीक्षितं ब्रह्मन् भगवान् यद् अभाषत /
नैतज् जानन्त्य् उपाध्यायाः किं न ब्रूयुर् विदुर् यदि (४॥२९॥५६)

rājovāca śrutam anvīkṣitaṃ
brahman bhagavān yad abhāṣata /
naitaj jānanty upādhyāyāḥ
kiṃ na brūyur vidur yadi (4.29.56)

rājovāca –King Barhi said, śrutam – was heard, anvīkṣitaṃ - see or remember, brahman – hey brahmin, bhagavān – lord, lordly, yad = yat = which, abhāṣata – spoke, naitaj = na (not) + etat (this), jānanty = jānanti = knows, upādhyāyāḥ - teachers, kiṃ - why, na – not, brūyur = brūyuḥ = instruct, vidur = viduḥ = understood, yadi – if

King Barhi said.
"What you said was heard and understood, O brahmin, lordly self. Those teachers do not know

this. Why did they not instructed me if they understood this? (4.29.56)

Detail

King Barhi addressed Nārad, as lordly self, *bhagavān*. This title is used to address the Lord or his great devotee. Although Barhi excused his previous teachers, he questioned their insight.

संशयो ऽत्र तु मे विप्र सञ्छिन्नस् तत्-कृतो महान् /
ऋषयो ऽपि हि मुह्यन्ति यत्र नेन्द्रिय-वृत्तयः (४॥२९॥५७)

saṃśayo 'tra tu me vipra
sañchinnas tat-kṛto mahān /
ṛṣayo 'pi hi muhyanti
yatra nendriya-vṛttayaḥ (4.29.57)

saṃśayo = saṃśayaḥ = doubt, 'tra = atra = concerning this, tu – but, me – my, vipra = O brahmin, sañchinnas = sañchinnaḥ = shredded, tat – that, kṛto = kṛtaḥ = did, mahān – greatest, ṛṣayo = ṛṣayaḥ = non-celibate qualified yogis, 'pi = api = also, hi – as a result, muhyanti = mystified, yatra – where, nendriyaa= na (not) + indriya (senses), vṛttayaḥ - matters

"For me, the doubt concerning this is shredded, O brahmin. Even the greatest of the non-celibate, but qualified yogis, are mystified by matters which are not comprehended by the senses. (4.29.57)

Detail

King Barhi integrated the information, and to some extent the experience, which was transmitted to him by Nārad. Barhi was in touch with some non-celibate but qualified yogis, the rishis. His conclusion was that their information on spiritual matters was faulty.

कर्माण्य् आरभते येन पुमान् इह विहाय तम् /
अमुत्रान्येन देहेन जुष्टानि स यद् अश्नुते (४॥२९॥५८)

karmāṇy ārabhate yena
pumān iha vihāya tam /
amutrānyena dehena
juṣṭāni sa yad aśnute (4.29.58)

karmāṇy = karmāṇi = cultural activities, ārabhate – performs, yena – by which, pumān – person, iha – in this life, vihāya – left aside, tam – that, amutra – hereafter, anyena – in another, dehena – by the body, juṣṭāni – development, sa = saḥ = he, yad = yat = that, aśnute - experiences

"Cultural activities performed by a person in this life, are left aside hereafter, but one experiences their development in another body in another life. (4.29.58)

Detail

There is some misunderstanding about how a person can derive the benefits of social kindness hereafter and in future lives. Some feel that if one is tagged for criminal actions, one can thwart the negative reactions by giving compensation to cover the liabilities of the acts.

Some feel that if one is credited for good behavior, one will enjoy happiness now and hereafter. These views are egocentric but they do not necessarily correspond to the course of nature.

Any act committed, the effects of which are not rendered before one is evicted from the body, will remain to be settled either hereafter or in a future life. These renderings take place at the convenience of Nature.

One has the upper hand if Nature sees it so. Otherwise, inconvenient events will occur. Those cultural activities which require a consequence in the physical world, will occur in the future but only when Nature constructs a history which facilitates their layout.

इति वेद-विदां वादः श्रूयते तत्र तत्र ह /
कर्म यत् क्रियते प्रोक्तं परोक्षं न प्रकाशते (४॥२९॥५९)

iti veda-vidāṃ vādaḥ
śrūyate tatra tatra ha /
karma yat kriyate proktaṃ
parokṣaṃ na prakāśate (4.29.59)

iti – thus, veda-vidāṃ = those who know the Vedic information, vādaḥ - doctrine, śrūyate – heard, tatra tatra = here there, ha – of course, karma – cultural activities, yat – what, kriyate – is done, proktaṃ - declared, parokṣaṃ - unknown, na – not, prakāśate – perceived

"Thus, it is declared by those who know the Vedic doctrine, which is heard here and there. But the cultural activities which were done no longer exist, nor are perceived here." (4.29.59)

Detail

Once it is performed, an event is no longer visible. And yet, its effects which have a psychic register are in the potential of history, to be rendered in the future on the physical plane.

The absence of performed physical actions only means that the physical display was suspended. Their subtle substance is present until that is resolved either by further physical acts or by psychic clash which cancels the motivations and intentions.

King Barhi had some doubts about the consequences of physical activities which could not be absolved at the time of their performance. For instance! If a man kills another and leaves the scene and is not arrested for the crime, how can one say that the laws of action and reaction operate in a satisfactory way?

नारद उवाच
येनैवारभते कर्म तेनैवामुत्र तत् पुमान् /
भुङ्क्ते ह्य् अव्यवधानेन लिङ्गेन मनसा स्वयम् (४॥२९॥६०)

nārada uvāca
yenaivārabhate karma
tenaivāmutra tat pumān /
bhuṅkte hy avyavadhānena
liṅgena manasā svayam (4.29.60)

nārada – Nārada, uvāca – replied, yenaivārabhate = yena (by which) + eva (as is) + ārabhate (commits), karma – cultural activities, tenaivāmutra = tena (by that) + eva (of course) + amutra (in the next life), tat – that, pumān – person, bhuṅkte – experiences, hy = hi = due to, avyavadhānena – no alteration, liṅgena – by the subtle body, manasā – by the mind, svayam – itself

Nārada said.
The same basis by which someone commits cultural activities in this life, serves to make the person experience the same with no alteration, through the subtle body and mind of the very self. (4.29.60)

Detail

Most cultural activities are witnessed by others but some are not obvious to anyone. Regardless, there is a psychic basis of intention and motivation. Though unseen, that psychic undergrowth supports the event and its reaction.

Some actions are similar to their psychic origin. Some are dissimilar. In either case, the psychic stub which is the support, remains as the cause of the original event and its reactive expression.

Death does not save anyone from a reaction, be it a positive or negative one, or even one which has a neutral content. The reply energy will surface and produce corresponding events, either hereafter or sometime in the history of the world.

Nature is not particularly interested in providing explanations or revelation, about how it solves social riddles. Nature functions in a *tit-for-tat* way. It may act visibly for someone to witness a reaction immediately after an action, but it may arbitrarily cause a tree to fall when no human observes it.

शयानम् इमम् उत्सृज्य श्वसन्तं पुरुषो यथा /
कर्मात्मन्य् आहितं भुङ्क्ते तादृशेनेतरेण वा (४॥२९॥६१)

śayānam imam utsṛjya
śvasantaṃ puruṣo yathā /
karmātmany āhitaṃ
bhuṅkte tādṛśenetareṇa vā (4.29.61)

śayānam – laying on a bed, imam – this, utsṛjya – leaving aside, śvasantaṃ - breathing, puruṣo = puruṣaḥ = person, yathā – as, karmātmany = karma (cultural acts) + ātmani (in self), āhitaṃ - completed, bhuṅkte – experiences, tādṛśenetareṇa = tādṛśena + (by a similar body) + itareṇa (by another body format), vā – or

Just as when laying on a bed, someone leaves aside breathing, so the cultural acts of the self are completed, and the self experiences in a similar body or in another format. (4.29.61)

Detail

Whatever someone did just before sleeping, is abandoned by that person for the time being, for as long as he/she did not resume awareness as the physical body. And yet that person who becomes aware of himself/herself, as the dream body continues acting in some way according to the psychic circumstance which occurs in the dream.

One is frequently compelled to cease social acts, but then one is compelled by some force to initiate acts on some other plane of existence. The self is influenced.

ममैते मनसा यद् यद् असाव् अहम् इति ब्रुवन् /
गृह्णीयात् तत् पुमान् राद्धं कर्म येन पुनर् भवः (४॥२९॥६२)

mamaite manasā yad yad
asāv aham iti bruvan /
gṛhṇīyāt tat pumān rāddhaṃ
karma yena punar bhavaḥ (4.29.62)

mamaite = mama (mine) + ete (these), manasā – by mind, yad yad = yat yat = whatever, asāv = asau = that, aham – I, iti – thus, bruvan – accepting, gṛhṇīyāt – taking, tat – that, pumān – person, rāddhaṃ - perfected, karma – social activity, yena – by which, punar = punaḥ = again, bhavaḥ - existence

Feeling in the mind that these are mine, with whom or whatever, that is accepted by that person, being perfectly suited according to social activity. That happens again and again in some existence. (4.29.62)

Detail

Each life has a starting point which can be counted from conception or from birth or else from adulthood. It occurs by the application of the sense of identity. This adjunct reaches out and clings to a social role where it can be of significance.

Nature establishes the situation. A self adjusts to it. Purañjan arrived at the southern Himalayas. There he found a beautiful woman who agreed to be with him for some time, for one hundred years. Coming into being, one is circumstantially force to accept the situation.

यथानुमीयते चित्तम् उभयैर् इन्द्रियेहितैः /
एवं प्राग्-देहजं कर्म लक्ष्यते चित्त-वृत्तिभिः (४॥२९॥६३)

yathānumīyate cittam
ubhayair indriyehitaiḥ /
evaṃ prāg-dehajaṃ karma
lakṣyate citta-vṛttibhiḥ (4.29.63)

yathānumīyate = yathā (so as) + anumīyate (inferred), cittam – mind, ubhayair = ubhayaiḥ = both, indriyehitaiḥ = indriya (psychological operations) + īhitaiḥ (by physical effort), evaṃ - thus, prāg = prāk = prior, dehajaṃ - created by the body, karma – cultural activities, lakṣyate – perceive, show, citta-vṛttibhiḥ = by the mento-emotional energy

As one can infer the state of mind by both types of sense operations, the psychological and physical ones, so what was done prior which was created by another body, shows through the cultural activities which are enacted by the mento-emotional energy. (4.29.63)

Detail

The physical reality has a psychic foundation from which physical events are enacted. There is a direct connection between the physical and the psychic, such that psychic actions which occur mentally and/or emotionally, can be traced either from or to physical operations.

When a person is physically focused, he or she may lose track of the psychic basis. He may falsely conclude or assume that what is physical, stands alone as the basis of an event.

The disappearance of the psychic source of a physical action merely means that the psychic involvement is out of range of detection. The assessment of a physical event should include the psychic underlayment. Only then is the investigation complete.

नानुभूतं क्व चानेन देहेनादृष्टम् अश्रुतम् /
कदाचिद् उपलभ्येत यद् रूपं यादृग् आत्मनि (४॥२९॥६४)

nānubhūtaṃ kva cānena
dehenādṛṣṭam aśrutam /
kadācid upalabhyeta
yad rūpaṃ yādṛg ātmani (4.29.64)

nānubhūtaṃ = na (not) + anubhūtaṃ (experience), kva – whenever, cānena = ca (and) + anena (this), dehenādṛṣṭam = dehena (by the body) + adṛṣṭam (not seen), aśrutam – not heard, kadācid = kadācit = sometimes, upalabhyeta – perceptible, yad = yat = which, rūpaṃ - form, yādṛg = yādṛt = whatever means, ātmani – in the self

That which is not experienced anywhere by this body, and what is not seen, nor heard, is sometimes perceptible in form by some other means in the self. (4.29.64)

Detail

The common reference for objects is the physical world. The majority of human beings and animals use that as the standard for calculation. The mistake humans make is that they stress the physical objects and neglect impressions regarding the psychic ones.

तेनास्य तादृशं राज लिङ्गिनो देह-सम्भवम् /
श्रद्धत्स्वाननुभूतो ऽर्थो न मनः स्प्रष्टुम् अर्हति (४॥२९॥६५)

tenāsya tādṛśaṃ rājal
liṅgino deha-sambhavam /
śraddhatsvānanubhūto 'rtho
na manaḥ spraṣṭum arhati (4.29.65)

tenāsya = tena (by this) + asya (of this), tādṛśaṃ - like that, rājal = rājan = O King, liṅgino = liṅginaḥ = subtle body, deha – physical body, sambhavam - existent, śraddhatsvānanubhūto = śraddhatsva (confident of it) + ānanubhūtaḥ (not perceived), 'rtho = arthah = something, na – not, manaḥ - in the mind, spraṣṭum – to comprehend, arhati – can do

By this discussion and regarding this topic, it is like this, O King. The subtle body and the physical one are existent. One can be confident of something even though it may not be perceived currently, even something which was not comprehended by the mind. (4.29.65)

Detail

Nārad requested that King Barhi, consider that both the subtle body and the physical one have value. Their interaction is current. Even when the subtle has an event which does not tally with the physical situation, that subtle aspect has relevance.

मन एव मनुष्यस्य पूर्व-रूपाणि शंसति /
भविष्यतश् च भद्रं ते तथैव न भविष्यतः (४॥२९॥६६)

mana eva manuṣyasya
pūrva-rūpāṇi śaṃsati /
bhaviṣyataś ca bhadraṃ te
tathaiva na bhaviṣyataḥ (4.29.66)

mana = manaḥ = mind, eva – as is, manuṣyasya = of someone, pūrva – formerly, rūpāṇi – forms, śaṃsati – determines, bhaviṣyataś = bhaviṣyataḥ = of one who will be, ca – and, bhadraṃ - lucky, te – to you, tathaiva – thus be sure, na – not, bhaviṣyataḥ - of one who will be

The mind's content from former forms determines how one will be. O lucky person, it should be used to figure if one will not be. (4.29.66)

Detail

The production of the landscape of time is based on whatever happened in the past. Nature does not display every origin. Much of what forms the basis of the present is invisible to those who are affected.

What happens currently, will be used to serve future events. Even though one has no evidence, these assumptions should be made. In considering what one may be in the future; one should understand that the procedure of time utilizes the subtle impressions which registered previously.

अदृष्टम् अश्रुतं चात्र क्वचिन् मनसि दृश्यते /
यथा तथानुमन्तव्यं देश-काल-क्रियाश्रयम् (४॥२९॥६७)

adṛṣṭam aśrutaṃ cātra
kvacin manasi dṛśyate /
yathā tathānumantavyaṃ
deśa-kāla-kriyāśrayam (4.29.67)

adṛṣṭam – not perceived, aśrutaṃ - not heard, cātra = can (and) + atra (here on earth), kvacin = kvacit = at some time, manasi – in the mind, dṛśyate – saw, yathā – as, tathānumantavyaṃ = tathā (so) + anumantavyaṃ (to be qualified), deśa – place, kāla – time, kriyāśrayam = kriyā (activity) + āśrayam (reliance)

Incidences not perceived nor heard on earth are sometimes seen in the mind. That is qualified by the place, time, and activity upon which they rely. (4.29.67)

Detail

It is possible to perceive the invisible subtle basis of an event. It may be a physical occurrence or a psychic environment. One should assume that the perception of a supernatural event is qualified by a place, time, and activity in some realm, even in the physical world.

Nārad wanted King Barhi to accept that whatever is done, will have a future impact. If it is not manifested on the physical plane, if it occurred only in the mind, it made a psychic imprint.

सर्वे क्रमानुरोधेन मनसीन्द्रिय-गोचराः /
आयान्ति बहुशो यान्ति सर्वे समनसो जनाः (४॥२९॥६८)

sarve kramānurodhena
manasīndriya-gocarāḥ /
āyānti bahuśo yānti
sarve samanaso janāḥ (4.29.68)

sarve – all, kramānurodhena = krama (step) + anurodhena (by order), manasīndriya = manasi (mind) + indriya (by senses), gocarāḥ - perception, āyānti – happen, bahuśo = bahuśaḥ = many methods, yānti – they logged, sarve = all, samanaso = samanasaḥ = with mind, janāḥ - persons

According to the sequence of sense perception, events are orderly stacked in the mind. The

incidences come into view by many causes, which are logged in the mind of the involved persons. (4.29.68)

Detail

Nature is ordered, such that what happens occurs in a specific sequence, according to how the original events were manifested and altered.

Nature has its timer. The limited entities too, carry a recorder which registers sensual events in the order of contact with the same.

This is complex but Nature operates chronological manifestations which take into account the complexity. A limited being cannot fully grasp what Nature calculates. He/She should accept Nature's sequenced productions as history.

सत्त्वैक-निष्ठे मनसि भगवत्-पार्श्व-वर्तिनि /
तमश् चन्द्रमसीवेदम् उपरज्यावभासते (४॥२९॥६९)

sattvaika-niṣṭhe manasi
bhagavat-pārśva-vartini /
tamaś candramasīvedam
uparajyāvabhāsate (4.29.69)

sattvaika = sattva (clarifying consciousness) + eka (one), niṣṭhe - position, manasi – in the mind, bhagavat – Supreme Lord, pārśva – in proximity, vartini - resting, acting, tamaś = tamaḥ = darkness, candramasīvedam = candramasi (in the moon) = iva (like) + idam (this), uparajyāvabhāsate = uparajya (being present) + avabhāsate – traversing

While experiencing the one clarifying consciousness which is established in the mind, and with the Supreme Lord resting in proximity, the confusion is like the dark influence traversing the moon. (4.29.69)

Detail

The mental operation which gives confusion regarding what is reality and what is substantial, is similar to the dark influence which moves across the moon. Whatever causes the shadow which transits the moon, should be accepted as a value. This is due to its effects on an observer. And yet, this occurrence should be understood as being relative in that it does not really affect the moon.

By reaching the spiritual plane of consciousness where there is one clarifying awareness and by being in touch with the Supreme Lord who is in proximity, one can simultaneously give very little value to the shadow events which affect the psyche. One should give optimum register to the Supreme Lord and to oneself as a perpetual self which is spiritual in nature.

नाहं ममेति भावो ऽयं पुरुषे व्यवधीयते /
यावद् बुद्धि-मनो-ऽक्षार्थ- गुण-व्यूहो ह्य् अनादिमान् (४॥२९॥७०)

nāhaṃ mameti bhāvo 'yaṃ
puruṣe vyavadhīyate /
yāvad buddhi-mano-'kṣārtha-
guṇa-vyūho hy anādimān (4.29.70)

nāhaṃ - not I, mameti = mama (my) + iti (thus), bhāvo = bhāvaḥ = being, 'yaṃ = ayam= this, puruṣe – in the person, vyavadhīyate – separated, yāvad = yāvat = so long as, buddhi – intellect, mano = manaḥ = mind, 'kṣārtha = akṣa (sight) + artha (what has value), guṇa – Nature influences, vyūho = vyūhaḥ = production, hy = hi = indeed, anādimān = anādimāt = without beginning

The feeling of *I-and-my*, as being this person which is not separated, will persist, so long as the intellect and mind is perceived as having value.

This is due to Nature's influences and productions, which are beginningless. (4.29.70)

Detail

The feeling of *I-and-my* will persist. One will feel as if one is not separate from the sense of possession which is applied to physical or subtle objects.

As long as the intellect and the mind are perceived as having value, their accounting and conclusions will be presented to the coreSelf within the mind. When the core is enlightened, it will perceive these presentations but it will give them a minimal value. According to the time and place, it will value them in reference to Nature's influences and productions.

सुप्ति-मूर्च्छोपतापेषु प्राणायन-विघाततः /
नेहते ऽहम् इति ज्ञानं मृत्यु-प्रज्वारयोर् अपि (४॥२९॥७१)

supti-mūrcchopatāpeṣu
prāṇāyana-vighātataḥ /
nehate 'ham iti jñānaṃ
mṛtyu-prajvārayor api (4.29.71)

supti – in sleep, mūrcchopatāpeṣu = mūrccha (unconsciousness) + upatāpeṣu (shock), prāṇāyana – check of breathing, vighātataḥ - interruption, nehate = na (not) + īhate (contemplate), 'ham = aham = I, iti - thus, jñānaṃ - experience, mṛtyu – dying, prajvārayor – in feverish state, api – too

In sleep, unconsciousness, and shock, there is interruption by check of breath, resulting in the lack of being *I*. This is experienced when dying and in a feverish state too. (4.29.71)

Detail

Is the *sense of I,* the personObserver, a reality? Does it exist perpetually? Will it terminate at the end of the body?

There is evidence that while the body lives, the *sense of I* is suspended periodically, where that personObserver fails to be itself and lacks the means of observation, which is the very function which is essentially itself.

If while sleeping, someone is addressed by someone who is awake, the sleeping someone may not respond. This is due to a temporary suspension of the *sense of I.* We know that it is temporary because the sleeping person may respond as soon as he/she is awakened.

If while unconscious, someone is addressed, the unconscious someone will not respond. This may be due to a temporary suspension of the *sense of I,* with a corresponding loss of objectivity. It may be temporary because the unconscious person may respond as soon as the unconsciousness ceases. It happens however, that some unconscious persons do not recover. These die while in the unconscious state. What then, is the reality of the *sense of I.*

While in a state of shock, someone may not respond when he/she is addressed. Or that person may respond in an unintelligent way. Then there is uncertainty due to the lack of administrative use of the *sense of I.* Such a person may pass from the physical body, ending any possibility of physical response.

The use of a physical body as a demonstration of individuality is put to question by any suspension of the *sense of I.*

Breath operation is involved. The question is. Does breath energize the subtle body as it does the physical one? We know that suspension of breath could cause death of the physical system. What should one conclude about its effect on the psychological aspects?

The mystery of objective consciousness continues. Whatever is subjective, and which is simultaneously conscious, is the signal of reality. That has no dependence on supportive features. This causes the inquiry as to the usefulness of subjectivity.

गर्भे बाल्ये ऽप्य् अपौष्कल्याद् एकादश-विधं तदा /
लिङ्गं न दृश्यते यूनः कुह्वां चन्द्रमसो यथा (४॥२९॥७२)

garbhe bālye 'py apauṣkalyād
ekādaśa-vidhaṃ tadā /
liṅgaṃ na dṛśyate yūnaḥ
kuhvāṃ candramaso yathā (4.29.72)

garbhe - in the embryonic stage, bālye – in childhood, 'py = api = as well, apauṣkalyād = apauṣkalyāt = because of immaturity, ekādaśa – ten senses and one mind, vidhaṃ - type, tadā – then, liṅgaṃ - subtle body, na – not, dṛśyate – is seen, yūnaḥ - of a youth, kuhvāṃ - apparent development, candramaso = candramasaḥ = moon, yathā – so as

In the embryonic stage and in childhood as well, because of immaturity, the ten senses and the single mind are of a type according to the time, such that the subtle body is not fully experienced in youth, just as is the case of the apparent development of the moon. (4.29.72)

Detail

As during the full iridescent phase, the face of the moon is seen in full, so in the adult stage of the physical body, its maximum potential is evident. Otherwise like during partial or full shadowing of the moon, when the physical body is unable to respond to the full capacity of the subtle one, the entity finds that it cannot make the physical system comply with some subtle commands.

When a boy uses a man's glove, the boy's fingers do not fill each finger-slot. Similarly, the subtle body is not matched fully to an immature physical form. This is due to the diminished facilities in an infant form or elderly body.

The full demonstration of a subtle body is muted when it is interspaced in an infant or elderly physical form. During the maturity of the form, the maximum coordination occurs, such that the entity feels complete in the peak of the adult years. However, even in the adult stage, the subtle body has other facilities which do not correspond to anything the physical body can do.

To use the other facilities which only the subtle body can express, one should shift the attention to the psychic plane. This may be done by performing austerities of sense control or by taking drugs or potent herbs or by making or becoming influenced by vibrations which shift the focus of the self into mystic planes of consciousness.

अर्थे ह्य् अविद्यमाने ऽपि संसृतिर् न निवर्तते /
ध्यायतो विषयान् अस्य स्वप्ने ऽनर्थागमो यथा (४॥२९॥७३)

arthe hy avidyamāne
'pi saṃsṛtir na nivartate /

dhyāyato viṣayān asya
svapne 'narthāgamo yathā (4.29.73)

arthe – in what has value, hy = hi = due to, avidyamāne = not present, 'pi = api = also, saṃsṛtir = saṃsṛtiḥ = course of existence, na – not, nivartate – ceases, dhyāyato = dhyāyataḥ = effortless mental focus, viṣayān – sense objects, asya – of this, svapne – in dreaming, 'narthāgamo = anartha (unwanted) + āgamaḥ (becomes manifest), yathā – as

What has value, even when it is not present in the course of existence, may not cease to exist. This is because of the effortless mental focus on sense objects, such that in dreaming even the unwanted things become manifest. (4.29.73)

Detail

One can be affected even by events which are not present to one's sense perception. This is because the lack of an energy in one level of existence, does not prevent the subtle effects of that object from penetrating and influencing what happens elsewhere.

Some involuntary focus on unwanted things occurs. This causes one to be influenced by circumstances which one may dislike but which leak into the plane of consciousness where one's attention is focused. This is how a person is haunted by an event which he/she can neither identify nor recognize.

एवं पञ्च-विधं लिङ्गं त्रि-वृत् षोडश विस्तृतम् /
एष चेतनया युक्तो जीव इत्य् अभिधीयते (४॥२९॥७४)

evaṃ pañca-vidhaṃ liṅgaṃ
tri-vṛt ṣoḍaśa vistṛtam /
eṣa cetanayā yukto
jīva ity abhidhīyate (4.29.74)

evaṃ - thus, pañca – five, vidhaṃ - object, liṅgaṃ - subtle body, tri-vṛt = three aspects, ṣoḍaśa – sixteen, vistṛtam – expanded, eṣa = eṣaḥ = this, cetanayā – with psychology, yukto = yuktah = combined with, jīva – limited individual self, ity = iti = thus, abhidhīyate – considered

Thus, the five objects which are the subtle body, has three aspects expanded into sixteen features. This psychology is combined with the limited individual self. That should be considered. (4.29.74)

Detail

The five objects are.

- odors
- flavors
- colors
- surfaces
- sounds

These are express in three features which are the attitudes of Nature. The highest feature renders the *clarifying perception.* The median one inspires *passionate action.* The lowest has a *de-energizing effect* on beneficial action.

The psyche is the combination of the limited individual self and the facilities of Nature, which show in sixteen features as the mind as a whole psychic mechanism or as an intellect analysis mechanism, the five sensual targets, the five senses for grasping what is desired and the five enthusiasms or psychological powers.

The lingam is the subtle body which contains sixteen features and which is tagged as the person. This complex forms as a psychic organism consisting of three aspects which pervade the system.

Five of the sixteen features are the sense consumptions; odors, flavors, colors, surfaces, and sounds. These occur inside and outside the physical body.

Another five consist of the organs which detect and gather information about what is objective. These are.

- nostrils
- tongue
- eyes
- skin
- ear

There are also another five rangers. These operate psycho-biological detection operations. They are the smelling sense, the one of taste, the one of vision, the one of touch and the one for hearing. Finally, there is the single complex action of the mind. This is the intellect which gathers sense data, rates it and forms conclusions. The entire composite has survival as the objective.

अनेन पुरुषो देहान् उपादत्ते विमुञ्चति /
हर्षं शोकं भयं दुःखं सुखं चानेन विन्दति (४॥२९॥७५)

anena puruṣo dehān
upādatte vimuñcati /
harṣaṃ śokaṃ bhayaṃ duḥkhaṃ
sukhaṃ cānena vindati (4.29.75)

anena – by this, puruṣo = puruṣah = person, dehān – physical forms, upādatte – assumes, vimuñcati – sheds, abandons, harṣaṃ - joy, śokaṃ - distress, bhayaṃ - fear, duḥkhaṃ - displeasure, sukhaṃ - happiness, cānena = ca (and) + anena (by this), vindati – experiences

By this (subtle body), the person assumes and sheds physical forms. Joy, distress, fear, displeasure, and happiness, is what he experiences by this. (4.29.75)

Detail

Even though there is a continuity from one adult body to an infant one, which in turn develops into a new adult body, which again begets an infant form, the basis for this physical development and display, is the psychic energy which though unseen through physical perception, is real nevertheless.

The assumption of a physical self begins not with physical components but with an emotional one, psychological feelings. In the exchange of feelings between a deceased someone and a living physical body of someone else, the potential parent, there is the beginning of being a physical body.

While a deceased person no longer has physical power, he or she has more intensified feelings. This energy easily mixes with or fuses into the feelings of someone who has a physical body. In that physique of the potential parent, the deceased person's feelings can cause physical movement.

Once a deceased person is fused with the emotional energy of a potential parent, that deceased someone feels the joy, distress, fear, displeasure, and happiness of that physical person's body. This continues until there is the development of a fetus, which is expelled to survive as a newborn infant.

यथा तृण-जलूकेयं नापयात्य् अपयाति च /
न त्यजेन् म्रियमाणो ऽपि प्राग्-देहाभिमतिं जनः (४॥२९॥७६)

yathā tṛṇa-jalūkeyaṃ
nāpayāty apayāti ca /
na tyajen mriyamāṇo 'pi
prāg-dehābhimatiṃ janaḥ (4.29.76)

yathā – as, tṛṇa jalūkeyaṃ = caterpillar, nāpayāty = na (not) = apayāti (release), apayāti clutches, ca – and, na – not, tyajen = tyajet = detach, mriyamāṇo = mriyamāṇaḥ = at death, 'pi = api = so, prāg = prāk = previous, dehābhimatiṃ = deha (physical body) + abhimatiṃ (my-ness, identification as), janaḥ - person

As a caterpillar does not release but clutches to a leaf, so at death, someone does not detach from the previous body. This is due the person's application of *my-ness*. (4.29.76)

Detail

In theory, someone on the verge of death should detach itself from the physical body. People sometimes announce that a certain human left the body. This is rarely the case however. Usually, the person is left aside by the body. The body becomes unusable, and unresponsive. It is more like the person is discarded by the body.

While a body dies, unless its death is sudden and instant, the person finds that he/she cannot release himself/herself from the body. This release is involuntary. It is a psychological disconnection which happens only when the physical system no longer responds to the willpower commands which are mental or emotional actions.

When those actions are no longer recognized by the physical body, when that physical system no longer executes those orders, the person involved finds itself to be something other than a physical body. He/She discovers the self to be only a psychic someone with no physical compliment.

The remnant self which survives the physical body's death, is the subtle body of that person. Since that person did not identify itself as such, it feels inconvenient and reduced, when it can no longer order physical actions. Its physical utility is not responsive.

The power to detached from a physical body just before its death was mentioned in spiritual literature but only for advanced beings, only for great yogis, and people who were rated as divinities or mystics.

The power to kill one's physical body, by using mere willpower, is beyond the scope of most human beings. Usually, the body is killed by something other than the willpower command of the person. The individual psychic self is one of the realities which are involved in the life of a physical body. It does not have the power to kill the body through an act of volition.

Sometimes however, someone may assist some natural action which would kill a body. Then by applying a little willpower, the body may die. An example is when a person faints or is about to faint. If he or she becomes aware of the condition, he/she may voluntarily interrupt the breathing process causing termination of oxygen to the body, which is already oxygen-deprived, because of some other action, or the lack of an action. That is a rare opportunity however. It depends on other involuntary factors. It is not an independent killing action by willpower.

यावद् अन्यं न विन्देत व्यवधानेन कर्मणाम् /
मन एव मनुष्येन्द्र भूतानां भव-भावनम् (४॥२९॥७७)

yāvad anyaṃ na vindeta
vyavadhānena karmaṇām /
mana eva manuṣyendra
bhūtānāṃ bhava-bhāvanam (4.29.77)

yāvad = yāvat = until, anyaṃ - some other, na – not, vindeta – gets, vyavadhānena – by doing, karmaṇām – cultural activities, mana = manaḥ = mind, eva – sure, manuṣyendra = manuṣya (human beings) + indra (O ruler), bhūtānāṃ - living beings, bhava – state of being, bhāvanam - cause

He does not get some other body except through past cultural activities. It is the mind for sure, O king of human beings, which is the cause of these states of the living beings. (4.29.77)

Detail

The assumption of a new body, which begins as a sperm organism and an ovum, actually began as an emotional presence in the psyche of the parents. It has objectivity as a disembodied someone on the astral level, but that is sublimal. Its subjectivity alone, is on display in the parents' bodies. It exists there only as psychological energy.

The connection between the disembodied self and the potential parent is emotional only. That relationship was based on cultural involvement which happened previously.

As Nārad stated, one can get a new body, through past cultural activities. The energy in the psyche, which is there as a result of previous social acts, is the basis for becoming an infant of somebody. The entity involved does not need to be aware of his/her previous acts. The energy which developed from those acts, has the power to attract the self to new situations, in which its energy exerts an influence. It may be subjective or instinctive. That does not prevent it from having an influence.

यदाक्षैश् चरितान् ध्यायन् कर्माण्य् आचिनुते ऽसकृत् /
सति कर्मण्य् अविद्यायां बन्धः कर्मण्य् अनात्मनः (४॥२९॥७८)

yadākṣaiś caritān dhyāyan
karmāṇy ācinute 'sakṛt /
sati karmaṇy avidyāyāṃ
bandhaḥ karmaṇy anātmanaḥ (4.29.78)

yadākṣaiś = yadā (when) + akṣaiḥ (by rehashing), caritān – fun activities, dhyāyan – absorbed in, karmāṇy = karmāṇi = actions, ācinute – investing, 'sakṛt = asakṛt = always, sati karmaṇy = sati karmaṇi = compelling social activities, avidyāyāṃ - uninformed, bandhaḥ - held in check, karmaṇy = karmani = activities, anātmanaḥ - not for the coreSelf

By rehashing fun activities and being absorbed in actions, always investing in more compulsive social acts, due to being uninformed, he is held in check by the activities which are not in the interest of the coreSelf. (4.29.78)

Detail

Regurgitating fond memories causes the formation of new impetus to become involved in fresh activities. These impressions mix with the imprints from other events to create even more compulsions. This increases the degree of distraction from self-focus. It is not in the interest of the coreSelf.

अतस् तद् अपवादार्थं भज सर्वात्मना हरिम् /
पश्यंस् तद्-ात्मकं विश्वं स्थित्य्-ुत्पत्त्य्-प्यया यतः (४॥२९॥७९)

atas tad apavādārthaṃ
bhaja sarvātmanā harim /
paśyaṃs tad-ātmakaṃ viśvaṃ
sthity-utpatty-apyayā yataḥ (4.29.79)

atas = ataḥ = thus, tad = tat = this, apavādārthaṃ = apavāda (cancel) + arthaṃ (value), bhaja – worship, adore, sarvātmanā = with all of self, harim – God who removes distress, paśyaṃs = paśyan = viewing, tad – of that, ātmakaṃ - composed of, viśvaṃ - the cosmos, sthity = sthiti = maintenance, utpatty – creation, apyayā = apyayāḥ = annihilation, yataḥ - from whom

Thus, regarding this, cancel the value given to it. Instead, with all of the self, worship Lord Hari, who removes distress. View the cosmos as his self, as the maintainer, creator, and annihilator from whom all this exist. (4.29.79)

Detail

The value given to whimsical thinking and impulsive feelings should be nullified by an effective psychic action, where the core focuses instead on Lord Hari, who is the one to remove distress.

This God should be regarded as the cosmos, as the maintainer, creator, and annihilator from whom all this exist. Hence one should refrain from adopting a possessive hold on whatever one encounters in the creation.

Due to his excessive involvement with the queen, Purañjan thought only of being entertained by the lady. He did not stop to consider the origins.

मैत्रेय उवाच
भागवत-मुख्यो भगवान् नारदो हंसयोर् गतिम् /
प्रदर्श्य ह्य् अमुम् आमन्त्र्य सिद्ध-लोकं ततो ऽगमत् (४॥२९॥८०)

maitreya uvāca
bhāgavata-mukhyo bhagavān
nārado haṃsayor gatim /
pradarśya hy amum āmantrya
siddha-lokaṃ tato 'gamat (4.29.80)

maitreya – Maitreya, uvāca – said, bhagavata - of those who are devoted to the Supreme Lord, mukhyo = mukhyaḥ = best, bhagavān – God, nārado = nāradaḥ = Nārada, haṃsayor = haṃsayoḥ = of two swan-like beings, gatim – situation, pradarśya – revealed, hy = hi = certainly, amum – him. āmantrya – invited, siddha-lokaṃ = to Siddhaloka realm of perfected being, tato = tataḥ = then, 'gamat = agamat = departed

Maitreya said:
"The best of those who are devoted to the Supreme Lord, the one Nārada, revealed the situation of the two swan-like beings. Then inviting him (King Barhi) to the Siddhaloka realm of perfected beings, Nārada departed. (4.29.80)

Detail

An invitation to siddhaloka is a blank request if the invitee did not achieve yoga proficiency. This invitation meant that in the near future, Barhi would complete the practice or will be translated to a higher state by Nārada or by another qualified being.

प्राचीनबर्हीं राजर्षिः प्रजा-सर्गाभिरक्षणे /
आदिश्य पुत्रान् अगमत् तपसे कपिलाश्रमम् (४॥२९॥८१)

prācīnabarhī rājarṣiḥ
prajā-sargābhirakṣaṇe /
ādiśya putrān agamat
tapase kapilāśramam (4.29.81)

prācīnabarhī – Barhi, rājarṣiḥ - wise yogi King, prajā – people, sargābhirakṣaṇe = sarga (collective) + abhirakṣaṇe (protect), ādiśya – instructing, putrān – sons, agamat – went, tapase – doing sensual disciplines, kapilāśramam = kapila (Kapila) + āśramam (hermitage)

"The wise yogi-king, Barhi, instructed his sons about protecting the people. He went to do sensual disciplines at the hermitage of Kapila. (4.29.81)

Detail

At the hermitage of Kapila, Barhi perfected the yoga practice.

तत्रैकाग्र-मना धीरो गोविन्द-चरणाम्बुजम् /
विमुक्त-सङ्गो ऽनुभजन् भक्त्या तत्-साम्यताम् अगात् (४॥२९॥८२)

tatraikāgra-manā dhīro
govinda-caraṇāmbujam /
vimukta-saṅgo 'nubhajan
bhaktyā tat-sāmyatām agāt (4.29.82)

tatraikāgra- = tatre (there) + eka (singular) + agra (focus), manāḥ - mental, dhīro = dhīraḥ = person with sensual balance, Govinda – God Krishna, caraṇāmbujam = caraṇa (feet) + āmbujam (lotus), vimukta – freedom from, saṅgo = saṅgaḥ = worldly association, 'nubhajan = anubhajan = worshiping devoutly, bhaktyā – by loving dedication, tat – with him, sāmyatām – similar existential condition, agāt – achieved

"There, with singular mental focus, being with sensual balance, he was at the lotus feet of Govinda, the God Krishna. Being free from worldly association, Barhi devotedly worshipped Krishna with loving dedication. He achieved an existential condition which was similar to that of Krishna. (4.29.82)

एतद् अध्यात्म-पारोक्ष्यं गीतं देवर्षिणानघ /
यः श्रावयेद् यः शृणुयात् स लिङ्गेन विमुच्यते (४॥२९॥८३)

etad adhyātma-pārokṣyaṃ
gītaṃ devarṣiṇānagha /
yaḥ śrāvayed yaḥ śṛṇuyāt
sa liṅgena vimucyate (4.29.83)

etad = etat = this, adhyātma – what concerns the supreme self, pārokṣyaṃ - mysterious something, gītaṃ - poetically declared, devarṣiṇānagha = deva (supernatural controllers) + ṛṣiṇā (yogi philosophers) + anagha without fault, yaḥ - whosoever, śrāvayed = śrāvayet = should hear, yaḥ - whosoever, śṛṇuyāt – from hearing, sa = saḥ = he, liṅgena – by the subtle body, vimucyate - released

"This information is about the supreme self, which is mysterious but was poetically declared by the supernatural controllers and the yogi philosophers, who are faultless. Whosoever hears this, whosoever tells others of it, is released from the influence of the subtle body. (4.29.83)

एतन् मुकुन्द-यशसा भुवनं पुनानं
देवर्षि-वर्य-मुख-निःसृतम् आत्म-शौचम्
यः कीर्त्यमानम् अधिगच्छति पारमेष्ठ्यं
नास्मिन् भवे भ्रमति मुक्त-समस्त-बन्धः (४॥२९॥८४)

etan mukunda-yaśasā
bhuvanaṃ punānaṃ
devarṣi-varya-mukha-
niḥsṛtam ātma-śaucam
yaḥ kīrtyamānam
adhigacchati pārameṣṭhyaṃ
nāsmin bhave bhramati
mukta-samasta-bandhaḥ (4.29.84)

etan = etat = this, mukunda – Mukunda Krishna, yaśasā – fame, bhuvanaṃ - this existence, punānaṃ - clearing, devarṣi – yogi-philosopher among the gods, varya – best, mukha – from mouth, niḥsṛtam – announced, ātma-śaucam = purified self, yaḥ - whosoever, kīrtyamānam – announcing the reputation of, adhigacchati – returns, pārameṣṭhyaṃ - relating to the Supreme Person, nāsmin = na (not) + asmin (this), bhave – in this existence, bhramati – wanders, mukta – liberated, samasta – total, bandhaḥ - bound

"This conversation about the fame of Mukunda Krishna is the clearance of this existence. Among the gods, it was announced from the mouth of the best of the yogi-philosophers. It purifies the self of whosoever hears it. He does not return. It announces the reputation of the Supreme Lord, such that one does not wander but is fully liberated. (4.29.84)

अध्यात्म-पारोक्ष्यम् इदं मयाधिगतम् अद्भुतम् /
एवं स्त्रियाश्रमः पुंसश् छिन्नो ऽमुत्र च संशयः (४॥२९॥८५)

adhyātma-pārokṣyam idaṃ
mayādhigatam adbhutam /
evaṃ striyāśramaḥ puṃsaś
chinno 'mutra ca saṃśayaḥ (4.29.85)

adhyātma – what concerns the essential self, pārokṣyam – mysterious something, idaṃ - this, mayādhigatam = mayā (by me) + adhigatam (heard), adbhutam – wonderful, evaṃ - thus, striyāśramaḥ = striyā (by the woman) + aśramaḥ (shelter), puṃsaś = puṃsaḥ = of the man, chinno = chinnaḥ = separation, 'mutra = amutra = life hereafter, ca – and, saṃśayaḥ - doubt

"What concerns the mysterious essential self was explained by me. Thus, the symbolism of lifestyle of the woman and the man, and their separation hereafter, is of no doubt." (4.29.85)

Index

D

E

M

About the Author

Michael Beloved (Yogi *Madhvāchārya)* took his current body in 1951 in Guyana. In 1965, while living in Trinidad, he instinctively began doing yoga postures and tried to make sense of the supernatural side of life.

Later in 1970, in the Philippines, he approached a Martial Arts Master named Arthur Beverford. Michael explained to the teacher that he was seeking a yoga instructor. Mr. Beverford identified himself as an advanced disciple of Rishi Singh Gherwal, an Ashtanga Yoga master.

Beverford taught the traditional Ashtanga Yoga with stress on postures, attentive breathing, and brow chakra centering meditation. In 1972, Michael entered the Denver Colorado Ashram of *kundalini* yoga Master Harbhajan Singh. There he took instruction in *bhastrika pranayama* and its application to yoga postures.

In 1979 Michael formally entered the disciplic succession of the Brahmā-Madhava-Gaudiya Sampradaya through *Swāmī* Kirtanananda, who was a prominent sannyasi disciple of the great Vaishnava authority *Swāmī* Bhaktivedanta Prabhupada, the exponent of devotion to Krishna.

However, yoga has a mystic side to it, thus Michael took training and teaching empowerment from several spiritual masters of different aspects of spiritual development. This is consistent with Krishna's advice to Arjuna in the *Bhagavad Gītā*:

Most of the instructions Michael received were given in the astral world. On that side of existence, his most prominent teachers were *Swāmī* Shivananda of Rishikesh, Yogiraj *Swāmī* Vishnudevananda, *Bābāji Mahasaya* - the master of the masters of *Kriyā* Yoga, Yogeshwarananda of Gangotri - the master of the masters of *Raja* Yoga (spiritual clarity), and Siddha *Swāmī* Nityananda, the Brahmā Yoga authority.

The course for kundalini yoga using *pranayama* breath infusion was detailed by Michael in the book *Kundalini Hatha Yoga Pradipika*.

Michael's preliminary books relating to meditation are *Meditation Pictorial, Meditation Expertise,* and *Meditation ~ Sense Faculty* (co-author). Every technique (*kriya*) mentioned was tested by him during *pranayama* breath infusion and *samyama* deep meditation practice.

This is a result of over fifty years of meditation practice with astute subtle observations intending to share the methods and experiences. The information is published freely with no intention of forming an institution nor hogtying anyone as a disciple.

This book runs the gauntlet of the incidences which occur while being a physical body. A physical being is involved in losing battle which he must endure until the body's death. If he is successful, he loses in the end. If he fails, he loses anyway. And yet, for those who tap into the psychic side of life, there is a bright light at the end of the tunnel. That is the discussion in this book.

Publications

English Series

Bhagavad Gītā English

Anu Gītā English

Markandeya Samasya English

Yoga Sutras English

Hatha Yoga Pradipika English

Uddhava Gītā English

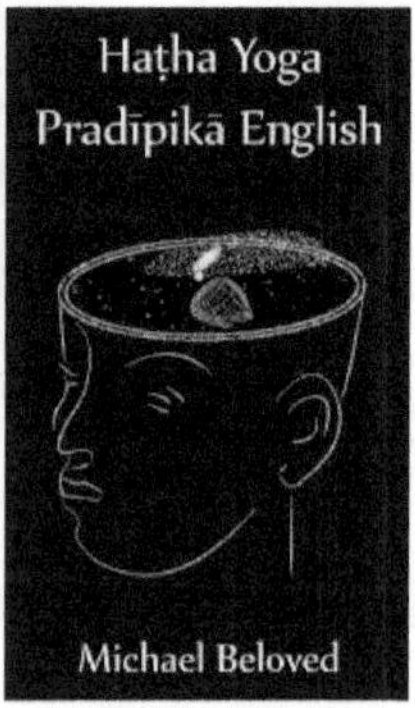

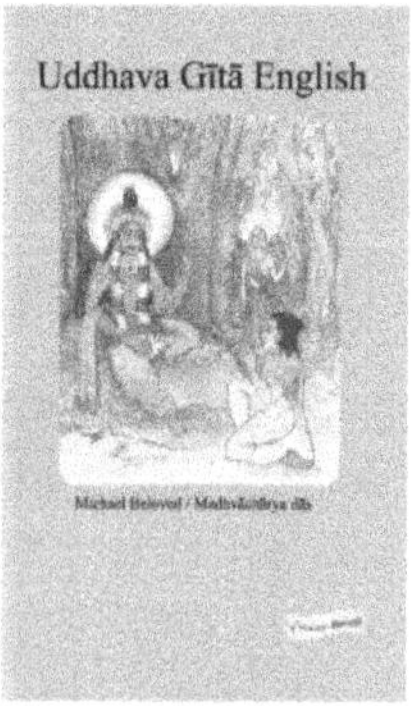

These are in precise and exacting English. Many Sanskrit words which were considered untranslatable into a Western language are rendered in precise, expressive, and modern English.

Three of these books are instructions from Krishna. **In *Bhagavad Gītā* English** and **Anu Gītā English**, the instructions were for Arjuna. In the **Uddhava Gītā English,** it was for Uddhava. *Bhagavad Gītā* and Anu Gītā are extracted from the *Mahabharata*. Uddhava Gītā was extracted from the 11th Canto of the Srimad Bhagavatam (Uddhava Gītā Bhagavata Purana). One of these books, the **Markandeya Samasya English** is about Krishna, as described by Yogi Markandeya, who survived the cosmic collapse and reached a divine child in whose transcendental body, the collapsed world existed.

Two of this series are the syllabus about yoga practice. The *Yoga Sutras* of Patañjali is elaboration about ashtanga yoga. Hatha Yoga Pradipika English, is the detailed information about *asana* postures, *pranayama* breath- infusion, energy compression, naad sound resonance and advanced meditation. The Sanskrit author is Swatmarama Mahayogin.

My suggestion is that you read ***Bhagavad Gītā* English**, the **Anu Gītā English, the Markandeya Samasya English,** the *Yoga Sutras* English, the Hatha Yoga Pradipika and lastly the **Uddhava Gītā English**, which is complicated and detailed.

For each of these books we have at least one commentary, which is published separately. Thus, one's particular interest can be researched further in the commentaries.

The smallest of these commentaries and perhaps the simplest is the one for the Anu *Gītā*. We published its commentary as the Anu Gītā Explained. The *Bhagavad Gītā* explanations were published in three distinct targeted commentaries. The first is *Bhagavad Gītā* Explained, which sheds lights on how people in the time of Krishna and Arjuna regarded the information and applied it. *Bhagavad Gītā* is an exposition of the application of yoga practice to cultural activities, which is known in the Sanskrit language as karma yoga.

Interestingly, *Bhagavad Gītā* was spoken on a battlefield just before one of the greatest battles in the ancient world. A warrior, Arjuna, lost his wits and had no idea that he could apply his training in yoga to political dealings. Krishna, his charioteer, lectured on the spur of the moment to give Arjuna the skill of using yoga proficiency in cultural dealings including how to deal with corrupt officials on a battlefield.

The second Gītā commentary is the Kriya Yoga *Bhagavad Gītā*. This clears the air about Krishna's information on the science of kriya yoga, showing that its techniques are clearly described for anyone who takes the time to read *Bhagavad Gītā*. Kriya yoga concerns the battlefield which is the psyche of the living being. The internal war and the mental and emotional forces which are hostile to self-realization are dealt with in the kriya yoga practice.

The third commentary is the Brahma Yoga *Bhagavad Gītā*. This shows what Krishna had to say outright and what he hinted about which concerns the brahma yoga practice, a mystic process for those who mastered kriya yoga.

There is one commentary for the **Markandeya Samasya English**. The title of that publication is Krishna Cosmic Body.

There are two commentaries to the *Yoga Sutras*. One is the *Yoga Sutras* of Patañjali and the other is the Meditation Expertise. These give detailed explanations of ashtanga Yoga.

The commentary of Hatha Yoga Pradipika is titled Kundalini Hatha Yoga Pradipika.

For the Uddhava *Gītā*, we published the Uddhava Gītā Explained. This is a large book and requires concentration and study for integration of the information. Of the books which deal with transcendental topics, my opinion is that the discourse between Krishna and Uddhava has the complete information about the realities in existence. This book is the one which removes massive existential ignorance.

Meditation Series

Meditation Pictorial

Meditation Expertise

CoreSelf Discovery

Meditation Sense Faculty

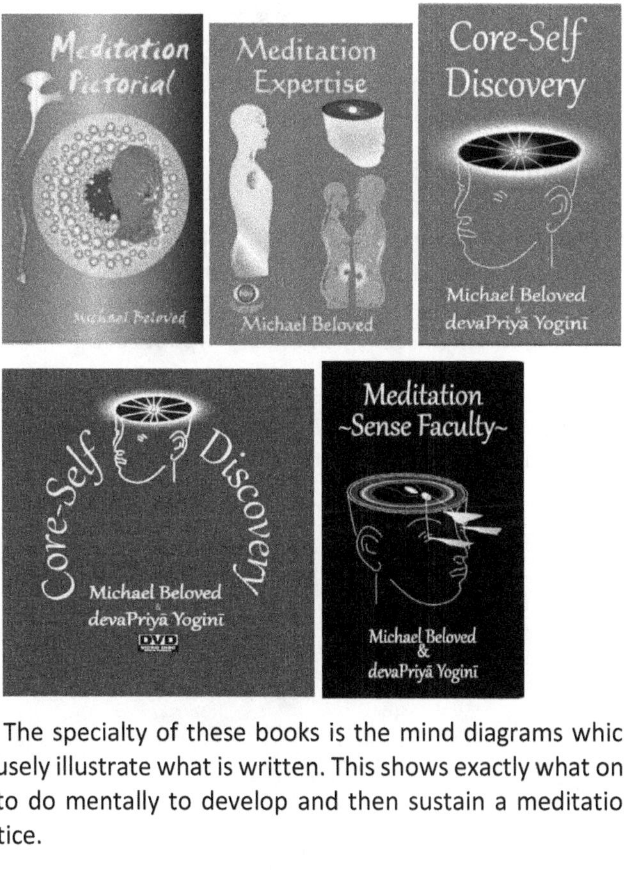

The specialty of these books is the mind diagrams which profusely illustrate what is written. This shows exactly what one has to do mentally to develop and then sustain a meditation practice.

In the **Meditation Pictorial**, one is shown how to develop psychic insight, a feature without which meditation is imagination and visualization, with no mystic experience.

In the **Meditation Expertise**, one is shown how to corral one's practice to bring it in line with the classic syllabus of yoga which Patañjali lays out as the ashtanga yoga eight-staged practice.

In **CoreSelf Discovery**, (co-authored with *devaPriya Yogini*) one is taken though the course of *pratyahar* sensual energy withdrawal which is the 5th stage of yoga in the Patañjali ashtanga eight-process complete system of yoga practice. These events lead to the discovery of a coreSelf which is surrounded by psychic organs in the head of the subtle body. This product has a DVD component.

Meditation ~ Sense Faculty (co-authored with *devaPriya Yogini*) is a detailed tutorial with profuse diagrams showing what actions to take in the subtle body to investigate the senses faculties. The meditator must first establish the location and function of the observing self. That self must be screened from the thoughts and ideas which usually hypnotize it.

These books are profusely illustrated with mind diagrams showing the components of psychic consciousness and the inner design of the subtle body.

Explained Series

Bhagavad Gītā Explained

Uddhava Gītā Explained

Anu Gītā Explained

The specialty of these books is that they are free of missionary intentions, cult tactics and philosophical distortion. Instead of using these books to add credence to a philosophy, meditation process, belief, or plea for followers, I spread the information out so that a reader can look through this literature and freely take or leave anything as desired.

When Krishna stressed himself as God, I stated that. When Krishna laid no claims for supremacy, I showed that. The reader is left to form an independent opinion about the validity of the information and the credibility of Krishna.

There is a difference in the discourse with Arjuna in the *Bhagavad Gītā,* and the one with Uddhava in the Uddhava *Gītā*. In fact, these two books may appear to contradict each other. In the *Bhagavad Gītā*, Krishna pressured Arjuna to complete social duties. In the Uddhava *Gītā*, Krishna insisted that Uddhava should abandon the same.

The Anu Gītā is not as popular as the *Bhagavad Gītā* but it is the conclusion of that text. Anu means what is to follow. In this discourse, an anxious Arjuna request that Krishna should repeat the *Bhagavad Gītā* and again show His supernatural and divine forms.

However, Krishna refuses to do so and chastises Arjuna for being a disappointment in forgetting what was revealed. Krishna then cited a celestial yogi, a near-perfected being, who explained the process of transmigration in vivid detail.

Commentaries

Yoga Sutras of Patañjali

Meditation Expertise

Krishna Cosmic Body

Anu Gītā Explained

Bhagavad Gītā Explained

Kriya Yoga Bhagavad Gītā

Brahma Yoga Bhagavad Gītā

Uddhava Gītā Explained

Kundalini Hatha Yoga Pradipika

corePerson ~ Krishna Sāmkhya

Yoga Sūtras

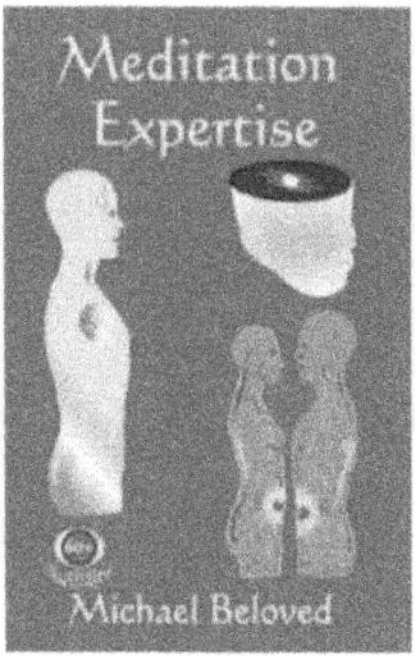
Meditation Expertise
Michael Beloved

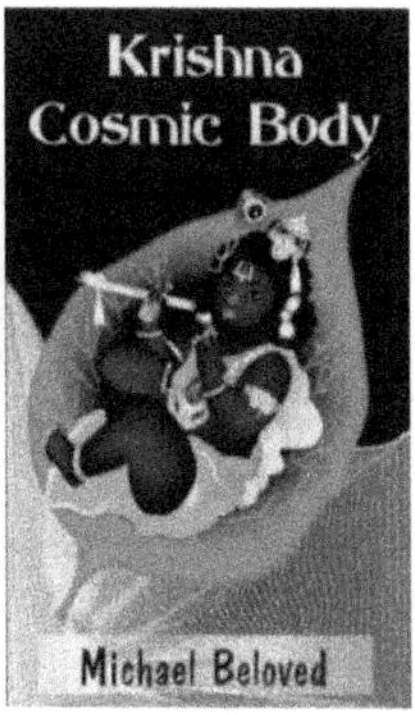
Krishna Cosmic Body
Michael Beloved

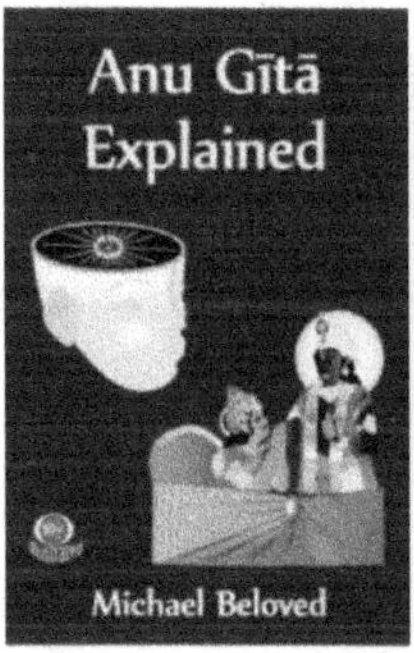
Anu Gītā Explained
Michael Beloved

Bhagavad Gītā Explained

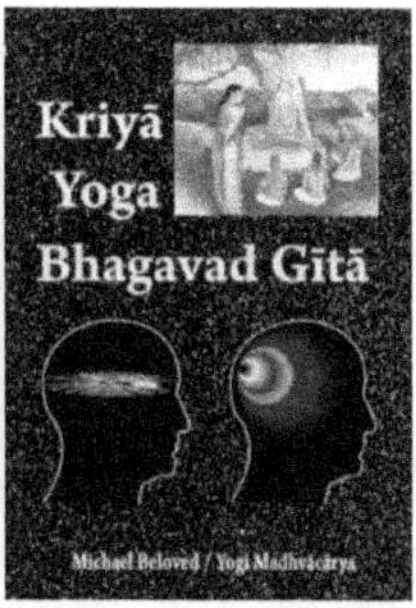
Kriyā Yoga Bhagavad Gītā

Brahma Yoga Bhagavad Gītā

Uddhava Gītā Explained

Kuṇḍalinī Haṭha Yoga Pradīpikā
Michael Beloved

***Yoga Sutras* of Patañjali is** the globally acclaimed textbook of yoga. This has detailed expositions of yoga techniques. Many kriya techniques are vividly described in the commentary.

Meditation Expertise is an analysis and application of the *Yoga Sutras*. This book is loaded with illustrations and has detailed explanations of secretive advanced meditation techniques which are called kriyas in the Sanskrit language.

Krishna Cosmic Body is a narrative commentary on the *Markandeya Samasya* portion of the Aranyaka Parva of the *Mahabharata*. This is the detailed description of the dissolution of the world, as experienced by the great yogin Markandeya who transcended the cosmic deity, Brahma, and reached Brahma's source who is the divine infant, Krishna.

Anu Gītā Explained is a detailed explanation of how we endure many material bodies in the course of transmigrating through various life-forms. This is a discourse between Krishna and Arjuna. Arjuna requested of Krishna a display of the Universal Form and a repeat narration of the *Bhagavad Gītā* but Krishna declined and explained what a siddha perfected being told the Yadu family about the sequence of existences one endures and the systematic flow of those lives at the convenience of material nature.

***Bhagavad Gītā* Explained** shows what was said in the Gītā, without religious overtones and sectarian biases.

Kriya Yoga *Bhagavad Gītā* shows the instructions for those who are doing kriya yoga.

Brahma Yoga *Bhagavad Gītā* shows the instructions for those who are doing brahma yoga.

Uddhava Gītā Explained shows the instructions to Uddhava which are more advanced than the ones given to Arjuna.

Bhagavad Gītā is an instruction for applying the expertise of yoga in the cultural field. This is why the process taught to Arjuna is called karma yoga which means karma + yoga or cultural activities done with yogic insight.

Uddhava Gītā is an instruction for applying the expertise of yoga to attaining spiritual status. This is why it explains jnana yoga and *bhakti* yoga in detail. Jnana yoga is using mystic skill for knowing the spiritual part of existence. *Bhakti* yoga is for developing affectionate relationships with divine beings.

Karma yoga is for negotiating the social concerns in the material world. It is inferior to *bhakti* yoga which concerns negotiating the social concerns in the spiritual world.

This world has a social environment. The spiritual world has one too.

Currently, Uddhava Gītā is the most advanced and informative spiritual book on the planet. There is nothing anywhere which is superior to it or which goes into so much detail as it. It verified that historically Krishna is the most advanced human being to ever have left literary instructions on this planet. Even Patañjali *Yoga Sutras* which I translated and gave an application for in my book, **Meditation Expertise**, does not go as far as the Uddhava *Gītā*.

Some of the information of these two books is identical but while the *Yoga Sutras* are concerned with the personal spiritual emancipation (*kaivalyam*) of the individual spirits, the Uddhava Gītā explains that and also explains the situations in the spiritual universes.

Bhagavad Gītā is from the *Mahabharata* which is the history of the Pandavas. Arjuna, the student of the *Gītā*, is one of the Pandavas brothers. He was in a social hassle, and did not know how to apply yoga expertise to solve it. On the battlefield, Krishna gave a crash-course on yogic social interactions.

Uddhava Gītā is from the *Srimad Bhagavatam (Bhagavata Purana),* which is a history of the incarnations of Krishna. Uddhava was a relative of Krishna. He was concerned about the situation of the deaths of many relatives, but Krishna diverted Uddhava to the practice of yoga for the purpose of successfully migrating to the spiritual environment.

Kundalini Hatha Yoga Pradipika is the commentary for the Hatha Yoga Pradipika of Swatmarama Mahayogin. This is the detailed process about *asana* posture, *pranayama* breath-infusion, complex compressions of energy, naad sound resonance intonement and advanced meditation practice.

This is the singular book with all the techniques of how to reform and redesign the subtle body so that it does not have the tendency for physical life forms, and for it to attain the status of a siddha.

corePerson ~ Krishna Sāmkhya is from the Uddhava Gita. It renders the Sāmkhya teaching of Krishna, which was given to Uddhava. It is distinct from other Sāmkhya itemization teachings which abound in India. To understand the Bhagavad Gita, one should study this.

It departs from the Upanishads in that it renders value to the person factor, the purusha, Unlike Advaita Vedanta and even Buddhism, it does not erase or undermine the person. And yet it does not over-value the coreSelf.

These books are based on the author's experiences in meditation, yoga practice and participation in spiritual groups:

Specialty

Spiritual Master

sex you!

Sleep Paralysis

Astral Projection

Masturbation Psychic Details

death You!

Experience You!

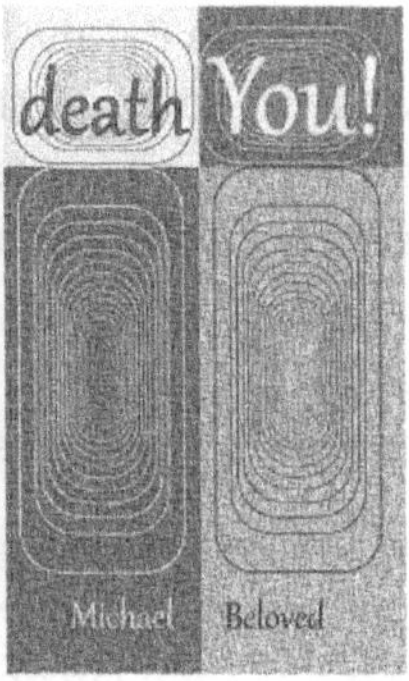

In **Spiritual Master**, Michael draws from experience with gurus or with their senior students. His contact with astral gurus is rated. He walks you through the avenue of gurus showing what you should do and what you should not do, so as to gain proficiency in whatever area of spirituality the guru mastered.

sex you! is a masterpiece about the adventures of an individual spirit's passage through the parents' psyches. The conversion of a departed soul into a sexual urge is described. The transit from the afterlife to residency in the emotions of the parents, is detailed. This is about sex and you. Learn about how much of you comprises the romantic energy of one's would-be parents!

Sleep Paralysis clears misconceptions so that one can see what sleep paralysis is, and what frightening astral experience occurs, while the paralysis is being experienced. This disempowerment has great value in giving you confidence that you can, and do exist, even if one is unable to operate the physical body. The implication is that one can exist apart from, and will survive, the loss of the material form.

Astral Projection details experiences Michael had even in childhood, where he assumed incorrectly that everyone was astrally conversant. He discusses the lifeForce psychic mechanism which operates the sleep-wake cycle of the physical form, and which budgets energy into the separated astral form which determines if the individual will have dream recall or no objective awareness during the projections. Astral travel happens on every occasion when the physical body sleeps. What is missing in awareness is the observer status while the astral body is separated.

Masturbation Psychic Details is a surprise presentation which relates what happens on the psychic plane during a masturbation event. This does not tackle moral issues or even addictions but shows the involvement of memory and the sure but hidden subconscious mind which operates many features of the psyche irrespective of the desire or approval of the self-conscious personality.

death You! is derived from the author's current experience in the psychic existence. It is not a text for supporting religion or for making indoctrination. It presents your likelihood when you are eventually deprived of using the physical body which you now identify as.

Experience You! is a translation and commentary on the allegoric tale about a fabled King Puranjan. This person never existed but the analogy about him, was grafted into the life of King Barhi. Out of compassion, it was told by Narad, a great yogi whose exploits are described in the Mahabharata and Puranas. This is from Canto 4 of the Srimad Bhagavatam. It laces into the life of every human being, as to how one becomes familia with an intellect and lives with that as the main calculating principle which assist one to negotiate the life of the physical body. There is much insight into the psyche of a living being in this fabled story.

inVision Series

Yoga inVision 1

Yoga inVision 2

Yoga inVision 3

Yoga inVision 4

Yoga inVision 5

Yoga inVision 6

Yoga inVision 7

Yoga inVision 8

Yoga inVision 9

Yoga inVision 10

Yoga inVision 11

Yoga inVision 12

Yoga inVision 13

Yoga inVision 14

Yoga inVision 15

Yoga inVision 16

Yoga inVision 17

Yoga inVision 18

Yoga inVision 19

Yoga inVision 20

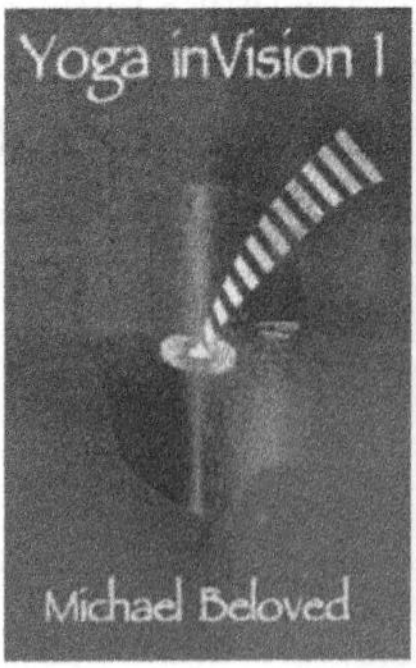

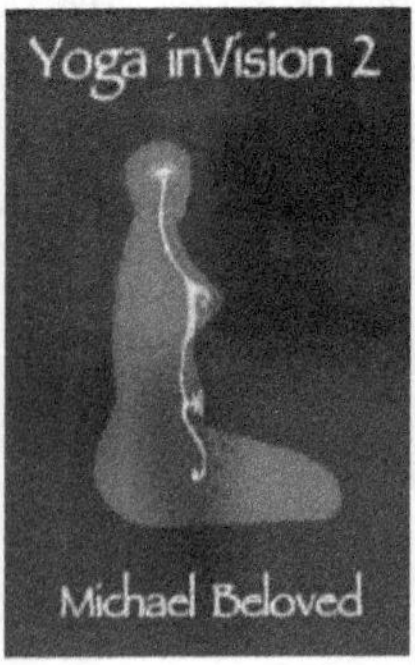

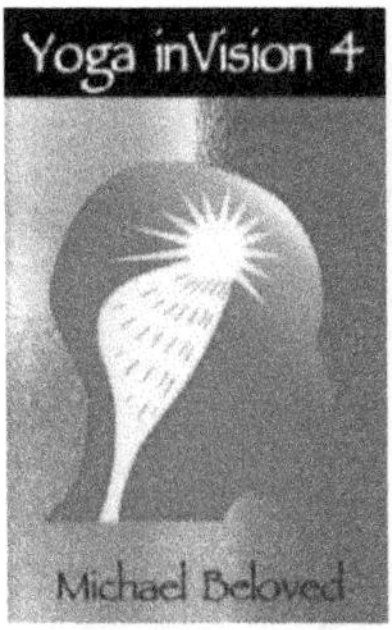
Yoga inVision 4
Michael Beloved

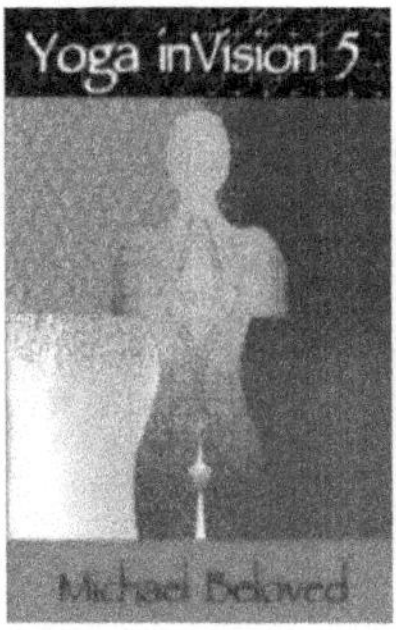
Yoga inVision 5
Michael Beloved

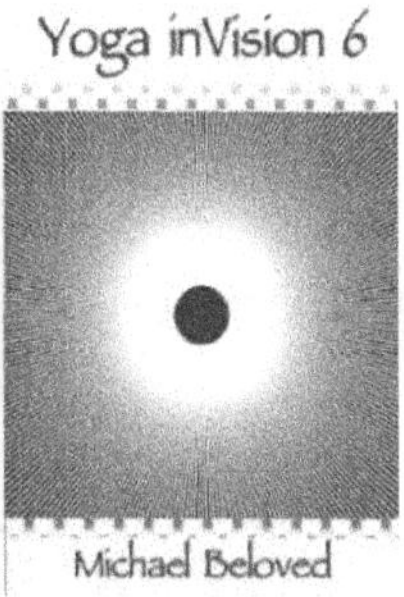
Yoga inVision 6
Michael Beloved

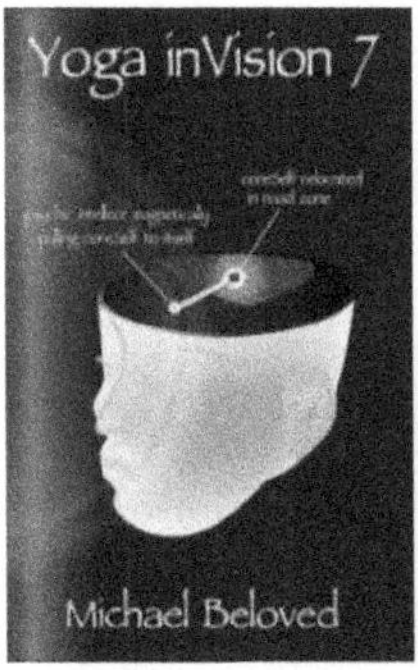
Yoga inVision 7
Michael Beloved

Yoga inVision 8
Michael Beloved

Yoga inVision 9
Michael Beloved

Yoga inVision 10
Michael Beloved

Yoga inVision 11
Michael Beloved

Yoga inVision 12
Michael Beloved

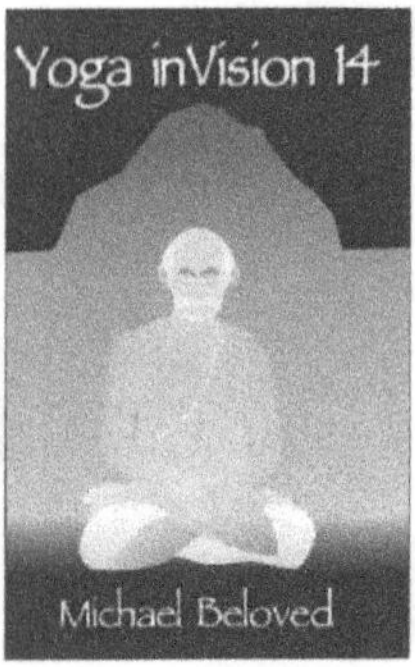

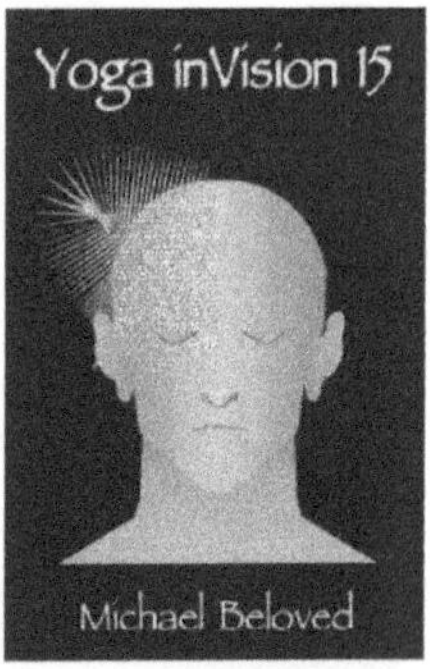

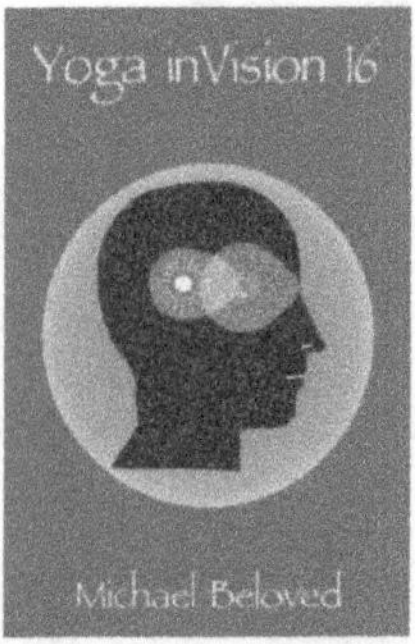

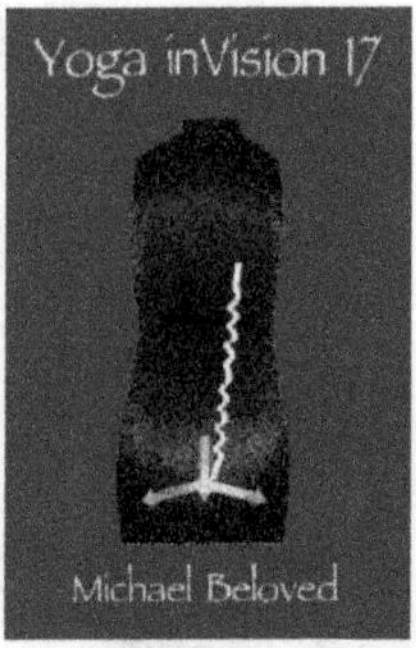

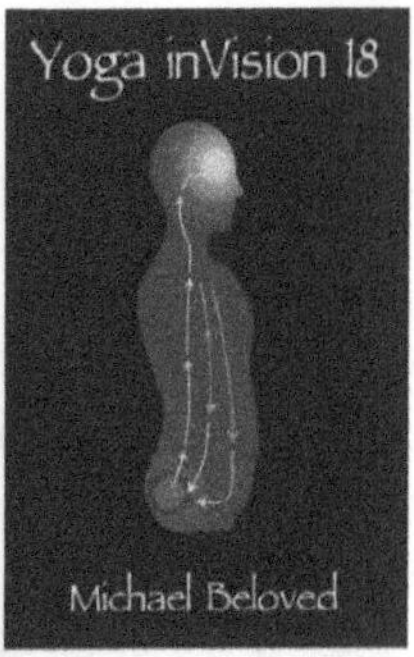

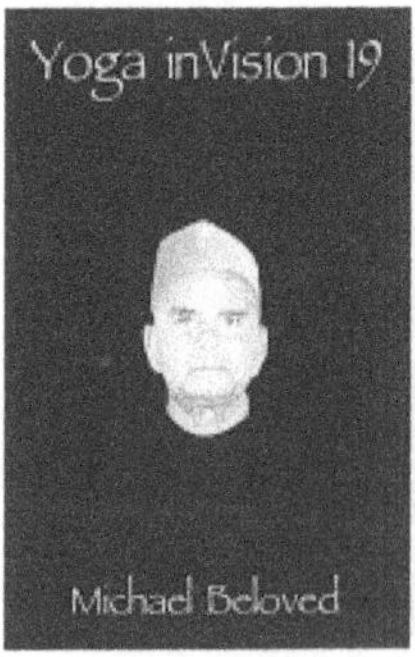

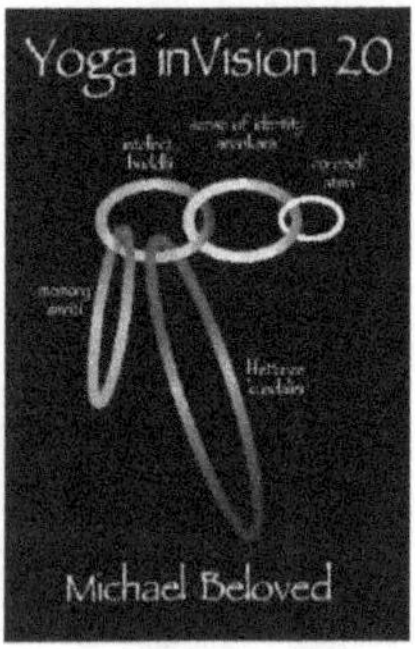

Yoga inVision 1, the first in this series, describes the breath infusion and meditation practices during the years of 1998 and 1999. There are unique, once in a lifetime, as well as recurring insights which are elaborated. inFocus during breath infusion, and the meditation which follows, is an adventure for any yogi. This gives what happened to this particular ascetic.

Yoga inVision 2 reports on the author's experiences from 1999 to 2001. Each day the experience is unique, illustrating the vibrancy of practice. Many rare once-in-a-lifetime perceptions are described.

Yoga inVision 3 reports on the author's experiences from 2001 to 2003.

Yoga inVision 4 reports on the author's experiences from 2006 to 2009.

Yoga inVision 5 reports on the author's experiences from 2006 to 2008.

Yoga inVision 6 reports on the author's experiences in 2010.

Yoga inVision 7 reports on the author's experiences in 2011.

Yoga inVision 8 reports on the author's experiences in 2011.

Yoga inVision 9 reports on the author's experiences in 2012.

Yoga inVision 10 reports on the author's experiences in 2012.

Yoga inVision 11 reports on the author's experiences in 2012.

Yoga inVision 12 reports on the author's experiences in 2012-2013.

Yoga inVision 13 reports on the author's experiences in 2013-2014.

Yoga inVision 14 reports on the author's experiences in 2013-2014.

Yoga inVision 15 reports on the author's experiences in 2014.

Yoga inVision 16 reports on the author's experiences in 2014-2015.

Yoga inVision 17 reports on the author's experiences in 2016-2017.

Yoga inVision 18 reports on the author's experiences in 2017-2019.

Yoga inVision 19 reports on the author's experiences in 2019-2021.

Yoga inVision 20 reports on the author's experiences in 2021-2022.

Online Resources

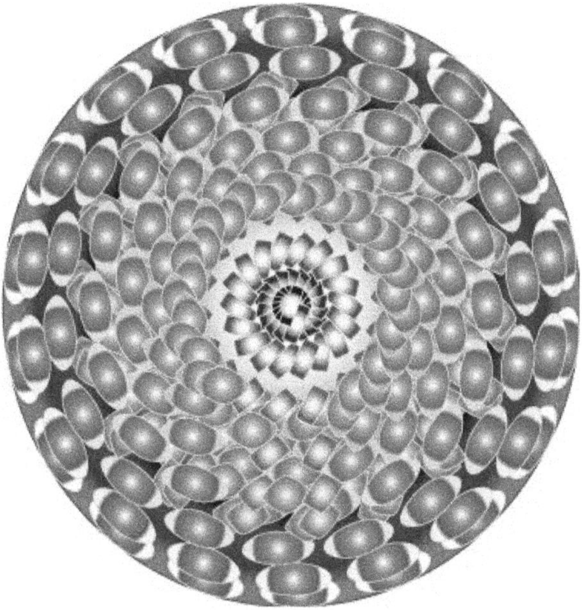

Email: michaelbelovedbooks@gmail.com

axisnexus@gmail.com

Website: michaelbeloved.com

Forum: inselfyoga.com

Posters: zazzle.com/inself

www.ingramcontent.com/pod-product-compliance
Lightning Source LLC
Chambersburg PA
CBHW072336090426
42741CB00012B/2811
* 9 7 8 1 9 4 2 8 8 7 5 7 7 *